Why Teenagers Act the Way They Do

■ *DR. G. KEITH OLSON*

Books

Loveland, Colorado

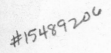

DEDICATION

To Ryan,
whose unfolding personality
is a source of constant delight
to his thoroughly biased dad.

Why Teenagers Act the Way They Do

For the sake of privacy all people named in the case histories in this book are composites, with names and details sufficiently altered to make them unidentifiable.

Credits
Edited by Nancy M. Shaw
Designed by Judy Atwood
Cover Photo by Joe Coca

All scripture quotations in this publication are from the Holy Bible, New International Version. Copyright © 1973, 1978, 1984 International Bible Society. Used by permission of Zondervan Bible Publishers.

Library of Congress Cataloging-in-Publication Data
Olson, G. Keith.
  Why teenagers act the way they do.

    1. Adolescent psychology.   2. Personality.
I. Title.
BF724.047 1987   155.5   87-8385
ISBN 0-931529-17-4 (soft)

Printed in the United States of America

Why Teenagers Act the Way They Do

■ ACKNOWLEDGMENTS

A book like this is never the result of one person's effort. In this case the final product is the result of many hours of loving and devoted work from many wonderful people committed to the task of equipping parents, youth ministers, teachers and counselors for more effective work with teenagers.

Acknowledgment must first be given to Rolfe LaForge, the originator of the Interpersonal Check List which serves as the theoretical and statistical basis for much of this book. His original research during the 1950s and his efforts since that time are greatly appreciated.

Two very competent and hard-working associates in Family Consultation Service hand scored almost 2,000 Interpersonal Check List answer sheets and plotted those results. For agreeing to take on and complete that laborious task, I am grateful to Karen J. Lenell, M.A., and Pamela Dahlin.

Designing and executing the program for statistically analyzing the research data were far beyond my capabilities. My grateful appreciation goes to Keith Peterson for his methodical and thorough treatment of the data which were produced by this research.

Editors really can be an author's best friend! I am deeply indebted to Nancy Shaw who has lovingly taken my thoughts and words and transformed them into language which is more articulate and striking than my own. Her continuing encouragement and excitement for this project provided marvelous emotional and motivational support when it was crucially needed. And to Lee Sparks, I am grateful for sharing the vision for this project. His initial stimulus to begin, his regular support to stay on course and his continuing efforts (though largely unsuccessful!) to help me meet deadlines have been invaluable assets in completing this project.

Writing this book has caused periodic disruption in my regular therapy schedule. Appreciation is genuinely expressed to my clients who graciously understood and were flexible in rescheduling appointments. Many youth ministers have contributed to this book through their candid disclosures about the adolescents in their families and youth groups. Many of the case studies cited in this book come from these accounts. Deep appreciation is also expressed to many adolescent clients who have courageously opened themselves to me during their therapy process. Of course, all case studies presented in this book have been camouflaged and details have been altered to protect the identities of the adolescents.

Finally, my love and deepest thanks are extended to Betty and Ryan—whose loving patience supported and encouraged me to complete this task, even though it meant many lost hours of contact with their husband and dad.

Contents

■ P a r t   O n e

Factors That Influence Personality Development

■ Part Two

Personality Types: How to Identify and Work With Different Types of Adolescents

■ PART ONE:

Factors That Influence Personality Development

Introduction

Several youth workers thoughtfully considered their seminar leader's question, "How does your youth group respond to your attempts to start a meeting?" After a few moments, one of the youth workers began to share:

> *Helen settles down almost immediately with a quiet and thoughtful look on her face. Sylvia looks around and begins to mimic what I've said to everyone who will listen. When Mark becomes irritated with her immature behavior, he tells her to straighten up. David usually bustles with activity, making sure everything is ready. Rachel quietly but carefully edges her chair away from the rest of the group. During all of this, Susan and Carlos, oblivious to what is happening around them, continue their muffled conversation. Each of the kids in my group reacts differently. And some weeks none of them act like they did the week before. Why do these teenagers act the way they do?*

After struggling with her pain and shedding many tears of frustration, the caring parent expressed her concern to the young youth minister:

> *How can I get my daughter to share her feelings and frustrations with me? I know she's going through tremendous stress at school, but she seems to reject everyone's attempts to help her. Why can't she be like her older brother who organizes everything and everybody around him? or like her youngest sister who talks to me incessantly about anything? I just don't know how to help her. I'm not even sure of what she needs help with. Why are teenagers so different? Why do they act the way they do?*

Parents and people who work with adolescents struggle with the same question: Why do teenagers act the way they do? Even though you seem to work with the same problems and the same teenagers over and over again, the situations are always different. Different teenagers have different needs at different times during their lives. And these differences are normal.

The purpose of this book is to help youth workers, parents and other adults understand and meet the needs of teenagers. Part One explains why teenagers are different. It describes the different stages of development and investigates the many factors that may influence or shape adolescents' personalities. Part Two describes the eight personality types, how they operate and how you can work with these young people to meet their basic needs.

To deepen your understanding and enhance your ability to help teenagers more effectively, it is important to gain a clear understanding of how personalities develop. The three chapters in Part One briefly introduce the internal and external forces that interact to influence personality. Your understanding of these interactions will help you work with young people and with one another to meet the needs of those whom you seek to serve.

It is important to realize we are not alone in our efforts

to understand today's adolescents. With the normal developmental problems of the teenage years complicated by struggles with eating disorders, alcohol and drugs, it feels good to know we have support from others who care. Developing a support system of interested adults can tap energies that go beyond the ability of any individual effort. When young people experience this kind of concern, they are introduced to the concept of love that reaches beyond itself. Like the children you seek to serve, you too are touched by a love that reaches out. No, we are not alone in this task. We have our children, we have each other, and we have the spirit of Jesus Christ who is concerned for all of us.

Adolescence IS a Part of God's Plan

While watching our church youth choir perform during a recent Sunday evening service, my wife and I observed a remarkably diverse display of individuals. Although we knew several of these 12- to 18-year-old young people, we felt we were observing an awkwardly mismatched group of 10- to 25-year-olds, struggling to bring order and harmony to their musical presentation.

Virtually every type of body was represented. Twelve-year-old Susan stood in the front row near the left end. Her 5-foot, barrel-shaped frame duplicated her mother's and older sister's shape. Near the onset of puberty, Susan presented little indication of developing femininity. This sweet child nervously turned from side to side in rhythm with the music as she sang.

In stark contrast stood 5-foot-11 Carlotta in the back row. At age 14 she had not yet had time to adjust to her rapidly elongating frame. Thin, plain and somewhat awkward, her face reflected her intensity. She was working hard to get the words right and sing on key. With her eyes riveted on the director and her mouth wide, she carefully enunciated each word and performed as near to perfection as possible.

In the center of the second row, beautiful, 16-year-old Sylvia drew and held our attention. Her shapely 5-foot-5 body complemented her remarkably attractive face that was framed in soft flowing curls. As she responded to the rhythm of singing "unto the Lord," she was totally unconscious of her suggestive movements.

Eighteen-year-old Martha was a picture of grace and maturity. Her poise and apparently natural self-control suggested a pleasant ease and comfort about herself. Her self-confidence, femininity and gentle spirit were reflected in her worshipful singing.

Then there was Randy. His 6 feet of tanned and muscular masculinity dominated the center of the back row. His light brown hair topped a handsome, well-featured face that sparkled with self-confidence. Virile energy and young male bravado emanated from this confident and exuberant 18-year-old.

Quite a different picture was presented by 15-year-old Phillip. We had difficulty remembering where he stood in the youth choir. Phillip's posture, gestures and facial expressions were basically unremarkable. His black horn-rimmed glasses were evidence to his serious, studious nature. His build was slight, he sported a few more than the average facial pimples, and his body language indicated he preferred to stand *behind* the person next to him.

Harvey stood in the second row near the right end. At age 13 and only a little over 5 feet tall, Harvey was Susan's male counterpart. He weighed in at an excessive 180 pounds. Because of his size, movements were laborious and limited in range. Even his arms failed to hang naturally by his sides. Self-conscious and fearful of making mistakes, he moved as little as possible, lest he attract attention to himself. Little expression ever broke through his face, and his mouth seemed frozen in a slightly open position.

We cannot leave out 14-year-old Mitch. Standing next

to Harvey, he seemed quite unnoticeable. Even though he and Harvey were the same height, Mitch still appeared dwarfed. But as we continued our observation, we knew we had found a gem. Mitch was a good-looking boy with an average build, and his face beamed with personality. Through an abundance of freckles and a captivating grin, his sparkling eyes warned us of the mischievousness that lay within.

Viewing this panorama of adolescence caused us to question God's rationality, sense of order and degree of forethought in designing his creation. But scripture reminds us that God designed humanity as he wanted us to be. Psalm 139:13-16a assures us of his loving presence at the time of our conception and during the whole process of our formation. David writes:

> *For you created my inmost being; you knit me together in my mother's womb. I praise you because I am fearfully and wonderfully made; your works are wonderful, I know that full well. My frame was not hidden from you when I was made in the secret place. When I was woven together in the depths of the earth, your eyes saw my unformed body.*

How good it is for us to know that our Lord is so intimately involved in our lives and in the lives of our teenagers, even from the time of conception.

We may wonder at times if adolescence is a departure from God's intended design. Some have even questioned whether this developmental stage is a sort of transitory psychosis, or temporary insanity. Bruce Narramore responded to that question when he wrote *Adolescence Is Not an Illness*, his book on how to parent teenagers.[1] We can trust God's design not to contain developmental flaws. No mass recall of certain human models is in order. In Genesis 1:27 and 31a, we find our Creator's reassuring stamp of approval. "So God created man in his own image, in the image of God he created him; male and female he created them . . . God saw all that he had made, and it was very good." Human beings, even during the adolescent stage, pass God's strict standards for quality control.

Many of the differences my wife and I noticed among the members of our youth choir represented the impact of the different stages in adolescent development. We can describe adolescence most accurately as a period of *dramatic transition* and *wide variation*. A junior higher is physically, mentally, psychologically and morally very different from a college sophomore. Yet, both are adolescents. Youth pastors, Sunday school teachers and parents who have close contact with junior high through college-age teenagers can verify how different these young people are from each other. Did you ever try to program a meeting that would hold the attention of your 13-year-olds and, at the same time, intellectually challenge the 19-year-olds? Maybe you've tried to plan a family outing that would captivate your junior higher's interest and also offer your college freshman a worthwhile experience? The difficulty of these tasks arises because even though both children are adolescents, they are in different stages of adolescent development.

Let's examine the three stages of development we group together under the general banner of adolescence. Each stage is marked by its own psychological tasks, physical characteristics, intellectual and moral traits and appropriate behaviors. The three stages are listed below with their approximate ages:

- Early adolescence (ages 12 to 14),
- Mid-adolescence (ages 15 to 16), and
- Late adolescence (ages 17 to 21).

■ *Early Adolescence*

Most junior highers are early adolescents. They are experiencing a transition from childhood into adolescence and may display characteristics of both stages of development. Many young people in this age group mourn the loss of their childhood. They find they must let go of some of their pleasures of the past like being carried to bed, sleeping with stuffed animals and enjoying relative freedom from responsibility. As growth into adolescence continues, however, these lost experiences are replaced by the anticipation and excitement of new freedoms, expanded boundaries and enjoyable activities that come with the teenage years.

Adolescents' bodies, as well as their lives, are changing. In fact, physical changes actually bring on adolescence. A sudden growth spurt is followed by the onset of puberty. Girls go through their first menstrual cycle, and boys experience their first ejaculation. Dramatic hormonal and other glandular changes initiate the development of secondary sexual characteristics. Girls begin breast development, pelvic changes and body hair growth. Boys develop facial and body hair, active sweat glands, voice changes and an increased potential for physical strength. These physical changes set the stage for many other early adolescent characteristics.

The primary psychological task for early adolescents is to begin developing their identity as separate and unique individuals. Failure to accomplish this task results in role diffusion, or an inability to determine "just who I am" or "what I stand for." Fourteen-year-old Jeremy realizes he acts one way at home and another way at school. He acts still differently at church and even differently again with his team on the playing field. He has no central concept of who he really is. Nothing serves as a common thread to unite all of his roles. No sense of self gives his life special value as an individual. To move further toward normal adolescent development, Jeremy needs to establish a more clearly defined identity.

Junior highers are beginning to advance from concrete thinking toward thinking more abstractly. "If . . . , then . . . " sequences take on more meaning. For example, "*If* I don't do my homework, *then* I can't pass the test."

As 12-year-old Sherry has moved from childhood into her early adolescent years, she can think through the possible consequences of her actions. This skill gives her the ability to make wiser decisions. She now can avoid embarrassing and even dangerous situations. Her problem-solving skills are still limited, but the beginnings of abstract thought are apparent. As a result, early teenagers, like Sherry, have the ability to ask more difficult questions about their relationships with both God and the church.

Michelle is a 13-year-old eighth grader who generally enjoys life. She is very active with her friends at school and church. She spends hours on the phone, talking over every detail of the day's happenings with her closest buddies. The sun rises when she gets together with her group and sets when she must return home for dinner and homework. It's not that she doesn't love and enjoy her family. It's just that the value of her friends' stock has far surpassed that of her family's on the relationship market. She is so focused on her own activities, feelings and thoughts that she frequently forgets to think about the people around her.

Generally, Michelle likes herself; however, she feels somewhat uncomfortable around people. She went through puberty about 18 months ago and hasn't yet adjusted to the changes in her physical appearance. Instead of running away from her, boys now pursue her. She rides an emotional roller coaster. Insignificant events can cause her to cry or wonder if life has any meaning. At other times she flies high and feels confident she can accomplish any goal she chooses. Michelle is a normal early adolescent. Her behavior reflects the physical changes and psychological dynamics occurring within her.

■ Mid-Adolescence

Most high school freshmen, sophomores and juniors are in mid-adolescence. By the time teenagers reach ages 14 or 15, the physical changes occurring since the onset of puberty have slowed down. The mid-adolescent is more comfortable with his or her new body. Continuing development of the secondary sexual characteristics further enhances the young person's identity as male or female. The ability to enter into and maintain relationships also increases. During this stage the intense focus on same-sex peer groups begins to diminish, and in its place surfaces a strong need to find special, more intimate relationships. Boys and girls become intensely interested in the opposite sex and are eager to establish romantic attachments.

The ability to form intimate relationships as an expression of their developing identity is the primary psychological task of mid-adolescents. Failure in this task seriously impedes teenagers' growth in self-confidence and their ability in adulthood to establish stable marriage relationships. Teenagers must *learn* how to give of themselves and how to receive from others. They must allow themselves to be known while getting to know others.

The individuation process, in which teenagers separate themselves from their parents, continues through mid-adolescence. At this point many young people join groups which advocate values, beliefs or behaviors which are different from those of their parents and the church. Teenagers' formations of identity get an additional boost if the parent or church finds their adolescent's particular group not only different but also threatening. Then the young people experience an even stronger sense of difference and individuality from their parents.

Mid-adolescence continues the intellectual and moral changes that began during the early adolescent years. The 14- to16-year-old is capable of more complex and abstract thoughts than the younger teenager. Asking deeper-reaching questions, seeing through illogical arguments and thinking more critically about what they are told to believe make living and working with mid-adolescents a challenge. (God sometimes uses these young people to help us recognize just how little we know.)

The critical nature of mid-adolescence can certainly try

an adult's patience. But we need not overreact to teenagers' criticisms. Even though they may not allow us to see it, teenagers are at least as critical of themselves as they are of us. Their bravado, apparent self-assuredness and energetic exuberance often hide their deeply felt insecurities and self-doubts.

A glimpse at 15-year-old Jason presents a picture of a fairly typical mid-adolescent. As a sophomore in a four-year high school, Jason feels academically and socially much more comfortable than he did as a freshman. He has accustomed himself to the high school routine, the larger campus and being around 2,500 other kids all day. Increased feelings of security also come from his now well-established circle of buddies with whom he spends most of his free time.

Like most teenagers, Jason seeks recognition for being particularly good in some activity. He's not really fond of sports. But he does play an above-average game of tennis, and his abilities have earned him a spot on the school's tennis team. With little courage or confidence in his popularity, he hesitates to run for an elected office. But he does enjoy membership in the French club and serves as its publicity chairman.

Jason thinks about girls a lot. He enjoys watching them and wonders what they think about, especially what they think about him. He often fantasizes and pictures himself in a romantic, loving relationship. The two relationships he did have with girls make these fantasies almost irresistible. Sometimes he fantasizes about petting sessions and sexual involvement, and he has experimented with masturbation. These brief experiences provide stimulating memories and an intense desire to have more girlfriends in the future.

Feelings of guilt and anxiety accompany Jason's fantasies and petting experiences. He is a Christian who isn't quite sure what is and is not okay in God's eyes. And he certainly doesn't want his parents or anyone else to know about his fantasies, masturbation or experiences with girls.

Like many mid-adolescents, Jason constantly struggles through uncharted waters and feels very alone. He believes some of what he does is wrong and commits to stop. But his resolve crumbles under the intensity of his sex drive. He prays for forgiveness, hoping that God will somehow understand that he really does mean to obey.

Jason doesn't feel good about his relationship with his parents. His mother's mannerisms irritate him. He thinks his dad is okay, but he doesn't seem to share any common interests with Jason. An occasional baseball game, fishing trip and project in the yard sum up the times they spend together. He knows his dad loves him, but Jason feels uncomfortable when he tries to talk with his dad about important personal matters. When he wants to go out with friends or a date, he expects a grilling from his parents:

"Where are you going?"

"Who are you going with?"

"When will you be home?"

"Are there going to be any adults there?"

"Have we met the kids you're going with?"

"Have you finished your homework?"

He finds this questioning almost more hassle than the experience is worth. Jason's current life experiences are typical of many mid-adolescents.

■ Late Adolescence

The final stage in adolescent development is usually the longest. It lasts from about age 17 until sometime during the early 20s. As adolescents move toward independence from their need for parental support, they complete their final transition into early adulthood. Young people typically rebel less during this stage, unless they are struggling with the process of individuating from their parents. They feel more confident and secure within their own identity and usually develop meaningful relationships with others, including the opposite sex. Increasing intimacy marks these relationships, and signs of commitment become evident.

Late adolescents become increasingly involved in their future. They recognize, usually for the first time, that their decisions today can dramatically impact their tomorrows. This orientation toward the future and their increased ability to develop commitment to relationships indicate diminishing egocentricity that is normal during this last stage of adolescence. Finally, young people can see beyond themselves. They can understand and care about how others feel and think. They can now say no to themselves for another person's benefit.

Career decisions take on new importance.

"Shall I go to college? Where should I attend? community college? state university? Or should I go to a Christian college?"

"Maybe I ought to join the military or go to a trade school. Or should I just get a job and earn some money?"

Late adolescents begin to realize that their answers to these and other important questions will impact their lives in the future.

This ability to consider the pros and cons of many options and to think in "If . . . , then . . . " patterns allows older adolescents to take more responsibility for their lives. Their increased ability to think abstractly enables them to make better and more mature decisions. They are more likely to resolve conflicts and prevent problems *before* they occur.

Their developing thinking abilities also pave the way to more maturity in their spiritual lives. The movement from concrete to abstract thought patterns equips young people with the ability to develop a broader understanding of God, salvation, sin, forgiveness, sanctification, the Trinity, eternity and many other difficult spiritual concepts. The Apostle Paul reminds us: "Now we see but a poor reflection; then we shall see face to face. Now I know in part; then I shall know fully, even as I am fully known" (1 Corinthians 13:12). While on this earth, we will never fully comprehend the nature of God, but it is our responsibility and privilege to increase our understanding of him. In his delightful book *Your God Is Too Small*, J.B. Phillips alerts us to some of the dangers of defining God in a too limited, concrete fashion.[2] Encourage your older adolescents to ask questions, raise apparent inconsistencies and express their doubts. This process is necessary for them to procure *real*, not just cliché, answers. Failure to mature intellectually and spiritually seriously restricts young people's abilities to adopt a theology that will stand up to the stresses of their adult lives.

Shirley, a 20-year-old college junior, is a late adolescent. She went to community college for two years while living at home with her parents and two younger brothers. She now attends a state university and lives in an on-campus dormitory. To help support her education, she works in the campus cafeteria during the school year and plans to get a summer job in her hometown.

Shirley and her parents went through several difficult times during her early and mid-adolescent years. She was rebellious and critical of most everything her parents stood for and did. Though she always got along well with her youngest brother, she showed little tolerance for her brother George, only two years her junior. They fought and argued constantly throughout her teenage years. After her year away, Shirley has grown to appreciate George and even enjoys talking to her parents. She now feels much less defensive when they offer advice or ask questions about her activities.

Dating has been a major part of Shirley's adolescence. Since her second year at community college, she has been going with Roger. This is her third long-term relationship lasting over one year. They have been dating seriously and are considering the possibility of marriage. Both she and Roger are Christians, and they strive to base their relationship on Christian principles. But because they are strongly attracted to each other, they have difficulty restraining their sexual impulses. They pray for forgiveness for the few times their heavy petting has resulted in sexual intercourse and commit to each other to say no. But their mutual decision remains imperfect.

Shirley is unsure about many things. The simple answers she learned during childhood just aren't adequate for life as she is experiencing it now. Her spiritual experiences and theological orientation are challenged in the classroom almost daily. Her personal morality differs painfully from some of her own wishes and desires. Life is stretching her as she matures toward adulthood.

Adolescence is a time of extreme and rapid change. Knowing whether young people are in early, mid- or late adolescence helps us understand which behaviors are appropriate. This basic understanding of the stages of adolescence helps us examine some of the family, social, biological and spiritual factors that shape children's growth into different adolescent personality types. The next two chapters will describe how personalities are affected by drives, needs and wants. We will also explore common defense mechanisms and how they are used to relieve anxiety. These indicators and discoveries will help us increase our awareness of the spiritual and psychological problems young people in our youth groups may encounter as they progress through these developmental stages.

CHAPTER 2

Families and Other Influences Are Used in God's Plan

Between early and late adolescence, tremendous changes occur in a person's intellectual, emotional, physical and spiritual development. But maturation doesn't account for all of the differences among adolescents. Why are some 13-year-olds more like grade school children while others look and act like young adults? Why do some 15-year-olds rebel at every suggestion, inquiry, direction and discipline given by their parents while others feel quite tolerant and accepting? The answers to these and similar questions can be found in the young person's genetic inheritance, family environment and personal history.

God uses everything in our lives to bring about the full expression of his image. The writer of Hebrews identifies

Jesus Christ as the "author and perfecter of our faith" (Hebrews 12:2). As our creator, Christ is also the perfecter of our whole person. The Apostle John tells us, "Through him all things were made; without him nothing was made that has been made" (John 1:3). Christ's perfecting of us continues eternally. Adolescence is a part of his design and process for developing perfection within us. Our loving God uses whatever resources are available to accomplish his purposes.

Unfortunately, however, many of the individual differences we observe in young people cannot in good faith be attributed to God. He receives credit for many phenomena he neither deserves nor wants. Our peculiar quirks and individual habits often result from our own decisions and reactions to life's experiences. Problems, plus the unhealthy feelings, attitudes, thoughts and behaviors normally exhibited in adolescence, are viewed as breakdowns in young people's abilities to respond and adapt to a complex and difficult world.

As teachers, parents, youth leaders and counselors, we often meet adolescents whose present behaviors concern us about their well-being. To help these young people, we must understand them and their behavior. How did they get to be this way? What message does this type of behavior send to us? What does their behavior say about them? What unmet needs do they express? In this chapter we will discuss some of the major environmental and historical factors that determine how a person develops through the adolescent years. Specifically, we will focus on:

- Genetic inheritance
- Family environment
- Relationship history
- Developmental history
- Health history
- School history
- Socio-economic and cultural environment
- Spiritual history

■ *Genetic Inheritance*

The question of genetic inheritance determining an individual's personality and behavior patterns continues to be an issue. Some psychologists believe personality characteristics are largely determined by a person's genetic endowment. Other psychologists believe personality differences develop as a result of the individual's interaction with the environment. Commonly known as the "nature versus nurture controversy," this is one of the oldest and most difficult questions to resolve. Most psychotherapists and other human behavior scientists believe it is not an all-or-none type of issue. *Both* nature and nurture contribute to the formation of human personality.

We have already read that God is present at the time of conception (Psalm 139:13-16). He is in the womb as the fetus forms and grows. God is conscious of the genetically carried traits of the egg and sperm transferred to this new life. God is active and lovingly involved in this miraculous process; he is not passive. God was present in the creation of the young people with whom we live and work.

Our genetic inheritance provides some limits or ceilings to our physical and mental capacities. We inherit certain organ systems that are strong and resilient and other systems which are not so strong. Some adolescents have strong bones and a weak respiratory system. Others possess a strong nervous system and an easily disturbed digestive system. We can trace some of our observable strengths and weaknesses back to our inheritance.

In the same way, certain personality traits can also be inherited. For example, some young people are born with a high energy level. This energy undoubtedly affects the adolescent's interest patterns, activity levels, friendship preferences and degrees of motivation.

But during adolescence we seldom see the pure effects of inheritance. Parenting, relationships, nourishment, illnesses, and the sum of life's experiences powerfully impact each person's personality and behavior patterns. The *specific* effects of inherited characteristics are difficult to isolate.

■ *Family Environment*

The family unit is often cited as the single most powerful influence on a child's life. The amount of teaching, modeling, correction and influencing that occurs within the family environment far surpasses the input from other sources and greatly influences the adolescent's adaptation to his or her world.

The Generation Gap. Differences between parents and their children are usually most dramatic when young people are going through adolescence. This is commonly known as the generation gap. Young people frequently complain: "You don't understand. You don't really listen when I try to tell you what is important to me. You don't know what it's like being a kid today."

Parents often reply: "You're right. I don't understand everything about you! I don't understand why you dress the way you do. I don't understand why you listen to music that destroys your eardrums. And I don't *want* to understand your kind of behavior!"

When children are in adolescence, their parents usually enter middle age. The combination of these two life stages complicates the generation gap. While young people experiment with new behaviors, stretch their limits and take risks, their parents become more conservative. While youth experience exuberance and idealism, parents realistically evaluate the status of their finances and health for their later years. Young people see no end to life and instinctively rebel against its boundaries. But their middle-aged parents see friends and relatives dying, recognize a feeling of "It's too late" and learn to respect life's cautions and limitations. Is it any surprise there is conflict as the energy of adolescence collides with the realism of middle age?

The Style of Parenting. A major shaping force in the family environment is the style of parenting. How parents choose to teach, discipline and influence their children impacts not only the family atmosphere, but also how their children view the world and themselves. Parents who consistently express love and affection, support firm limits, and provide meaningful consequences for misbehavior establish an optimal family environment for their children.

Dysfunctional (impaired) parenting is often the root of adolescents' problems. Youth workers or teachers can understand teenagers' struggles by observing how the parents operate. Several classic dysfunctional parenting styles produce unhealthy reactions in adolescent children.[1]

The Perfectionistic Parent. When parents continually demand perfection, their young people falsely learn they can never be good enough. These adolescents are usually discouraged, feel inadequate and experience deep self-hate. Many exhibit extreme depression and often harbor repressed hostility toward their parents. Their anger, however, is usually aimed at a safer target—themselves.

The Rejecting Parent. Rejecting parents attack not only what young people do, but who they are. Because these teenagers feel unloved by their parents, they don't expect love from others. When adults reject their children's efforts to demand attention, these young people may react negatively and destructively in delinquency and other antisocial behavior.

The Overprotective Parent. These parents continue to help their children when assistance is no longer necessary. Some seek to control because they are insecure and afraid to let go. Others restrict their children from life's experiences because of their own unconscious angers and fears. Overprotected teenagers feel smothered, constricted and doubted. They grow up to believe they are inadequate and helpless.

The Overindulgent Parent. These parents continually give things to accomplish their goal. Some try to compensate for their own childhood impoverishment. Others are afraid of saying no or seek to control their maturing children. But whatever their motivation, these parents set themselves up to feel used.

"All he does is want, want, want."

"Doesn't she appreciate anything?"

"You think money grows on trees!"

Their children pay an even costlier price. With no practice in planning and waiting for things they want, these young people never learn how to deal with normal frustrations. They have difficulty developing accountability and responsibility. Overindulgent parents actually sabotage their adolescents' development into maturity.

The Overpermissive Parent. Overpermissive parenting produces children with no tolerance or ability to adjust to others. Never having to deal with consistent rules and limitations, these young people disregard others' feelings, needs and rights. They often experience the pain of discouragement and alienation.

The Severe Parent. Excessively strict limits and cruel forms of punishment almost always produce severe psychological problems in the children of these parents. Many times internal difficulties will erupt into delinquency or other inappropriate behaviors, creating even more pain for these teenagers and their families. Other times a crushed spirit and a complete loss of self-confidence will result from severe parenting.

The Inconsistent Parent. Variations in parenting standards and expectations can be destructive to children. When discipline is severe and then mild, when rules are strict and then lenient, when expectations are exacting and then nil, young people have difficulty developing a strong moral and ethical basis for their lives. The blurring of right and wrong inhibits their conscience development. These parents train their young people to become cunning manipulators by unconsciously encouraging them to work arbitrary and unpredictable rules around to their benefit.

The Faulty Parent Model. The Bible warns us about the disastrous effects of criminal, antisocial and immoral parental behavior upon children. Numbers 14:18 states: "The Lord is slow to anger, abounding in love and forgiving sin and rebellion. Yet he does not leave the guilty unpunished; he punishes the children for the sin of the fathers to the third and fourth generation." Faulty parents model values that justify illegal and immoral behavior. The sins of the father are truly passed from one generation to the next.

The Double-Binding Parent. Young people feel crippled by double-binding parents. Double-binding places children in no-win situations.

> *"We want you to make your own choice in this matter."*
> **But the parents also say,**
> *"It's about time you show us a little maturity."*

> *"We're proud of how well you're doing on your new job."*
> **But the parents also say,**
> *"Maybe it's our fault you won't lift a finger around the house."*

Living with a steady diet of dual messages produces rage, guilt, resentment and confusion. There is no way to please these parents and proceed through a normal, healthy adolescence at the same time.

A word of caution: Parents may function within one or more of these plus some positive styles of parenting. When you observe adolescents' parents, take notes over a period of time in different circumstances to get a *complete* picture of how parents operate.

Use of Parental Authority. Another aspect of parenting that impacts young people is how parents *use* their authority. The role and acceptance of parental authority is evident in scripture. In his letter to the Ephesian church, Paul wrote: "Children, obey your parents in the Lord, for this is right. 'Honor your father and mother'—which is the first commandment with a promise—'that it may go well with you and that you may enjoy long life on the earth' " (Ephesians 6:1-3).

The next verse suggests that parental authority can be either destructive or constructive for our teenagers. "Fathers, do not exasperate your children; instead, bring them up in the training and instruction of the Lord" (Ephesians 6:4). By observing how teenagers relate to other adult authority figures, we gain understanding about how their parents handle authority.

Too much or too little parenting definitely affects young people's interaction with others. Let's examine four common patterns for expressing parental authority.

Authoritarian Pattern. Authoritarian parents view human nature as basically sinful. They believe in complete parental authority and tight behavior control. Children are to obey and not cause problems. To obtain absolute conformity and complete obedience, authoritarian parents resort to numerous pressures, threats, coercion, guilt tactics and sometimes rewards. Teenagers often respond with passive conformity, outright rebellion or silent withdrawal. Young people's emotions may include extreme anger, frustration and resentment in addition to fear, depression and despair. Teenagers may also feel helpless and alienated.

Permissive Pattern. At the opposite end of the spectrum from authoritarian parents are permissive parents. Since these parents believe that human nature is basically good, they treat their children as equals. Eliminating *all* controls and limits, these parents believe their children will naturally choose positive behavior. They rely on parental authority in only extreme situations. Parental input is limited to love, praise, cooperation, promises and encouragement to foster positive attitudes and feelings.

Due to a lack of interaction with limits or authorities, these children often exhibit anger, rebellion and withdrawal. With no opportunities to develop inner controls, these children find it difficult to say no to themselves or their desires. They typically experience rage, resentment and frustration along with anxiety, fear and depression. Many also feel extremely alienated from others and the world around them.

Authoritative Pattern. Authoritative parents are similar to but not as extreme as authoritarian parents. They believe their children are valuable creations in God's image, but they also see them as sinful and in need of control. These parents value both their own authority and their children.

Rewards and punishments, cooperation and consequences, praise and fear are used interchangeably to develop acceptable behavior in their children. Typical reactions of their children range from passivity to rebellion, but may include conformity, cooperation, and assertiveness when parents have nurtured successfully. Again, emotions run the gamut from anger to joy and from fear to security.

Democratic Pattern. Democratic parents are similar to, but not as extreme, as permissive parents. They believe humanity is basically good yet capable of destructive behavior. Children are respected as equals who generally behave well, but who sometimes need and are offered limits and guidance. There is a sensitivity to teenagers' needs to express feelings, set their limits and make decisions for themselves. Clear communication is essential for both parents and their young people. These parents use encouragement, consequences, love and group cooperation to help their children develop healthy attitudes, appropriate feelings and positive behavior. Parents and children *share* authority. Teenagers' typical behaviors include conformity, cooperation, assertiveness and healthy rebellion. These children often experience anger and fear. But with support from a loving family, they develop security, love and self-respect.

On a continuum from the most to the least use of authority, the relationship of these four patterns is illustrated in Chart 1.

Chart 1
Continuum for Expressing Parental Authority

GREATEST USE OF AUTHORITY   *LEAST USE OF AUTHORITY*

←——————————————————————————→

Authoritarian   Authoritative   Democratic   Permissive

Please note: Both extremely authoritarian and extremely permissive parents tend to produce the same undesirable behaviors and emotions in their children. The more moderate forms of authoritative and democratic parenting usually produce the most favorable results.

Family Communication. When poor communication patterns exist *within* a family, teenagers will probably have difficulty relating to others *outside* the home. By talking with parents or observing the family's interaction at meals or after church, we pick up valuable clues about why young people are struggling. Be sure to observe the three dimensions of family communication:

● the *amount* of communication in the family,
● the *quality* of communication in the family, and
● the *content* of communication in the family.

One of the most common cries of adolescents is: "No one understands or listens to me. No one cares about what I think or say!" Many teenagers come from families where little communication occurs. Mom may be frustrated and question her role as wife and mother. She feels trapped in both her job and her marriage. She fights depression, struggles for an identity and wonders what her future holds. Dad sees his value as money provider, but beyond this role is unsure of his importance. He shares little of significance with the rest of the family and spends his free

time watching television and doing chores around the
house and yard.

Teenagers watch their parents go through life sharing
little with each other or the rest of the family. These parents rob their teenagers of opportunities for learning how
to communicate. Since no one at home seems interested,
these young people develop a sense of alienation and isolation. Mistakenly, they see themselves as uninteresting and
bland. This poor self-concept follows them to school,
youth group and even to places like the athletic field. Inadequate amounts of communication within the family
limit adolescents' self-concepts and their abilities to interact within healthy relationships.

Some families communicate sufficiently, but their style
is impaired. The *way* they talk with each other, not the
amount of conversation, is the problem. For example, in
some families *sarcasm* is the primary method for making a
point, and someone is always the butt of the joke. The
price for this kind of humor is usually a chunk of someone's dignity. People who relate with sarcasm often feel
insecure and defensive. They indirectly let others know
their feelings with a laugh or joke squeezed in to cover up
their primary message. When victims of sarcasm react
openly to the underlying message, they are often attacked
with even more sarcasm. "I didn't realize you were so sensitive." "My, my, aren't we touchy today!" At other times
individuals may deny their sarcastic messages. "I was only
kidding. Can't you take a joke?" When a family member
uses sarcasm, others feel angry and hurt, and want to hurt
back. They experience communication as a dangerous and
painful game of subterfuge, camouflage and outwitting the
other.

Lecturing, another impaired communication style, assumes the speaker is superior to the listener. Instead of
sharing views, discussing perceptions and inviting other
solutions, communication is a closed, one-way process.
Parents assume the role of drill instructor with their children. Young people are told, either openly or implicitly,

that their thoughts, feelings, attitudes and perceptions are neither valued nor wanted. They are taught that they have little of meaning or importance to say. Gradually, they also assume they are not smart enough to speak up, either at home or elsewhere.

A third unhealthy communication style involves *accusing and blaming.* Instead of investing creative energy into finding solutions to problems, destructive energy is poured into finding out "who dunnit" and extracting a confession. Children grow up believing their personal worth is determined by the perfection of their performance. Since mistakes make them vulnerable to attack, they are avoided or concealed at all costs. These children avoid responsibility because taking it proves too risky and too painful. These children anticipate incrimination from other adults; therefore, they avoid teachers, youth leaders and other people who could help and care for them.

Avoiding conflict or *placating* characterizes the final dysfunctional family communication pattern.

"It's going to be all right. Just you wait. You'll see."

"Now, I'm sure he didn't mean anything by that. Surely you just misunderstood."

"I don't think we should talk about this anymore. Everyone's getting upset. Let's talk about something pleasant."

Fear of rejection, loss of love or pain of alienation can initiate placating behavior. Children in these families grow up believing confrontation is bad. Sometimes they never learn how to use anger constructively. They are robbed of opportunities to experience family growth through learning how to cope with and process anger. This avoidance of conflict reinforces their fears of confrontation.

These impaired communication patterns have been presented in a manner that helps us remember them:

*S*arcasm

*L*ecture

*A*ccusation

*P*lacating

Unhealthy communication styles **SLAP** people, causing them psychological pain.[2]

We have looked at problems of inadequate amounts and impaired styles of communication which negatively affect teenagers' self-concepts and relationships. The third potential problem with family communication is the possibility of destructive content in the communication that does occur. Telling a lie is probably the most destructive type of communication known to us. When lies become part of a family's interaction, negative results take place.

● Distance is created between family members.

● The individual telling the lie expresses distrust in himself or herself, in the other person and in their relationship.

● The person being told the lie is led into confusion about what is real. The lie presents a falsehood cloaked as reality.

This contradictory and confusing process is sometimes called "crazy-making behavior" because of its effect on everyone involved. When teenagers grow up in families where lies are the norm, these young people often develop a pattern of manipulating and deceiving others. They have not learned what the Bible teaches: "Then you will know the truth, and the truth will set you free" (John 8:32). With no experience in openness and honesty, young people are severely stunted in their ability to form meaningful relationships with peers and adults alike.

Families struggle with another area of content in communication. Depth of meaning within family conversations varies in all homes. In a surprising number of families, the most meaningful issues are avoided regularly. John Powell, S.J., has outlined five levels of communication to help us identify the depth of sharing evident in a young person's family.[3] Note the sample comments in Chart 2, clarifying what we might experience at each level.

Chart 2
Powell's Five
Levels of Communication

Level 5: Clichés.
"How are you?"
"Nice day, isn't it!"

Level 4: External facts.
"Tom rode his bicycle to the dentist."
"Jane got all A's on her report card."

Level 3: Personal ideas, judgments, opinions.
"I believe Tom was trying to take
some of the pressure off Mother
and her taxi service."
"I think Jane's report card indicates
how hard she is working."

Level 2: Feelings and emotions.
"I am so proud of Tom's maturity
for taking responsibility for his own
transportation."
"I am pleased that Jane is taking
school seriously."

Level 1: Peak communication.
These are spontaneous moments
when perfect mutual empathy and
understanding take place, when
each person truly knows and ap-
preciates the other person and his
or her point of view.

With each descending level of communication, individuals reveal more of themselves to each other, and more intimacy is shared. When teenagers are raised in families where dialogue seldom reaches level two or even level three, young people are usually restricted in their ability to communicate meaningfully with peers or adults.

Remember, find out the *amount* of communication, the *style* of communication and the typical *content* of communication within teenagers' families. All these facets of family communication help us understand why teenagers relate to others as they do. This knowledge will also assist us in developing helping strategies for our young people.

Birth Order. The birth order, or ordinal position, of children is another important aspect of teenagers' family environments. A fascinating body of psychological research indicates that birth order of children has a strong impact on their future personality development. In other words, firstborns tend to resemble each other, as do middle children, youngest children and single children.

During adolescence, firstborn children are usually high achievers. They want to please adults and find that academic success brings praise and reward. They make good leaders and exercise their abilities in elected offices they have won. Officers (especially presidents) in school, club and church organizations are firstborn more often than children from any other family position.

Firstborns carry a great amount of tension within them. Their need for perfection drives them to succeed. Fear of personal incompetence and failure drains their energy. They work continuously to control their emotions as well as their actions. Generally, they prefer to rely on their own strengths rather than depend on other people. They think in a logical and highly rational manner.

Second-born or middle children need to feel secure about belonging within their family. Rather than compete with an older sibling where he or she is already "the best," these children select their own specialty. They often involve themselves in athletics or hobbies and carry on an active social life. Their desire for a unique position within the family partially explains the radical differences we sometimes see between children next to each other in the family. Second-born or middle children tend to be more flexible than older brothers or sisters because they have to adjust to living with both.

As youngest children enter adolescence, they have usually accumulated a wealth of relationship experiences. Older siblings as well as parents have been eager to perform services for them and meet their needs. Many youngest children become adept at eliciting helpful, caretaking and even rescuing behaviors from their friends and adults. Although these young people sometimes become self-centered, manipulative and demanding, they often develop into cooperative and amiable teenagers who seem to get along with everyone. Their early-life experiences of having people eager to interact with them often bear fruit in healthy self-concepts. They learn they are attractive to others and often develop social behavior that wins popularity for them.

Single children are essentially firstborns who never had to adapt to younger siblings; they are also the youngest child. These children usually develop many firstborn characteristics. But without the experience of daily interaction in the home, these young people miss out on learning how to relate with others, especially other children. During adolescence their greatest struggle is with peer relationships; however, many of these single children blossom as they mature into adulthood.

By knowing the family position of our young people, we add one more valuable piece of information to our repertoire of knowledge. Kevin Leman's *The Birth Order Book* offers more in-depth information about this aspect of family environment.[4]

Impact of Death or Divorce. Families disrupted by divorce or death present additional considerations in understanding the impact of family environment upon teenagers. Young people show the effects of these dramatic changes in their behaviors, feelings and attitudes.

When one parent leaves, children almost always feel somewhat responsible. "If only I had been a better kid, things would have worked out." "If I hadn't caused so much constant hassling, Dad would have stayed."

There is an ongoing wish to patch things up between parents. Many children try to step into a mediating role between their divorcing or divorced parents. They assume the heavy burden of responsibility for their parents' decisions and place it on their own teenage shoulders. Their ensuing guilt, frustration and anger leave these young people in great need of help from other adults.

When stepparents and other siblings are added to the family environment, even more adjustment is required. While living with just one parent, young people probably assume more responsibility at home, sometimes even as additional money-earners. This sense of being needed sometimes increases adolescents' self-worth. When the parent remarries, this position of importance and value is seriously threatened. Passage of time and generous amounts of love and reassurance from both parents help adolescents adapt to this new adjustment within their family structure.

■ Relationship History

It has been said, "If you want to know what someone is like, look at his friends." Our associates reflect much of our values, beliefs and attitudes. All of us are strongly impacted by our peer group, but never as much as during adolescence. Prior to puberty, however, young people have had from 10 to 12 years of experience with relationships. During this time dozens of people have influenced their lives. Learning about teenagers' past and present relationships will help us understand more about teenagers' personalities and behaviors.

Who were the important players in the history of their relationships? Most psychotherapists feel that early-life events have a stronger effect on how personalities develop than events occurring later. Teenagers are largely the product of the particular mix of people who make up their relationship histories. Some of these people have been intimately involved in a youth's life for many years, and some may have been involved for only a few brief moments. Some have been vested with significant power, authority, control or influence, while others have played only minor or limited roles in helping shape the adolescents we know today.

Family Relationships. Certainly, parents play the most significant role in a child's life. No other people have greater impact on how a child will move into adolescence than the mother and father. The degree and type of input parents have on their children was more fully discussed in the previous section on family environment.

Siblings are also important players in a young person's development. The "social laboratory" of living and learning with brothers and (or) sisters teaches a young person many beliefs about the self and others that will be carried throughout life.[5]

"How well does the adolescent get along with her peers?"

"Is he willing to compromise?"

"Does she always have to be the boss, or can she sometimes be just one of the workers?"

"Is there a willingness to give as well as the freedom to receive?"

"Can he initiate social activity, or is he only able to respond when invited?"

The significance of all interpersonal behavior we observe in a teenager can be more fully understood once we know about the young person's siblings and the history of their interaction.

Grandparents, aunts, uncles, cousins and other relatives also influence a teenager's personal and social development. Sometimes a relative from the extended family provides valuable and life-saving support for a child when there are glaring inadequacies within the youth's immediate family.

Fourteen-year-old Tim is an excellent example of how God uses distant relatives. When Tim was four months old, his alcoholic father deserted him and his mother. Tim's mother kept him with her. But in her own search for support and companionship during the next 10 years, she sought out and lived with several different men. Most of these were in their late adolescence or early 20s. Few had stable jobs or enough money to help out financially, so his mom ended up supporting them, too. None had any parenting skills or experience. Fortunately, a few did express some genuine affection for Tim. But to most of them, Tim was just in the way. His needs and infrequent requests for someone to play with were rejected as unnecessary hassles and intrusions. He also witnessed frequent sexual activity between his mom and her boyfriends. Drug abuse was common in their apartment, and he was invited to participate on numerous occasions. Violence between his mother and her guests was not unusual, and Tim was injured several times while trying to defend his mom.

During a weekend trip to his aunt's home, some serious bruises were discovered on Tim's back, legs and arms. After much gentle probing, Tim broke down and told about the violence that had occurred four days before. He was scared—afraid of what his mother would do if she found out he told someone. He felt guilty and ashamed for betraying her. After a medical examination and a series of family conferences, the court took legal action to remove young Tim from his mother's home.

During the past four years Tim has lived with his aunt and uncle. He has a stable home environment, nourishing food and a family with whom he can interact. Tim made a Christian commitment and regularly takes an active part in his cousins' youth group at church. The family also encourages Tim's involvement in professional counseling. His counselor hopes to help him resolve the pain and anger resulting from his early life experiences and adjust to his current family involvement.

What would have become of Tim if his relatives had not intervened on his behalf? We cannot know the answer to that question. But we do know he has a much better chance for healthy adolescent development because they extended their love to him.

This is a beautiful, heart-warming story. Unfortunately, relatives can also be the source of unhappiness. Children sometimes find themselves caught up in relatives' quarrels, competitions and gossip. Many find themselves trapped between two people or families they love with the relatives cruelly demanding that the child choose sides. These painful experiences and horribly negative lessons children learn are sure to impact their readiness and desire for relationships during adolescence.

Peer Relationships. Teenagers value their friends. The peer group is supreme in interpersonal influence over adolescent behavior, attitudes and perceptions. So how do teenagers become involved with particular peer groups? Why does Barbara choose to be with the cheerleaders while Peter opts for the academic dropouts? How could Terri seek out the popular group while her brother Keith selected the cowboys? We must remember there is no one or exact answer to these questions.

A young person doesn't begin relating with friends at puberty. From the curious gazes of infancy through the uncertain interactions of toddlers, children make their first attempts at friendship by merely recognizing the presence of others. As they develop common interests and curiosity, they strive to involve each other in what is going on. Age and cooperative social skills develop further, and soon they express preferences for certain people and interests. All of a young person's previous experience with peers helps shape the style of his or her personal relationships during the teenage years.

None of us can know himself or herself in a vacuum. One of the most valuable sources for a teenager's developing self-concept is the feedback or personal reactions that come from peers. A teenager knows that he or she is socially attractive or unattractive by the responses received from others. Randy, for example, has learned from his friends that he is fun to play ball with. But since he doesn't receive many party invitations, he believes others really don't like him very well. Judy knows she is physically attractive because of the looks and comments she receives from other people. She has also learned people lose interest quickly after she opens her mouth to speak.

Some young people learn that their personality or character lacks something because they never quite fit in with an attractive or popular group. Others discover they are fun and interesting because they experience the popularity and consistent, easy acceptance of others. Knowing the past and present friendship patterns of your young people will help you understand and assist them during their adolescence.

Relationships with Other Authority Figures. Another part of adolescents' relationship histories concerns their reactions to authority figures other than parents. Children interact with neighbor adults, teachers, coaches, pastors, police officers, doctors and other authority figures throughout their preadolescent years. This exposure to a wide variety of adults in many different authority positions plays a major role in shaping teenagers' attitudes and perceptions of authority.

"Is authority something I should seek or avoid?"

"Can I generally trust authority figures?"

"What kinds of people usually seek positions of authority?"

"Does authority usually ruin a person?"

Answers to these and other questions typically come from young people's childhood and adolescent experiences.

By the time young people reach their adolescent years, they have learned very well whether school is a place where teachers care or don't care about them. By then, they also have determined whether police are good or bad people. Most adolescents have an opinion about whether pastors are righteous or phoney. Some trust government officials, while others turn a deaf ear to anyone who even sounds like a politician.

The effects of these biases dramatically impact the behaviors of teenagers. Rebellion is a natural part of normal adolescent development. The health and constructive nature of their rebellion is determined by the history young people have with authority figures. Both violent rebellion and adolescent passivity are products of unhealthy relationships with authority figures. Teenagers act out the pain and rage from these past experiences against other adults or against themselves during the adolescent years. Both patterns can have tragic and permanent results in most teenagers' personality development.

■ *Developmental History*

Much is written about adolescence being an important stage of human development. Actually, every age range represents a developmental stage. Psychologists believe human growth is an ongoing process that begins at conception and ends at death. A Christian perspective suggests that human development continues through eternity.

Understanding why your teenagers act the way they do is incomplete without an awareness of their developmental history. One of the major principles of developmental psychology is that people's successful passage through any one stage of development is largely dependent upon how well they resolved the issues of previous stages. Each stage has its own developmental tasks. The more fully the tasks of one stage are accomplished, the better prepared people are to work on the tasks of the next developmental stage. Therefore, the successful completion of the adolescent developmental tasks discussed in Chapter 1 is either limited or enabled by how well young people have accomplished the tasks for previous developmental stages.

Psychologist Erik Erikson has given us the most accurate and helpful design for understanding developmental stages.[6] Examining these earlier life stages for clues will help us better understand the behavior, attitudes, values and perceptions we see in our teenagers. Remember, the specific ages cited are approximations. And each person progresses through each stage at a different pace.

Infancy. The first stage lasts from birth through the first year. The primary psychological developmental task of the infant is to develop a basic trust in the world as a safe place in which to live.

"Am I going to be okay here?"

"Are my basic needs going to be met consistently so that I can stay alive?"

"Can I depend on the people around me for adequate support and nourishment?"

These are the questions which must be answered in a sufficiently positive manner to allow satisfactory progress to the next stage.

Failure to gain adequate trust results in an all-encompassing fear and suspicion. "Hyper-alertness" and paranoia during adolescence often have their roots in severe disruption of children's infancy. Inadequate care, insufficient nourishment, rejection, lack of affection and inconsistent parenting teaches infants not to trust the world in which they live. However, when care, nourishment, love, affection and parenting are adequately consistent, infants learn they can rely on their world to be safe and dependable.

Toddler Years. The second stage lasts from age 2 through age 3. The primary developmental task for children in this stage is to gain confidence in their ability to exercise some control over themselves and their environment. Developing a degree of autonomy, or self-government, requires some movement away from the complete dependence of infancy.

"Am I able to do some things on my own?"

"Can I determine when and at what pace I will do certain things?"

"Can I exert my will against the will of others and sometimes win?"

"Can I trust myself to move away from dependency?"

These questions must be answered positively for children to continue their progress psychologically.

Failure to develop adequate trust in their autonomy, or their ability to govern themselves, leads children into self-doubt. Teenagers who are insecure in their abilities to do things on their own may have had problems with self-government as a toddler. Parental overprotection or withdrawal of support teaches toddlers to doubt their abilities and depend on others. Opportunities to try new skills, move at their own pace and experiment with doing tasks their own way fosters confidence within toddlers.

Preschool Years. The third stage begins at age 4 and extends through age 5. The developmental task for children at this age is to gain confidence in their ability to initiate activities.

"Is it okay for me to start doing something without always having to ask for permission?"

"Am I capable of initiating an important action by myself?"

"Is it wise for me to always wait for someone else to speak before I join in?"

Before further psychological development can proceed, these questions of self-direction must be resolved.

Failure to develop confidence in their ability and right to initiate activity leaves children with a deep sense of guilt about themselves. Teenagers who see themselves as only followers may have experienced serious frustrations during their preschool years. Severe restrictions, impatience, refusal to answer questions and treating children like nuisances lead them to feel guilty about themselves. But when children are encouraged to try new activities, ask questions and share new ideas, they build a strong faith in their ability to initiate activities and express valuable thoughts.

Elementary School Years. The fourth stage is positioned immediately prior to early adolescence and lasts from about age 6 through age 11, or when puberty begins. During this time children need to be industrious, gain confidence in their abilities to make things happen, produce good work and complete tasks.

"Am I capable of doing something worthwhile?"

"Is my work good enough to be noticed?"

"Can I complete worthwhile projects in a manner that accomplishes anything of significance?"

Gaining confidence in their ability to do things well is a must for children before they advance into adolescence.

Failure to develop industriousness leaves young people inferior to their peers. Teenagers may fail to try their hardest because they doubt their ability to succeed and get things done. Their range of confidence may be very narrow. They may attempt only simple tasks. Limiting activities and projects with negative parental statements teaches children to think of themselves as inferior. However, encouragement to make things, build projects and accomplish tasks helps children trust in their own abilities and industry. Generous expressions of appreciation, thanks and praise during this life stage bear positive fruit during adolescence.

Chart 3 is a summary of Erikson's four stages of psychological development which lead to adolescence.

■ Health History

Teenagers are extremely conscious of their bodies. Much of their identity is wrapped up in their physical image. "I'm fat." "I'm athletic." "I'm strong." "I'm attractive." All of these comments contain much more information about the person's self-concept than just a physical description. Teenagers know that the visual impression they make largely determines how their peers think of them. "What you see is what you get" is a common assumption in the way adolescents perceive each other.

Chart 3
Erikson's Preadolescent Stages of Development

Age Range	Task	Explanation
Birth to 1 Year	Trust vs. Mistrust	"The world is safe and dependable." *or* "The world is dangerous and insecure."
2-3 Years	Autonomy vs. Self-Doubt	"I can do it myself!" *or* "I need someone to do it for me."
4-5 Years	Initiative vs. Guilt	"It is okay for me to start doing this." *or* "Someone else better start it; I'll follow."
6-11 Years	Industry vs. Inferiority	"I can accomplish things." *or* "I'm too afraid to try."

The fifth developmental stage encompasses the adolescent years. Teenagers making a positive adjustment during this stage have satisfactorily resolved the tasks associated with earlier developmental stages. Similarly, young people struggling or failing to accomplish the psychological challenges of adolescence may have insufficiently resolved their earlier developmental tasks. Notice the specific problem behaviors or attitudes; these will provide clues about where the core of the problem lies and which developmental task needs more work.

An important aspect of teenagers' relationships with their bodies is their health history. A history of strength and vitality is a valuable asset in developing a competent self-concept. On the other hand, teenagers with histories of illnesses, injuries or a general lack of vitality tend to possess weak self-concepts and see themselves as ineffective and dependent. These young people are less likely to develop strong leadership characteristics. They do not see themselves as valuable, nor do they feel capable or motivated to offer contributions to their class, youth group or even their family.

Teenagers with a history of serious illness, physical handicap or debilitating injuries must find some way to adapt to their situation. They cannot rely on their physical strength or agility for their identity or self-esteem. They often find their personal value in intelligence, artistic ability or social skills.

Some teenagers with histories of physical problems develop the questionable skill of getting others to serve their needs. Convinced they cannot take care of themselves, these young people find meaning in their ability to manipulate others into attending to them. They develop dependent relationships—using their friends to do errands, study and spend time with them exclusively, rather than sharing and encouraging their friends to go to school, games, dances and church events.

■ *School History*

By the time young people reach junior high, they have had at least six years experience in school classrooms. As youngsters progress through their first years of school, they identify themselves according to their perceived capabilities in three areas of their school life: academics, athletics and social interaction. These self-perceptions have a great impact on their attitudes and behavior in school during adolescence.

Students learn to identify themselves as smart, average

or dumb by comparing their academic performance with that of their peers. By the time they reach junior high or high school, young people perform in a manner that agrees with their self-image. Many adolescents whose academic performance was poor in elementary school assume they are "dummies." They don't believe they can succeed in an academic environment. Just stepping onto a school campus is a signal for them to fail. Unconsciously, they fulfill their own prophecy with their performance.

In a similar manner, children who see themselves as average often try just hard enough to produce average academic results. They associate with other average students who mutually reinforce each other's self-concept as average. They are afraid of being unintelligent, but they become anxious when their performance exceeds their expectations. To reduce their discomfort, which is a masked fear of failure, they unconsciously decide to study less, make more careless errors in their work or in some other way lower their performance to a mediocre level.

Students who succeed academically during their early-school years grow to expect that kind of success from themselves. They are satisfied with nothing less. They take pride in their level of performance, even if on the surface they appear embarrassed and apologetic about their A's. These students can become overachievers and drive themselves too hard. As a result, they sometimes encounter severe levels of stress and anxiety. Their fear of failure and resulting devaluation and rejection drive them along the treadmill of academic demands. Psychologist David Elkind has written about the characteristics of these children and the dynamics of the society that produces them in his well-received book, *The Hurried Child*.[7] These teenagers fulfill and expand their learning potential. They usually tie their identities to their academic and intellectual performance.

Athletic performance is another important aspect of school history for many teenagers. Recess, free time and playground activities provide early-school athletic experiences for children. Physical strength, agility, speed and skills are tested, tried and compared in each of these arenas.

Children's histories of success and failure provide much direction to their adolescent mind-set about athletics. For many adolescents, athletic success provides positive self-identification and breeds a desire to enter competition in high school. It also builds positive evaluations of their abilities and expectations for success.

Elementary children who do not possess the gregariousness, speed, strength or coordination to succeed at baseball, basketball, football or other highly competitive sports feel too discouraged to compete in high school athletics. Some, however, do excel in tennis, golf or similar sports as they get older. Others find avenues other than sports for self-expression and personal identification.

Another major part of teenagers' school histories is their social experience. This history includes their interactions with classmates, older and younger children, teachers and administrators. Much has already been discussed about adolescents' social histories earlier in this chapter under the section on relationship history.

■ Socio-Economic and Cultural Environment

Adolescents' socio-economic environments and cultural heritage impact them in many ways. Children from similar social and economic backgrounds tend to draw together. Their experiences are similar, and they can easily identify with one another. These peer groups provide a setting for reinforcing common values, beliefs, attitudes and activities. Teenagers link themselves closer to their heritage through association with their cultural peer groups.

It is common for teenagers to associate closely with others from their economic, social and cultural background. Those who attempt to join other groups encounter resistance both from the group representing their heritage and from the new group they are trying to join.

Adolescents desperately need acceptance by their group. Young people attempting to move upward into a higher social or economic group exhibit strong self-confidence and courage. Those who seek membership in lower social or economic groups express a lack of self-esteem. They may have experienced rejection from previous peer groups.

The cultural heritage of teenagers provides a rich source of building blocks for identity development. The television miniseries *Roots* highlighted the value of knowing, understanding and appreciating the heritage of our ancestors. Pride in cultural heritage encourages teenagers to carry on the traditions of their families and neighborhoods. Shame or embarrassment about cultural heritage can lead teenagers toward strong rebellion against family values, traditions and customary behaviors. In seeking to understand adolescents' behavior, keep in mind their socio-economic level and their cultural heritage.

■ *Spiritual History*

Spiritual experiences can certainly influence teenagers' attitudes and moral choices. If the spiritual teachings derived from church experiences, denominational input and role models apply and work in real life, teenagers are likely to use what they have been taught. If their religious experiences allow continued growth as they mature intellectually, young people will find it easier to uphold their religious orientation.

Talk with your young people about their spiritual history. Help them recall the significant experiences and role models that impacted their early childhood and preadolescence. Encourage them to share their memories of spiritual experiences within the home. By listening carefully to their words and the feelings they choose to share, you will have a better understanding of your young people's spiritual history.

Early-life experiences definitely influence personality

development. While infants and small children check out the safety and security of their environment, they also investigate how their world responds to them. Early Christian education should emphasize God's care, love and protection. These nurturing themes should be repeated in Bible stories and Christian teachings that illustrate God's active protection and loving intervention in people's lives. Exposure to this kind of caring should help produce a healthy spiritual environment during these early years.

When you talk individually with your young people about their very-early spiritual experiences, check first to see if they were involved with church or any religious experiences. If they have no memories of early involvement, reassure these young people of their acceptability. Remind them that early spiritual experiences are not essential, only helpful for your understanding.

When young people do recall very-early spiritual experiences and teachings, help them focus on specific memories. Ask them questions that clarify their thoughts as much as possible. You might include some of these:

● Do you recall any specific spiritual experiences that occurred before you started attending school?

● If you attended Sunday school regularly, did you have an attendance chart on which you placed a star to say that you were present? How did you feel as you pasted your star on the chart? Did you feel special?

● Do you remember a specific lesson or experience that made you feel especially good? especially bad? Explain.

● What do you remember about prayer time? Did you or someone else pray before your snack time? Did you put your hands together or hold hands with the other children? Did you memorize prayers, or were they spontaneous? How did you feel about "talking to God"?

● Do you remember any special church activities or events? a Christmas pageant? an Easter sunrise service? Palm Sunday? a baptism? a dedication? What do you remember about the event? Did you have a special part in the activity? How did you feel about your experience?

● Did you have a special way to share your offering? Explain. How did you feel about giving money to God? to Jesus? to the church? Did you feel that your gift was a part of you?

● How did your Sunday school group celebrate birthdays? Did this experience make you feel special? How did you feel about the attention others gave you on your birthday?

● Which of these early-life experiences helped make you feel safe and secure?

● What do you remember about the people you met during these early life spiritual experiences?

● Is there any particular teacher, attendant or helper you remember in a special way? Did you feel good or bad about your relationship with that person? Why?

● Is there any incident or teaching that stands out in relation to a particular person? Explain.

● Do you recall any special person who made you feel safe and secure within your spiritual experiences? What did he or she do to make you feel this way?

It is hoped that some of these questions will allow your young people to reexamine their feelings about their very-early spiritual experiences. By recalling specific incidents and individuals, young people can see more clearly whether their early spiritual experiences met the safety and security needs they had at that time.

After listening to your young people share about their early years, talk with them about their memories of spiritual experiences during their elementary-school years. Primary and intermediate Sunday school classes need to provide interesting projects that illustrate biblical values and principles. Children need to see themselves as capable of working toward and accomplishing goals. They need to affirm their abilities to be productive and successful in completing tasks. Ask questions that help your teenagers clarify their memories of these elementary-school years within the church.

- What are some of the specific spiritual experiences you recall from these years?
- Did these experiences relate to a certain project, a special activity or a new responsibility for you? Explain.
- Did the church stress any particular types of spiritual activities? Did you participate in or assist with holiday events like the Christmas pageant or the process of collecting and delivering food baskets during the Thanksgiving season? Explain your experiences. How did you feel about those activities?
- What biblical teachings do you remember being emphasized? How did you feel about those teachings? Did you understand them? Did you *believe* what others told you? Did you *question* what others told you? Did you *do* what others told you?
- Which of these activities and experiences made you feel most productive and successful? Why?
- What special people do you remember as being particularly significant during this time? a Sunday school teacher? a minister? a youth volunteer? a parent? another child?
- What specific memory do you have of this individual?
- What interested you about this person? Was he or she interested in you?
- If you liked this individual, did he or she offer you praise and encouragement? Did he or she offer you new opportunities or experiences for growth?
- If you disliked them, were they judgmental, always talking about sin and continuously fault-finding in other people? How did their negative input influence your life during this time?

Try to determine which people and which experiences had the most impact during these elementary-school years. Be sure to reaffirm your teenagers' spiritual experiences they see as productive and successful. Remember to point out their spiritual growth as they developed into more responsible Christian young people.

After examining both early childhood and elementary-school age religious experiences, talk with your teenagers about their memories of spiritual experiences at home. Again, ask specific questions that will help them recognize what actually happened.

● Did your parents emphasize and encourage spiritual experiences in your home?

● Did both parents support spiritual experiences? belief in God? belief in Jesus Christ? regular church attendance? Bible reading, either individually or as a family? prayer at mealtimes or within family meetings?

● What do you remember about holiday celebrations in your home? Did family traditions evidence any spiritual emphases that were unspoken at other times? How did you feel about these special experiences?

● Did your family include you, or did you participate in any significant events such as baptisms, weddings or funerals? How did your parents handle these experiences? Did they explain or discuss the spiritual significance of these events, or was discussion of these matters left to the spiritual leaders who ministered to the family?

● Were your parents' lives consistent with what they taught you?

Remember, these questions are merely guidelines to further your understanding of what your young people have experienced and how these experiences may have affected their spiritual lives.

Talking about what was taught and shared during those early times at church and in the home might also provide important insights into young people's current spiritual development. If adults and leaders emphasized God's knowledge of our sinful acts and the rendering of a harsh punishment, young people may develop a desperate need for righteousness, holiness and a view of God emphasizing justice with its rewards and punishments. If there was emphasis on God's love and acceptance, however, this type of spiritual teaching will help children accept God's grace. As these young people develop into adolescence and experience times of stress, they can learn to accept themselves and rely upon a power beyond their own.

Listen to your teenagers as they share their memories and strongest emotional impressions of their early years related to church and spiritual activity at home. In ideal situations worship and spiritual service are consistent aspects of children's preadolescence. When children see and experience worship, prayer and church attendance as a normal part of their lives, they learn to attach value to an active spiritual life. If, however, there is exposure to unhealthy theology or impaired role models, adolescents may rebel against the spiritual teachings and habits to which they were exposed. Children who have had negative or unhappy spiritual experiences may reject their religious beliefs and practices as a part of their adolescent rebellion. But experiences that help children apply spiritual truths to their own lives will have more staying power during the adolescent years.

Role models also affect teenagers' spiritual development. When role models stress God's judgment and conviction, teenagers find it difficult to trust spiritual relationships. Fear of continued judgment and rejection is just too threatening for them to risk this type of relationship again. However, when role models stress God's sustaining love and unconditional acceptance during childhood, adolescents can trust in God's love and continual presence as revealed in these significant individuals. Knowledge of young people's spiritual history will help you understand their current spiritual development.

The obvious individual differences between teenagers have many sources. Is it any wonder that no two are alike? Any accounting of why adolescents are the way they are must give ample consideration to *all* of the forces which shape teenagers' personalities.

■ CHAPTER 3

What Makes Teenagers Tick?

Sauntering down the school hall toward his locker, 16-year-old José looked quite impressive. His well-muscled body bulged against his T-shirt which was stuffed tightly into his worn jeans. Dirty tennis shoes completed his attire. His purposeful slow gait, expressionless face and glazed eyes spelled out the intended message, "Macho bravado. I'm in control here!"

A cool October breeze played in Charlotte's long blond hair as she went through her solo cheer. Being selected cheerleader for the varsity squad was just about the most important event that had occurred in her life. Carefully she had watched the experienced cheerleaders and then meticulously duplicated their movements. She practiced long summer hours with her best girlfriend. She even enticed her parents to enroll her in two cheerleading camps before school started. Tryouts were scheduled, she competed and her dream came true! Nothing else seemed as important during her sophomore year. Cheerleading became her central focus for school and her social life.

Howard is a brain. He talks, eats and sleeps science and math. Little else exists for him. Most of the kids at youth group ignore him. They would much rather go water-skiing on Saturday than spend the afternoon studying cellular structures with Howard and his high-powered microscope. As a small child, Howard found playground and sports-related activities just too frightening and humiliating. Awkward, slow and self-conscious about his body, Howard felt much more comfortable with his books, calculators, computers and assorted scientific paraphernalia. His world revolves around things more than people. Howard has discovered that things are much more predictable. And with fewer surprises, he experiences less pain.

Barbara's youth pastor had a difficult time telling her parents how she was getting along in the group. When asked, he struggled to recall specific observations and memories of her involvement. He knew she was usually there, but what did she do? How did she act? Which people did she sit with? "Well, she's a nice girl . . . uh . . . She never causes problems. She seems to get along with the other kids . . . At least she doesn't have any enemies. I think she listens during the lessons, but she really doesn't participate or ask questions. I guess she's rather shy. Now that you ask me, I think Barbara succeeds extremely well at being present and not being noticed."

Each of these young people exhibit different, yet fre-quently observed, styles of adapting to the stresses of adolescence. Their adjustments to life exhibit wide varieties of defense mechanisms, self-concepts and views of the world. The first two chapters examined the nature of adolescent development and the various external and internal factors which alter its direction. In this chapter we will discuss some of the psychological dynamics that occur within teenagers. So let's take a look at what makes teenagers tick.

■ *Drives, Needs and Wants*

Sigmund Freud believed that essentially all behavior results from certain drives and needs within us. Other psychological theorists have supported this idea. While Freud wrote that it was the sexual and aggressive instincts which drive our behavior, Carl Jung taught that a universal life drive, present within each of us, motivates our behavior. Otto Rank focused on the human need for autonomy (self-government) and independence. Harry Stack Sullivan emphasized his theory that interpersonal needs motivate our behavior. Erich Fromm suggested that our needs for belonging with others and the needs within us stimulate our action.

Psychologist Abraham Maslow provides us with another perspective on development and human behavior.[1] His widely accepted work on motivation tells us that our needs are arranged in the form of a hierarchy, with the most basic needs being met first. Then the other, less basic needs can be satisfied. Let's take a look at what has come to be known as Maslow's Hierarchy of Needs. (See Chart 4.)

When parenting or working with teenagers, we try to understand which level of need they are expressing through their behavior. Once the primary need is identified, then we can respond to individual young people in the most beneficial manner. Starting at the most basic level, let's look at each need and examine the adolescent behaviors that typify that need.

Physiological Needs. This category includes all of the basic bodily needs like food, sleep, sexual release and physical activity. Adolescents are growing very quickly. Teenage boys are particularly famous for their gargantuan appetites—consuming cartons of ice cream, loaves of bread, jars of peanut butter or a grill full of hamburgers at one sitting.

Teenagers in our culture have most of their basic physiological needs adequately met, except their need for sexual release. Teenagers, boys especially, encounter sig-

Chart 4
Maslow's Hierarchy of Needs

Spiritual
(A need to
rise above the
boundaries
of oneself)

**Knowledge/
Understanding**
(To value knowledge
for its own sake)

Self-Development
(Personal growth;
fulfilling one's potential)

Esteem
(Status and self-respect;
feeling adequate and worthwhile)

Love and Belonging
(Warmth and affection,
acceptance, approval and connection
with others)

Safety
(Protection from
bodily harm and security)

Physiological
(Most basic needs:
food, sleep, sexual release and physical activity)

nificant frustration because society and religion provide
laws, rules and codes for delaying sexual intercourse until
marriage. As these mores continue to break down, however, more and more teenagers are seeking sexual release
through genital intercourse earlier in adolescence. Youth
ministry is charged with finding increasingly effective
means to help young people understand and follow the
biblical principles regarding sexual expression prior to
marriage. Since it is not the purpose of this book to
present a detailed scriptural or psychological study of
adolescent sexuality, you are encouraged to read *Counseling Teenagers*, which studies this subject on a deeper
level.[2]

When physiological needs are not adequately met,
teenagers' energies, thoughts and actions are directed
toward attaining their fulfillment. Higher-level needs are
normally delayed until physiological needs are met. But
even when adolescents focus on higher-level needs, they
still express their physiological needs. For instance, the
needs for love and belonging may be met by going out for
dinner or talking about food with the family or loved
ones. While seeking spiritual fulfillment, a teenager's
prayer may contain references about either the need for
food or, as in the case of fasting, a deliberate effort to
purge the mind of food-related thoughts.

Safety Needs. This category includes the need for
protection from bodily harm and the need for security
from threat to one's life. Many teenagers, especially those
who live within large cities, need to assure themselves of
their safety. To deal with threats of physical harm, these
young people join gangs, arm themselves, travel only in
groups and stay away from rival turf. Even in small towns
and suburban areas, adolescent bravado is motivated by a
need for safety. "If I can make you think I'm tough, then
you won't mess with me!"

Some teenagers fear nuclear war. When the world is in
or near a crisis, these young people become distraught and
lose their ability to function at higher mental levels. They

find it difficult to concentrate on school work and become dependent upon those around them. Similar reactions are often seen when a series of local robberies, rapes or even car accidents is reported. These typical examples of disruption occur in the higher-level needs when adolescents' safety needs are threatened or deprived.

Love and Belonging Needs. This category includes the needs for acceptance, warmth, affection, approval and relationships with others. Because peer acceptance is extremely important to teenagers, a great amount of psychological energy is invested at this level of Maslow's Hierarchy. When belonging in the peer group or the family is threatened, most adolescents react with panic, depression, anxiety, aggression or withdrawal. When relationships are threatened, adolescents struggle to find meaning in any of their accomplishments or future plans. All else fades into insignificance until the relationship crisis is resolved. Often it is the establishment of a new relationship that brings release.

Esteem Needs. The important needs in this category are feeling adequate and worthwhile. Status and self-respect are also included in the esteem needs. When physiological and safety needs are satisfied and when teenagers feel loved, they are motivated to strive for social status. They establish belief in their own personal value as an honor student, athlete, class officer, cheerleader, driver of the fastest car or whatever social position they see as meaningful.

Self-Development Needs. This category concentrates on the need for personal growth and the movement toward fulfilling one's created potential. While the physical needs include physiological and safety needs; love, belonging and self-esteem are classified as interpersonal needs. When young people are having their physical and interpersonal needs met, they can give more attention and energy to meeting their higher-level personal needs.

At this level teenagers strive for high grades, election to class offices or excellent job performance, *not* to be noticed by others, but for their own personal satisfaction. Their efforts fulfill their need to test and expand their personal limits. It's all part of finding answers to the question, "Who am I?"

Knowledge and Understanding Needs. These needs include the quest for information, just for the value of knowing. Some teenagers read, learn computer language and investigate natural phenomena for the pure joy of expanding their knowledge and understanding. Adolescents who function at this level study what they enjoy regardless of whether it is assigned in class. Operating at this need level enables young people to move beyond themselves and further into God's creation.

Spiritual Needs. These needs transcend, or go beyond, the boundaries of the self. Religious activities and aesthetic experiences are common forms of expression in seeking fulfillment of spiritual needs. For Christians, the goal is to become more Christlike. We seek to transcend, with God's grace and power, the limits of our own egos and bodies. In his letter to the Ephesian church, Paul wrote:

> *It was he (Christ) who gave some to be apostles, some to be prophets, some to be evangelists, and some to be pastors and teachers, to prepare God's people for works of service, so that the body of Christ may be built up until we all reach unity in the faith and in the knowledge of the Son of God and become mature, attaining to the whole measure of the fullness of Christ (Ephesians 4:11-13).*

To suggest that teenagers (or for that matter, anyone!) cannot seek fulfillment of their spiritual needs unless all six lower needs were satisfied would be be a serious misunderstanding. However, spiritual growth is probably altered when these lower hierarchical needs are frustrated or unmet. For many, corporate worship becomes an exercise in belonging as much as an experience of focusing on God. Youth-led Bible studies may be motivated more by esteem needs than by a need for spiritual service. It is rare to find a teenager strongly motivated at the level of spiritual needs.

Nevertheless, there is a need to know, to be known by and to be affiliated with God. All people need to be involved in an intimate relationship with God. Parachurch youth ministries often reach unchurched high schoolers with the message that God loves them and wants to be involved in their lives. And many young people respond eagerly and positively because such a response meets their needs.

Several years ago at age 15, Charles made a personal commitment to Christ. He was the middle of three children. His older brother was a straight-A student and active in his high school's student government. And his younger sister was the girl his parents had always wanted. Charles was an above-average student, a below-average athlete and a shy, late bloomer in his social relationships.

Charles' parents loved him, but somehow their message didn't get through, at least very convincingly to him. As the result of a chronic depression, his mother was unhappy and frequently expressed her anger in uncontrolled outbursts. Her negative emotions plus a lack of interest in taking care of the home were confusing signals to him. Though Charles received little affection or attention from his dad, he had always believed that his father loved him. It's just that his father was generally passive and quiet.

Charles experienced conflict with his parents beginning in junior high. This conflict continued through adolescence and into early adulthood. In his early 20s, Charles finally realized that his decision to receive Christ when he was only 15 was strongly motivated by his need for a father figure and a need to belong. His Christian fellowship group fulfilled his unmet need for a family, and God provided the active, involved fatherly love Charles was unable to receive from his own dad.

The interaction between spiritual needs and other human needs is common. Jesus' ministry was to the *whole* person. He healed both body and spirit. He fed the thousands with both spiritual and physical food. The apostles were brought not only into an intimate relationship with Jesus, but also into a close and mutually supportive association with each other. God is the creator of our whole being. He understands our needs. He knows what is required for us to function at our optimum level. "And my God will meet all your needs according to his glorious riches in Christ Jesus" (Philippians 4:19).

To say Charles' need for Christ was related to his need for belonging in a group and his need for a father in no way lessens the importance of his spiritual need for salvation. Rather, the linking of his spiritual and interpersonal needs reveals the intricate design with which God created him. It confirms the interrelationship between our body and spirit. And it affirms God as Creator and Lord of all.

Some seek a sharp distinction between our drives, needs and wants. These classifications are useful, but they are difficult terms to define. Applying these concepts to adolescent behavior is even more of a problem, but the following explanations and examples should help.

Drives are understood as inherited requirements for maintaining life itself. Drives primarily refer to the biological requirements for food, water, air, sexual release and stimulation. When these drives are not adequately met, the person becomes increasingly tense, irrational and finally dies. These are often called "primary drives." Parents of teenage boys see the primary drive of hunger operating daily.

Fifteen-year-old Bill rushes home from school. He drops his books at the nearest clearing as his automatic pilot sets his most direct course toward the kitchen. Until he attacks the refrigerator and devours its contents, he says nothing other than, "What can I have to eat?" Once his tension level caused by his hunger drive is reduced, he can relax and focus elsewhere. He can then say "Hi" to his mom and maybe even pick up his books and take them to his room.

Needs are also referred to as "secondary drives." They include a wide variety of psychological, social and spiritual requirements necessary for a fulfilling and rewarding life. Examples include the needs for self-esteem, belonging, approval from others and relationship with God. When these needs are not adequately met, life loses much of its meaning and interest.

Jill is a 12-year-old junior higher. On the morning of her Wednesday counseling appointment, she didn't want to go to school. She resisted, but her mother prevailed. Throughout the day she appeared listless, uninvolved and depressed. During her afternoon appointment she finally shared the reason for her pain with her counselor.

Over the weekend all three of her girlfriends had turned against her. Apparently one of her friends became angry and began spreading negative rumors about her. For three days her group had ignored her, snubbing her during lunch, before and after school and between classes. Her needs for belonging, acceptance and approval were not being met. She could not experience any joy in life or concentrate on her school work, even though her "primary" drives were being satisfied.

Wants operate in a somewhat different fashion from drives and needs. While the latter two "drive" behavior, wants "pull" behavior. Wants are not vital to either the person's existence or his or her fulfillment in life. Teenagers are *driven* by hunger, but they may *want* a cheeseburger and french fries. They *need* interpersonal relationships, but they *want* relationships with specific peers. A young person may *need* a jacket, but advertisements may convince this teenager that the latest fashion she *wants* is actually her basic need. When wants are not fulfilled, teenagers sometimes act as if their drives or needs were not satisfied. They can become extremely depressed, excitable, anxious or intense about getting what they want, actually believing they need it. Parents and those who work with youth can help them differentiate their wants from their drives and needs.

The following diagram depicts the effect of drives, needs and wants on a young person's behavior.

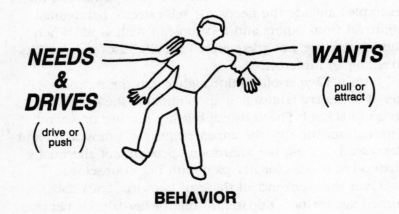

NEEDS & DRIVES

$\left(\begin{array}{c}\text{drive or}\\\text{push}\end{array}\right)$

WANTS

$\left(\begin{array}{c}\text{pull or}\\\text{attract}\end{array}\right)$

BEHAVIOR

Drives and needs "push" the teenager into action. Wants tend to "pull" or attract the young person into activity or toward a desirable goal or object.

■ Limits

The two stages during young people's development in which they encounter restrictive limits to their behavior are the toddler and the adolescent years. When children first learn to walk, they become more assertive in their speech and begin to proclaim their own will. At this point they encounter the verbal and physical restraints of their parents. They also learn to say no to themselves in an attempt to avoid painful consequences. Some of these unhappy consequences may result from parental action such as a loud, firm voice or a spanking. Other consequences may naturally follow the child's actions, for example, falling when trying to walk down the stairs or burning a hand when touching a hot stove.

Limits to what children want to do are also frequently encountered during adolescence. To successfully develop their own identity, teenagers must push away from their parents to see themselves as separate personalities. In their search and experimentation with new behaviors, interests and activities, young people encounter limitations established and enforced by their parents, school personnel, police and other authorities. The natural encounter between adolescents and authorities can be healthy and constructive or unhealthy and destructive.

Part of what determines the constructiveness or destructiveness of teenagers' confrontation with authority figures is how the adults handle their authority. When authority is handled positively, adolescents usually find a way of obeying without losing their dignity. Extreme or harsh authoritarian measures may require too much sacrifice of adolescents' autonomy and identification to comply with adults' demands. If the limits are inadequate or ineffectively enforced, however, adults do not provide teenagers with a sense of security. And young people will keep pushing against their limits until they find something or someone solid enough to depend on for stability.

Previous life experiences also affect how teenagers respond to limits determined by authority figures. Young people who have experienced their limits as friendly and helpful will accept them during adolescence more easily than those who have known strong frustration and discouragement. The decision not to rebel against authority is helped by the expectation that submission will bring positive results. Teenagers who have received positive affirmation and appreciation will find the encouragement to work with and not against authority figures. They will discover some of their identity through giving in and going along with authority figures as well as asserting against them.

Earning parents' trust by consistently following rules helps some young people attain more freedom and more relaxed limits. By allowing themselves to learn from adults, teenagers gain new skills which help them increase their confidence and personal esteem. In his letter to the Ephesian church, Paul reminds us, "Children, obey your parents in the Lord, for this is right. 'Honor your father and mother'— which is the first commandment with a promise— 'that it may go well with you and that you may enjoy long life on the earth' " (Ephesians 6:1-3).

The most challenging and difficult limits for teenagers to confront are their own personal limits. Since much of the adolescent task is to discover their own identity, teenagers must expand their capabilities, grow in their strengths and enlarge their realms of experience. Another equally important part of this task is discovering their personal limits. Young people need to know the extent of their strengths, persuasiveness, attractiveness, intelligence, spiritual sensitivity and skills. Adolescents will normally push to their limits, but they may experience depression, anger and some grief when they discover these limits. Adolescence is a period of great idealism and limitless possibilities. To find one's own limits is, at least symbolically, the first exposure to one's own death. Teenagers unconsciously resist an awareness of their limitations or death because they are still giving birth to their own identities.

During a recent discussion a local youth minister shared the story of twin boys in his youth group. He used this example to illustrate the trauma teenagers may experience when they confront their own limits. Robert and David were both juniors at the same high school. Both had been on the junior varsity track squad during their sophomore year, and both performed quite well in their events. Robert ran long-distance races, and David specialized in sprints and hurdles.

Both boys desperately wanted to be on the varsity squad during their junior year. Robert spent many long, hard hours during the summer, conditioning for the tryouts. He didn't know whether he would make the team, but he was determined to give his best effort. If he made the team, he would have the satisfaction of knowing he had earned his place. If he was sent back to junior varsity, he would still have the satisfaction of giving it his best.

David approached the situation quite differently. He worked out very little during the summer. His days were spent working part time at a fast-food restaurant, going to the beach and having a good time with his friends. On the surface it appeared he didn't desire a position as much as Robert. But he *did* want to be on the team. They differed in how they handled the stress of not knowing whether they were good enough for the varsity squad.

David hated the thought that he might fail and have to return to the junior varsity squad. To him, the humiliation and intense embarrassment of failure would be overwhelming. Focusing more on his performance than on his effort and spirit, he was afraid of what others might think. He also dreaded his own self-incrimination and personal rejection if he tried and failed. Therefore, he developed his own strategy. "If I try my best and fail, then I'll know I'm not good enough, that I'm a failure. If I don't try hard and then don't make the squad, I can think I would have been successful if I had worked hard."

Robert had sufficient self-acceptance to sustain his self-esteem even in the face of potential failure, but David felt too fragile to withstand such a blow to his ego. He had to leave a back door open. He set things up so he could rationalize his way out of possible embarrassment and self-rejection.

■ Pressures

In addition to recognizing personal limits, adolescence is also a stage when young people experience many strong pressures. As with limits, pressures come from the environment and from within the individual. We will examine two types of pressures.

The first and perhaps the most common pressure adolescents experience is the *pressure to conform*. The importance of the adolescent peer group as a socializing

force in teenagers' lives is well-documented. Acceptance,
belonging, esteem and, in some cases, protection are some
of the prizes sought by teenagers who conform to their
peer group's standards. Adolescents also feel significant
pressure to conform to the expectations of parents,
teachers and other adult authorities. Conforming to adults'
expectations brings approval, more privileges, more
independence and rewards in the forms of grades and
money.

Teenagers also place themselves under tremendous self-
imposed pressures. Even without direct action or instruction, these young people *perceive* pressures coming from
their peers or adults. And they pressure themselves to conform to those expectations to gain their anticipated
reward.

Fred recently celebrated his 16th birthday and succeeded in passing his drivers test last week. Knowing that
his parents reward responsibility with increased freedom,
Fred has conformed more than ever to their rules and
wishes. He has done his homework, arrived home on time
(even 15 minutes early!), completed his household chores
and taken part in family conversations. Why this miraculous transformation? Fred is pressuring himself to
conform to his parents' expectations in order to gain more
use of the family car.

The second type of pressure teenagers experience is
the *pressure to achieve*. Again, the origins of this pressure
are sometimes in the external environment and sometimes
within the individual. Teachers, administrators, parents and
even other adolescents create pressures for young people
to achieve at certain academic levels. Admission to certain
universities, eligibility to play sports, use of the car and
acceptance of valued peers are common rewards for
academic achievement.

The pressure to achieve relates to almost any area in
the lives of teenagers. Many young people respond to this
pressure by succeeding in athletics. Others seek to achieve
musically in choir, band or orchestra. Most try to earn

entrance into certain social groups.

Christian youth strive to accomplish spiritual goals and are encouraged to attain certain levels of righteousness. "But seek first his kingdom and his righteousness, and all these things will be given to you as well" (Matthew 6:33). Through commitment to Christ, many teenagers try to achieve the characteristics of the Holy Spirit. But righteousness is not something a person can achieve by his or her own efforts. It is a gift—a gift from God that offers rewards within its acceptance. For when a person actively seeks and accepts God's grace, he or she receives gifts that were not expected. Paul wrote to the Galatian church:

> . . . *the fruit of the Spirit is love, joy, peace, patience, kindness, goodness, faithfulness, gentleness and self-control. Against such things there is no law. Those who belong to Christ Jesus have crucified the sinful nature with its passions and desires. Since we live by the Spirit, let us keep in step with the Spirit (Galatians 5:22-25).*

■ How Limits and Pressures Block Drives, Needs and Wants

The following diagram indicates how limits and pressures block teenagers' drives, needs and wants.

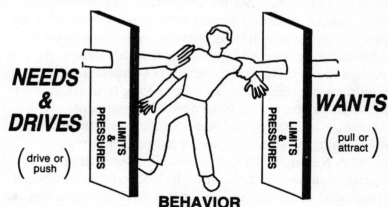

NEEDS & DRIVES
(drive or push)

LIMITS & PRESSURES

LIMITS & PRESSURES

WANTS
(pull or attract)

BEHAVIOR

Limits can completely or partially block the effect of *drives and needs* as "pushers" or drivers of behavior. For example, the hunger drive which causes the teenager to eat can be blocked by a lack of money. The pressure obese adolescents feel for peer acceptance often causes them to deny their hunger drive. The need for peer approval for staying out late is sometimes blocked by parents' curfew limits. A father's pressure on his child to achieve in sports may block his or her need to achieve in academics. In each of these examples, the limits and pressures completely stop, delay or alter the behavior that the drive or need would normally cause or "push" to happen.

Limits and pressures can also completely stop, delay or alter behaviors that are otherwise stimulated or "pulled" by teenagers' *wants*. Although Jim *wants* to ask Kelly out to dinner, not having a car seriously limits his dating opportunities. In addition, his desire for excellence in his studies (or his *want* for academic success) causes him to date less often. Again, the limits and pressures of no car and a need to study have blocked the relationship Jim *wants* to have with Kelly.

When drives, needs and wants are blocked by limits and pressures, emotional reactions such as frustration and anxiety can result. Anxiety most often occurs when teenagers' *drives and needs* are blocked. This anxiety is a reaction to the threat that life needs or other centrally important needs may not be adequately met. Anger and depression are common experiences when *wants* are completely or partially withheld. Anxiety is felt less often in these situations because life itself is not threatened. Adolescents are likely to feel angry when prevented from obtaining what they want. Strong or long-term frustration may result in feelings of bitterness or resentment.

Feelings of anxiety and anger cause much disruption within young people. To guard against feeling overwhelmed, teenagers, like children and adults, develop elaborate defense mechanisms. The collective experiences of frustrated drives, needs and wants have dramatic impact

on teenagers' self-concepts, their concepts of God and
their views of the world.

■ Defense Mechanisms

From the time Adam and Eve first sinned against God,
defending the self has had high priority in human behavior. Genesis describes the first defense mechanisms
used:

> *Then the eyes of both of them were opened,*
> *and they realized they were naked; so they*
> *sewed fig leaves together and made coverings*
> *for themselves.*
> *Then the man and his wife heard the*
> *sound of the Lord God as he was walking in*
> *the garden in the cool of the day, and they*
> *hid from the Lord God among the trees of the*
> *garden. But the Lord God called to the man,*
> *"Where are you?"*
> *He answered, "I heard you in the garden,*
> *and I was afraid because I was naked; so I*
> *hid."*
> *And he said, "Who told you that you were*
> *naked? Have you eaten from the tree that I*
> *commanded you not to eat from?"*
> *The man said, "The woman you put here*
> *with me—she gave me some fruit from the*
> *tree, and I ate it."*
> *Then the Lord God said to the woman,*
> *"What is this you have done?"*
> *The woman said, "The serpent deceived*
> *me, and I ate" (Genesis 3:7-13).*

Adam and Eve's defenses were quite elementary. First,
to protect their self-consciousness from each other's gaze,
they sewed fig leaves together. Then they hid from God
by crouching behind bushes. Their level of sophistication

quickly increased when God confronted them with their sin. Instead of accepting full responsibility for his actions and choices, Adam projected partial blame onto Eve for giving him the fruit. Eve must have thought Adam sounded extremely clever, for she responded with, "The serpent deceived me, and I ate."

Today's teenagers use defense mechanisms similar to those used by Adam and Eve.

● Defense mechanisms are designed to conceal selected details of the self.

● Defense mechanisms protect young people from feeling overexposed and self-conscious.

● Defense mechanisms protect individuals from internal conflict and feelings of anxiety and guilt.

● There are elements of truth within a defense mechanism which make it believable both to the teenager using it and to others with whom he or she comes in contact.

● In defense mechanisms there are elements of truth omitted or exaggerated beyond recognition.

● Defense mechanisms operate in either a partially conscious or totally unconscious manner.

In order to survive today's world, teenagers must make some use of their psychological defense mechanisms. Adolescents who do not have adequate mechanisms for defending themselves do not fare well. They suffer from extreme anxiety, guilt and inadequacy. They need help in building more effective methods for defending themselves.

Many young people depend much too heavily on their use of defense mechanisms. Excessive reliance on these defenses separates young people from the truth. Their perception of reality blurs and becomes distorted. Their behavior relates more to their defense needs than to reality.[3]

We will now define and look at examples of the psychological defense mechanisms commonly used by contemporary adolescents. Think of how each is used by teenagers in your home or youth group.

Acting out. Some teenagers release their anxieties and tensions more through active behavior than through talking and problem-solving. The behavior is often impulsive and frequently destructive.

Example: Seventeen-year-old Joseph is so frustrated with the lack of communication with his parents that he runs out of the house, jumps in his car and drives at high speeds to release his tensions. He endangers his life and the lives of others by his careless action.

Compartmentalization. Sometimes young people unconsciously operate with two different standards in two separate areas of their lives.

Example: Billy is 12 years old. On his paper route he regularly lies to make collections easier and to balance his account with the paper company. Billy is an active member of his Sunday school and his junior high church youth group. He fully agrees with the commandment not to lie; however, he never makes the connection between the way he handles his paper route and his moral and religious beliefs about telling the truth.

Compensation. When teenagers discover areas of inferiority within themselves, they seek to excel in areas of greater strength. With added focus on their area of strength, they become less aware of personal characteristics they see as inferior.

Example: Bruce is unable to earn good grades in his academic classes. But he has attained a reputation with his friends as being capable of fixing almost anything on their cars. His nickname? "Mr. Goodwrench!"

Overcompensation. These teenagers make an intense effort to improve or strengthen an area of known weakness or inadequacy.

Example: Eighteen-year-old Margaret is from a poor family who provided her with little training about how to act in social situations. Margaret overcompensates for her earlier social awkwardness by studying every book she can find on etiquette and social graces. She intends to major in home economics when she goes to college.

Compulsion. Adolescents sometimes feel a driving need to repeat certain behaviors or specific movements.

They experience an overpowering internal force to dupli-
cate the movement in just the right manner or the correct
number of times. Often this compulsion takes the form of
repeatedly "doing and undoing" an action, like locking
and unlocking a door numerous times. Unconsciously, this
compulsion is intended to protect the individual from
strong anxiety or panic reactions. Usually some symbolic
or logical association exists between the nature of the
compulsion and the content of what causes the rising level
of anxiety.

Example: Melanie, a 14-year-old freshman, became excessively conscious of germs when her younger brother
had a serious case of chicken pox. She began washing her
hands repeatedly, especially prior to each meal. She also
developed a curious habit of periodically exhaling with
force several times in sequence. Melanie was afraid she
might become ill and compulsively washed her hands to
protect herself from germs. Her forceful exhalations were
an attempt to rid her lungs of any contamination.

Denial of reality. Teenagers sometimes find certain
realities, thoughts, feelings, experiences and memories too
anxiety-producing. To protect themselves from an anxiety
overload, some refuse to accept the threatening thought or
feeling into their consciousness.

Example: Fifteen-year-old Tara learned that one of her
best girlfriends was killed the night before in a serious automobile accident.

"No! That can't be true. We talked on the phone just
last night. She can't be dead. I don't believe it!"

Displacement. Adolescents may experience a strong
emotional reaction toward someone who is threatening or
intimidating. Rather than risk further negative response
from that individual, their intense emotion is directed
toward a less-threatening person or object.

Example: Eva survived a rather harsh confrontation
with her swimming coach. Hurt and angry, she believed
the punishment she received was totally undeserved. Too
fearful to tell her coach how she felt, Eva unconsciously

redirected her anger at her little sister when she got home from practice.

Emotional insulation. This defense mechanism acts as an unconscious barrier to screen out or protect persons from severe anxiety. It reduces the intensity of a potentially damaging emotion.

Example: Vanessa competed in the county junior high spelling meet. She had her heart set on winning but failed to place even among the top five contestants. Her friends and family were amazed when she reported experiencing almost no pain or disappointment.

Fantasy. Adolescents normally experience an active fantasy life. When teenagers prefer fantasy to reality or when their fantasies detract from their ability to deal with reality, their fantasies become defense mechanisms.

Example: Sixteen-year-old Darrell is emotionally and socially immature. His awkward efforts to develop relationships with girls attract nothing more than their rejection. Rather than continue to develop better social skills, he now fantasizes that popular girls are irresistibly attracted to him.

Hypochondria. Belief in a real illness or the exaggeration of an illness requires a great amount of attention for apparent physical symptoms. This focus on illness helps adolescents avoid something more anxiety-producing or threatening.

Example: Because Beverly's father is in the military, her family has moved nine times during her 14 years. Beverly has had to face many new schools and classrooms. Being the "new kid" has caused her much anxiety, especially since she became an adolescent. As she dreaded her first day at yet another new school, she developed stomach cramps, nausea, diarrhea and dizziness, all apparent symptoms of the flu.

Ideas of reference. Some sensitive teenagers perceive others' laughter, jokes, gestures, facial expressions and quiet talking as directly related to them. Troubled individuals sometimes apply a personal reference to unrelated events that occur around them.

Example: Bobby knows he is not a good athlete. When he sees other kids in gym class talking quietly or laughing, he thinks they are talking about or laughing at him.

Intellectualization. Some young people avoid emotional pain by "thinking around the pain." They bypass their emotions by processing these difficult experiences in a completely intellectual manner.

Example: Seventeen-year-old Carlos just learned that his parents are getting a divorce. His concerned youth pastor asks how he is handling this difficult jolt. Carlos responds: "I'm just glad God is still on the throne. I know nothing happens that God doesn't know about. He is teaching me and stretching me through this experience, and I'll become stronger through it all. I'll probably be better able to help others in this kind of situation after I've gone through it myself."

Projection. With this defense mechanism, young people attribute to others the impulses, thoughts, feelings, attitudes and values they see within themselves, but reject as being too negative. Unable to accept these attributes as their own, they redirect their self-rejection onto the other person.

Example: Wanda becomes extremely irritated at anyone who exhibits jealousy. She is sarcastic, critical and openly hostile toward acquaintances who give the slightest indication of being jealous. Wanda is completely unaware of her own strong jealousies.

Rationalization. Many young people seek to become more comfortable with themselves and their behaviors by making excuses and explaining away any criticisms.

Example: "It was really good that I tried marijuana. After all, how could I witness effectively to drug users if I had never gotten high?"

Reaction formation. Young people afraid of certain impulses or feelings can prevent their awareness of those feelings by exhibiting exaggerated and intense behaviors that are directly opposite of those being rejected.

Example: Oscar is known as the friendliest and nicest boy on campus. But there is an uneasiness about his many thoughtful gestures. That's because they aren't real! Oscar is actually an angry young man with much repressed hostility. His excessively kind behavior serves as a guard against any exposure of his inner rage of which he is so fearful.

Regression. Adolescents sometimes withdraw from anxiety-producing situations by retreating to an earlier developmental period that was more comfortable and less demanding.

Example: Fifteen-year-old Tina demanded her freedom to date her 23-year-old boyfriend. However, when he invited her on a week-long vacation just with him, she became frightened. She became whiney, dependent, and increasingly demanding of attention and advice from her mother and father. She wanted her parents to protect her again by forbidding her to go.

Repression. This classic defense mechanism operates without the person's awareness of what is happening. Dangerous or anxiety-producing thoughts, feelings, attitudes, impulses and memories are forced into the unconscious. While in the unconscious, these elements still impact the person's thoughts, feelings and behaviors. However, since the whole process is unconscious, the individual doesn't know why he or she has those thoughts and feelings or why the behavior occurs.

Example: Wilma, age 19, struggles with strong homosexual fantasies and temptations. She doesn't remember her childhood experiences of being repeatedly sexually molested by her uncle. Those repressed memories unconsciously motivate her to avoid intimacy with men because she considers all of them dangerous.

Somatization. Internal conflicts and repressed feelings create intense stress. This stress sometimes causes breakdowns in the body organs and systems. When this occurs, physical symptoms develop. The term "psychosomatic disorder" is often used to refer to this type of problem.

A psychological problem is "somatized" or expressed through physical symptoms.

Example: Jerry is a bright and articulate debater. He wins many of his competitions and seldom has a poor performance. Prior to each event, however, he suffers for several days from severe gastric upset. Heartburn, stomach pain, cramps and diarrhea are common symptoms. If this pattern continues, Jerry may develop a serious ulcer.

Sublimation. Mental and physical energies are transferred from unacceptable feelings or unsuccessful efforts into other personally and socially acceptable desires and behaviors. Often this healthy defense mechanism can help teenagers function well in difficult situations.

Example: Perry had great success as a baseball pitcher until his junior year when he developed an arthritic elbow. No longer able to pitch, he redirected his efforts into coaching. Now he depends on his years of training and experience to help his teammates.

Suppression. This is another psychological defense which can be used in a healthy manner. It involves a conscious or semiconscious choice to delay action or put an issue "on hold" for a period of time.

Example: Vera just heard that her boyfriend has been dating one of her best friends. She is hurt and angry, but, she is presently studying for a college entrance exam which may determine her eligibility for certain universities. She decides to study now and deal with her troubled emotions and wandering boyfriend later.

Withdrawal. This is pure escape. It involves either physical or psychological movement away from an anxiety-producing situation.

Example: Melvin, a junior in high school, is failing. He feels no hope of making it to graduation. Often he is late for class. Sometimes he just doesn't show up. Even when he attends class, Melvin sits in the back of the room, slouched out of the teacher's view and daydreams about being somewhere else.

Psychological defense mechanisms are learned primarily

as a result of anxieties and frustrations that occur when a young person's drives, needs and wants are blocked by limits and pressures. Different teenagers develop their own styles of defense. The unique defenses they develop evolve partially from their own personality characteristics. Therefore, the defenses themselves impact the formation of adolescents' continuing personality development. The following diagram illustrates this reciprocal process.

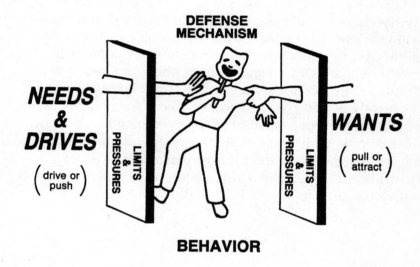

For a more thorough examination of defense mechanisms, see *Counseling Teenagers*.[4]

This chapter opened the door to understanding the internal world of teenagers. We examined how their needs, drives and wants provide motivation for what they do. We noted the strong impact that limits and pressures have on adolescents' behavior. And we also saw how young people develop defense mechanisms to handle the tensions and anxieties that occur when their needs, drives, and wants are frustrated by their limits and pressures. Examining the particular styles of defense teenagers use will also help us determine adolescents' personality types.

In summary, the first three chapters of this book introduced the fascinating study of *how personalities develop*. Our study of the eight personality types in Part 2 will reveal eight distinct responses to the complex array of forces and interactions to which teenagers are exposed. These eight personality types represent different styles of identity formation, ways of viewing the world, patterns of social interaction and structures for defending against anxiety and pain.

Remember, adolescence is a time of dramatic personality development. Therefore, many, if not most, teenagers will pass through several of these personality orientations as they grow through their adolescent years. Some will evidence aspects of several types at one point within their development. Be careful not to categorize teenagers too concretely as one type or another. Allow for richness in young people's personalities as they combine two or more orientations. With astute observation and educated listening, you will identify the primary personality style of particular adolescents and also see the variations within individual teenagers.

■ PART TWO:

Personality Types:

How to Identify and Work With Different Types of Adolescents

Introduction

*T*he members of the small support group listened intently to the young teacher as she described her unforgettable moment:

> *Most of the teachers in our building knew Kevin as volatile and stubborn. This young boy struggled for everything he wanted to achieve and rejected anything he couldn't master. His intense frustration pushed others away no matter how hard they tried to get close. His tense body and hostile temper were barriers to any kind of warmth others tried to share.*
>
> *Kevin's reaction to the visiting puppies took me totally by surprise. As I watched him kiss each glistening head, I marveled at how his shoulders had relaxed. Seating himself on the floor, he soon surrounded himself with the tiny balls of fur and was talking to each one as though it were a special friend.*
>
> *One look at my teaching partner, and I knew I wasn't alone in my surprise reaction to Kevin's behavior. The angry and aggressive*

preadolescent we knew had evolved into a
tender and caring child that stayed with us
for almost a week. After the puppies' visit we
got a glimpse of Kevin's sensitivity every once
in a while.

All of us develop our personality patterns as a way to handle the anxiety or stress we experience in our interactions with others. Some of us may vary our patterns a lot during our lifetime, especially during adolescence. Others may change very little. Generally, we are composites of several personality types, with one type dominating the others. It is rare to find anyone who operates in one personality style all the time for all of his or her life.

The obvious and unexpected change in Kevin's behavior illustrates how fallible our observations can be when we work with adolescents on a limited basis. Parents can also have moments of surprise. They may marvel when their normally abrasive teenager reaches out in tenderness to support a struggling brother or sister. And they are totally shocked when their responsible adolescent suddenly skips school for a day.

It is virtually impossible to judge or rate personality types as good or bad, right or wrong. Numerous factors influence our personality types. Since our culture values affection and dominance, we develop many responsible and power-oriented individuals. Hostile personality patterns operate quite well during war, but these aggressive characteristics cannot function effectively within a peaceful environment. In today's fast-paced world, flexibility in personality structure seems to be the key.

In Part One we explored the numerous factors that influence our individual personalities. In Part Two we will examine eight different personality types commonly found in adolescence. These eight types are not random ideas, but are based on research in developmental psychology,[1] using the Interpersonal Check List.[2] The eight personality types discussed in this book are the following:

Power-Oriented Personality
Competitive Personality
Aggressive Personality
Rebellious Personality
Self-Demeaning Personality
Dependent Personality
Conforming Personality
Responsible Personality

The Interpersonal Check List Profile (Chart 5) will help you understand how these eight personality types relate to each other.[3]

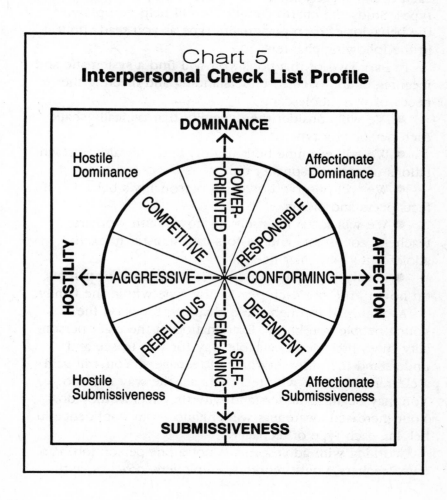

Each personality is positioned on a grid created by two scales. The vertical scale measures the degree of Dominance (top of scale) and Submissiveness (bottom of scale). The horizontal scale measures the degree of Hostility (left side of scale) and Affection (right side of scale). When these two scales intersect each other, they create four quadrants. Each quadrant reflects the dominant style of personal interaction for the personality types within that quadrant.

The grid is further subdivided into eight parts, with each octant representing one of the eight personality types. Study the chart carefully. It will help you picture the behavior of each personality type as you read about it in the following chapters.

In Part Two of this book you will find a systematic and meaningful approach to understanding and meeting the needs of your adolescents.

● We will consider the dynamics that typically shape each personality type.

● We will examine both healthy and unhealthy presentations of each personality type.

● We will observe how each personality's behavior affects peers and others.

● We will focus intensely on how youth workers, teachers, counselors and pastors can minister to each adolescent's particular needs.

● Finally, we will offer specific guidelines for parents on how to nurture each personality type within the family.

As you read through these chapters, focus on the young people you know. Examination of the eight personality types provides a valuable way for you to see and understand the different kinds of teenagers. You will gain a clearer picture of why teenagers act the way they do. You may begin to understand why they feel as they do. Your increased awareness will enhance your confidence in helping each type of teenager.

Working with adolescents is not a one-person job. Parents, teachers, youth workers, employers, coaches, and other adults need to work together to minister effectively to teenagers. When we work as a team to help young people develop healthy expressions of their personalities, we create a supportive environment not only for the teenagers involved, but for ourselves. Read both sets of guidelines so you may help each other as you work with the different adolescent personalities. This material is meant to be a resource for you in whatever relationships you have to teenagers.

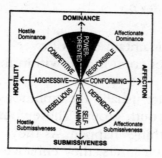

■CHAPTER 4

The Power-Oriented Personality

*T*eenagers who develop a power-oriented personality often appear to others as strong, confident and secure. Peers look up to them as "having it all together." Adults view these young people as surprisingly mature for their age. But upon closer evaluation, we find these adolescents have developed a defense system that merely gives the appearance of well-integrated strength. There is no denying the varying degrees of strength within these young people, but what they present to others is their "display" of strength.

Power-oriented teenagers are most comfortable when they feel strong and self-reliant. Although these young people are influenced by both affectionate and hostile characteristics, they are most concerned with dominance. They *need* to see themselves in control of their lives. They want the capacity to predict what will happen to them. Therefore, these young people do not welcome surprises. Even surprise birthday parties threaten power-oriented teenagers because of their loss of control. Young people with this personality type *must* maintain control over other people and activities to feel comfortable within their environment.

Power-oriented adolescents are usually the ambitious, goal-directed members of their youth group. These young people are the ones who make things happen. As they progress and successfully test their limits, they enhance their self-esteem. Ambition keeps them moving toward higher goals, and attaining those goals reinforces their feelings of personal worth and value. They also closely associate their importance as human beings with their performance and success.

■ *Development of the Power-Oriented Personality*

The use of power is an issue for all teenagers. It is a natural part of identity formation, the crucial developmental task of adolescents. Experiencing personal power by making their own choices or decisions contributes to young peoples' successful individuation (separation) from their parents. Without increasing self-control, teenagers do not mature. Without movement from dependency to active choices in life, adolescents do not grow into adulthood. Several factors can influence development of the power-oriented personality type.

First, most power-oriented defenses require high energy output. Therefore, good physical health and stamina are essential for sustaining this defense. Without proper nutrition, adequate rest and sufficient exercise, these adolescents have difficulty maintaining their strong power-related defenses.

Second, young people receive many forms of reinforcement for using power to enhance their self-esteem. Some gain outstanding grades and other academic honors for their ambitious study in schedules filled with college preparatory courses. Others attain popular acclaim, peer respect and special privileges as payoffs for their election to student government or offices within their class and youth group. Athletic achievements provide powerful respect and numerous honors to even more young people. Some adolescents' ambitious efforts in business may be reinforced by financial gain. The rewards for power are numerous and influential.

Third, teenagers are strongly affected by important adults in their lives. Parents provide the most powerful role models. For example, fathers and mothers who value achievement in their own lives often produce children who adopt that value as well. Other authority figures also impact teenagers who develop this power-oriented defense structure. Teachers, youth pastors, adult relatives and adult friends may model behaviors which affect teenagers' development. When these respected adults model power-oriented defense mechanisms, young people tend to imitate those same behaviors.

Fourth, many teenagers have experienced psychological and even physical pain and injury when they were not in control. Some young people have suffered from severe parenting throughout their childhood. Parents who struggle with alcohol, certain character disorders and abusive tendencies sometimes discipline their children so severely that they insure psychological injury. Harsh physical discipline, parental neglect, excessive roughness and mean or vicious teasing can lead to physical injury for the child. Experience assures us that physical injury is *always* accompanied by psychological damage. For these children, the inability to control their environment has had brutally painful and damaging results. They have learned a hard lesson by placing themselves under another's care or control. For these teenagers, *not* to be strong and powerful means to leave themselves vulnerable to danger, even from those people who say they love and care for them.

Many teenagers have created very painful situations for themselves by responding to an impulse during a lapse in self-control. While intoxicated or high on drugs, some have had car accidents or committed sexual or violent acts. Many pregnancies result from such incidents. Power-oriented adolescents develop their defense system as a direct result of experiencing pain, discomfort or injury during times when they were not in control. These teenagers believe self-control and control of their environment are *essential* for their security.

Fifth, some teenagers must develop strong determination, overpowering drive and inner stamina to survive and break away from parents who exercise excessive control. In some homes absolute compliance and obedience are required in virtually every detail of behavior. Some overprotective parents block every effort their children make to grow up. As a result, they discourage their children and teach them self-doubt. Deep feelings of guilt, burning resentment and intense anger result from these types of childhood experiences. If they are to succeed in life, these young people have to develop great resources of internal strength and courage to break these restrictive bonds. Personal power is the only way adolescents can break free to be their own person.

Certainly, there are more variables that can contribute to the development of power as a defense system. However, most teenagers who exhibit this personality type have been strongly influenced by one or more of these five contributing factors.

■ Healthy Forms of the Power-Oriented Personality

Teenagers who develop a controlled and balanced use of power usually succeed quite well as adolescents. Our society values and reinforces use of strength. Those who handle power in positive, constructive ways receive great esteem. Adolescents may find several positive expressions for their power-oriented defense systems.

The Leader. Leadership positions provide natural, constructive outlets for this type of adolescent. Phillip is a good example of how a power-oriented teenager can express his defensive style in a constructive leadership pattern. The oldest of four children, Phillip grew up in a loving, moderately strict home. His parents insisted on responsibility, honesty and adherence to other traditional values. Each child was responsible for certain required chores on a regular basis. School grades were important, though academic excellence was not stressed. The parents often told their children, "We just expect you to do your best." Not knowing exactly what his best was, Phillip grew up with the idea he probably could do better in most everything he tried.

As most oldest children do, Phillip tried eagerly to please his parents. Since traditional values were important in his household, he accepted them as his own. Phillip ordered his life around responsibility, integrity and strength. He absorbed and expressed the Christian values of helpfulness, generosity and care for others. He felt much better about himself when he was strong, useful and in control.

During junior high he began running for student body offices. He won the majority of his elections from that time through his senior year. Although campaigning for office made him uncomfortable, he did enjoy fulfilling the requirements for the job once he had won.

Phillip's church youth group provided another place for him to utilize his leadership gifts. He attended a small church where only a few people possessed real leadership qualities. Recognizing his gifts, the adults always chose Phillip when they needed youth group representation on their committees.

By Phillip's junior year in high school, he realized he felt best about himself when he was operating in some leadership capacity. He felt more confident when he was in control. Phillip recognized his discomfort around new people his own age, but he also felt uneasy in any unstructured group of his friends. With no leadership role to dictate his behavior, he didn't quite know how to act or what to say. He withdrew from close friendships and usually declined party invitations unless he had some prescribed role to fill.

Phillip depended more and more upon a leadership position for his feelings of self-esteem. Since his effectiveness in that role brought sufficient praise and respect, he seldom experienced any insecurity or self-doubt at a conscious level. For only brief moments did Phillip actually question whether people liked him for *who* he was. At these times of sensitivity he felt most people valued him only for what he could do for them. In response to those painful instances of loneliness and alienation, he quickly re-entered his leadership pattern where once again he regained a sense of self-value.

The Brain. Some power-oriented teenagers are not as concerned with the power of leadership. These young people just want to feel safe within themselves. If they can control their own world adequately, they can feel secure. That sense of security usually requires these power-oriented adolescents to maintain emotional distance from their peers. Stephanie's case gives us a clear picture of this expression of the power-oriented personality. Stephanie is a "brain."

Stephanie is the second of four children. She has an older brother who excels in athletics, a real star on the playing field. Her younger brother and sister are still in elementary school. The younger children are average academic students and are active in play and the organized activities normal for that age.

School has always been easy for Stephanie. As a child, she learned to read and write earlier than most children. Although she works hard at her studies, she believes in her natural ability to consistently earn straight A's. Teachers continuously praise her classroom behavior, making Stephanie and "teacher's pet" synonymous terms within her peer group.

As she progressed through junior high, Stephanie relied increasingly on her intelligence as the basis for her self-concept. Her self-esteem during high school depended almost entirely upon her continuing ability to perform academically. However, because she concentrated so hard on only one area of her life, problems appeared during her sophomore year. She began avoiding friends, parties and other social gatherings.

"I'd really like to go skating with you, but I've got to study for my chemistry exam tonight."

"I'd love to see that movie, too, but I have a French project due next week."

"Jill's birthday party sounds like a lot of fun, but I'm a little behind in algebra."

Stephanie withdrew more and more from her friends. Her studies replaced her social life. Now in her second year of high school, she feels too socially insecure to accept invitations to join her peers, and she is invited less often.

Stephanie created her own sphere of comfort. Greatly reinforced for her academic performance as a child, she made that the focus of her identity. But she went too far. By concentrating her energies on academics, she withdrew from the uncertainties of the interpersonal world of relationships.

Stephanie felt very competent and in control of her academic world. She knew what to expect. She could predict the outcome and had some control over her future as long as she focused on academics. If she studied diligently, she got A's. It was that simple.

But Stephanie didn't have that kind of control in her social environment. When she entered her social world, she was unsure of herself and others. She could not accurately predict what would happen and felt little control over her future. Several times during junior high, her friends shunned her. Like all kids her age, she went through some painful interpersonal experiences. To avoid that pain and anxiety, Stephanie retreated into her academic world where she had far more control.

At school, at home and at church, Stephanie was driven from within to be the best she could be. When asked about her greatest ambition, her immediate reply was, "I always want to be the best I can be at whatever I do." Stephanie's self-esteem and identity were balanced upon her personal evaluation of her performance in all areas of her life.

Phillip and Stephanie represent two patterns of the healthy power-oriented personality type. "Leaders" like Phillip seek personal comfort through having control over both themselves and others. "Brains" like Stephanie avoid anxiety by focusing on their own ambition and ability while avoiding the less predictable world of social interaction. As long as these patterns remain moderate and under control, they can be quite healthy.

■ Unhealthy Forms of the Power-Oriented Personality

When teenagers use their power-oriented defenses excessively, they lose the positive benefits of security for which their defense mechanisms have worked. Their behavior becomes unhealthy, and their interpersonal relationships suffer. Their attitudes, behaviors and perceptions of others become rigid and unyielding. As the pattern continues, these young people begin to lose touch with the reality of their world. Stephanie is a good example of someone whose increasing rigidity was slowly leading her to a poor adaptation within her adolescent world.

In this section we will examine two more case studies. Both of these teenagers also have power-oriented personalities, but these examples represent unhealthy extremes of this personality type.

The Dictator. As a young child, Cynthia was repeatedly teased and tormented by her two older brothers and their friends. She felt terribly alone and outnumbered. She had few opportunities to play with other children since in her neighborhood there was only one other small child, a little girl two years younger than Cynthia. Both of her parents worked full time, and there was little time to relax together as a family. Her parents accomplished most of the shopping, errands and other household chores on the weekends, leaving Cynthia to again defend herself from her brothers and their friends.

Cynthia learned early she had to be responsible for her own life and well-being. She also learned that when she was not in control of her life and those around her, she was vulnerable. For her, being vulnerable meant getting hurt and being helplessly angry.

Cynthia took what she learned to school. In each class she was confronted with 25 to 30 people who might take advantage of her. She started each school year restricting her friendships to only those children who allowed her to control the relationship. This pattern continued through-out junior high and into high school. Although she was reasonably well-liked and respected, most girls couldn't get close to her. Those who did soon found that everything had to go her way, which wasn't always negative. Cynthia had good ideas. She knew how to have fun, and she did nice things for her friends. It's just that she always had to maintain control.

Since her last year of junior high and now during high school, Cynthia's home life is turbulent. One of her broth-ers has moved out. Her remaining brother and both of her parents resent her efforts to control things at home. Tre-mendous power struggles have developed. Raised voices and flaring tempers reflect the tension. Her parents wonder if she will ever learn how to compromise and work with other people.

Cynthia experiences similar problems at church. She responds well to the thought of serving others. But she interprets being a servant similar to the way a dominant, authoritarian man interprets what it means to be "head of the household." For Cynthia, serving means to chair a committee, direct a project, lead a group or teach a class. Her interpretation of serving always incorporates being in charge of what is happening.

Cynthia's rigid demand for control increasingly limits her interpersonal effectiveness and fulfillment. She doesn't allow people close to her to grow and mature in their own ability to take care of themselves. She feels an immediate threat, insecurity and fear when others try to lead with their thoughts or actions. To dispel her anxiety, she automatically seeks to regain control of the situation.

The "dictator" is obviously an extreme of the "leader." There is rarely ill intent within the heart of the "dictator." Behavior like Cynthia's is motivated more by fear, pain, anxiety and sometimes anger. This young person's intensity rises merely as an attempt to protect his or her own sense of security.

The Perfectionist. Vincent was born in the United States just a few years after his parents immigrated from an Asian country. They live in an ethnic neighborhood in a West Coast city. His father is an engineer, and his mother owns and manages a small restaurant.

Vincent's parents sought counseling for him when he developed severe obsessions about germs and the persistent fear that he had lost his salvation. He also engaged in compulsive hand washing and other useless repetitive actions. His counselor began working with him during the last semester of his senior year.

Raised in a tightly structured, well-ordered home, Vincent had no brothers or sisters. The dominant parent was his mother, though both parents loved him very much. Vincent had been an easy child to raise. He obeyed his parents, required little correction and completed his chores with minimum reminding. Vincent continued to be a conscientious, successful student. In his church youth group Vincent emerged as a leader, willing to give much of his time and energy to that ministry. Throughout his adolescence he has shown few signs of outward rebellion. Family friends have always considered his parents fortunate to be raising such a fine son.

Early in life Vincent learned how to get his parents' and other adults' approval. He learned to give them what he thought they wanted from him. He offered academic excellence, proper manners, correct behavior and acceptance of responsibility as continual insurance for approval and praise from the significant adults in his life.

During his elementary school years Vincent committed his life to Christ. Since that time, he has dedicated himself to being a Christian. He sought God's approval in the same way he has gained approval from other authority figures. Hard work and diligent efforts served Vincent well until his last semester of high school when he began caving in from the weight of his own demand for personal perfection.

Being perfect was the only way Vincent could accept himself. Perfection was the one way he could gain visible, tangible proof of parental approval and God's acceptance. This concern about God's acceptance, mixed with a deep sense of personal guilt, caused his defense system to crack.

One special relationship contributed significantly to Vincent's feeling unacceptable. The summer before his senior year, Vincent dated a girl to whom he had been attracted for several months. By the end of the summer, they were involved in frequent petting sessions, sometimes engaging in manual stimulation of her genitals. After those experiences, Vincent felt extreme guilt. He feared his parents would be crushed if they found out what he had done, and he was sure he had let God down as well. He also fell short of his own ideals. Vincent based his perfection on maintaining perfect self-control. The act of partially giving in to his sexual desires represented a breach in his strong ability to control his impulses.

As with so many perfectionists, Vincent's guilt expressed itself in a self-punishing manner. With each new pimple and occasional cold sore, he was obsessed with a fear he had contracted some type of venereal disease. Positive his sin would somehow result in punishment, one obsession led to another. And soon Vincent was hopelessly involved in a complex maze of obsessions and compulsions, like the repetitive hand washing mentioned earlier.

Perfectionists are tyrants, dictators demanding absolute perfection primarily from themselves. They willingly

respond to their own command to be perfect but, like
Vincent, fail to understand that only through the grace of
God can perfection be given.

■ *Effects of Power-Oriented Behavior on Other People*

Each of the eight personality types discussed in this
book have developed different interpersonal defense
mechanisms. These defensive strategies are designed to
help the individual avoid anxiety. Since each personality
type strives for personal comfort and security in a different
manner, it is expected that each defense system will have
a different effect on other people.

Power-oriented behavior usually elicits one of two
types of responses. First, many respect and admire the
teenager who presents himself or herself with power.
Confidence, assertiveness and strong self-control are very
attractive to other young people who secretly wish they
could be sure of themselves. A young person who functions effectively with a power facade becomes a hero
worthy of high esteem. Dependency is gladly given to
one who appears better qualified to face life. In fact,
other young people often feel safer when they depend
upon someone else's strength rather than their own.

Second, when a teenager overemphasizes power
mechanisms, he or she may also receive some negative
reactions. Even when other teenagers are comfortable with
their own dependency, they may become angry and resistive if the power-oriented teenager controls or dominates
too much. Common reactions may include resistance, rebellion or even withdrawal.

The effective "leader" draws feelings of admiration and
trust from other adolescents. Many yield to his or her advice and decisions. The "brain" will certainly elicit feelings
of awe and respect. In fact, most teenagers feel inferior to
a peer with these competencies. Others' inferiority feelings
then widen the interpersonal gap and increase the power-

oriented teenager's feelings of security. It also reinforces his or her sense of importance and competence.

The "dictator" draws anger, frustration and resentment from most adolescent peers. Teenagers act out these unpleasant feelings in rebellion and withdrawal. Only the most dependent adolescents will tolerate being dominated to such an extent. A "perfectionist" will normally elicit only frustration and lack of understanding from his or her peers. Friends who would like to help are kept at a distance. Only the perfectionist can help himself or herself.

A power-oriented teenager views others as weak and less capable than they really are. This error in perception of others is one more way this type of teenager seeks to reinforce his or her own sense of personal value and importance. Depending upon how intense this characteristic is in the young person, it intensifies the reactions of either respect or anger from others.

■ Guidelines for Working with Power-Oriented Adolescents

The teenagers described in this chapter use power as their primary defensive maneuver. Interpersonal and personal problems often occur because of the way they handle power. Their perceptions and uses of power are at the root of their difficulties. Misuse of power can limit fulfillment in life and may cause distance between themselves and others.

You can help these young people whether you are a youth pastor, volunteer youth sponsor, teacher or counselor. *Listen* to what their behavior says about them. What do they fear? What are their hopes? What internal conflicts do they experience? How do they reduce their anxiety? When do they feel most comfortable? When and how do they use power to an excess?

Use the following suggestions to help you work with your power-oriented teenagers. Some suggestions may apply directly, and you may choose to adapt other ideas to the specific adolescents with whom you work.

1. Ensure power-oriented teenagers opportunities to experience their own power. These adolescents feel best about themselves when they experience their own strength or competency. They base their self-esteem largely upon how frequently and adequately they experience their own power. Therefore, it is important to ensure them of those opportunities. Don't remove the one experience that gives them good feelings about who they are. Instead, harness the strength God created within them. Help them find positive and constructive avenues to express their strength. Guide them to use their gift in ways that help others as well as enhance themselves. Encourage them to value their gift of personal strength for the good they can produce for everyone.

2. Help young people recognize and reinforce their healthy uses of power. These young people need to learn how to differentiate between positive, constructive uses of power and unhealthy, defensive uses of power. Be alert to opportunities that help adolescents better understand their use of power and how it limits their own lives and the lives of others.

Remember, when you confront young people's defense mechanisms, you will often meet with defensive responses. Don't let those responses discourage you. Gently make yourself heard. Help teenagers understand how the other person might feel in response to their expressions of power. The ability to step into another's shoes is an important skill to develop. As young people gain the ability to differentiate between healthy and unhealthy uses of power, significant growth can happen. Then they can seek to reduce their negative uses of power and continue to express their power in positive ways.

3. Let these teenagers experience being "just a part of the team." Power-oriented teenagers need to learn how to work *with* their peers, not just *lead* them. At school and in the youth group, place power-oriented teenagers on working and decision-making committees, making a special effort to prevent their chairing or heading the committee. Leadership by committee can reduce power-oriented teenagers' needs to be in charge because decisions are made by a consensus of opinion. This type of experience forces these adolescents to use interpersonal skills rather than their "tried and true" power mechanisms. It encourages them to find other ways of relating. And it offers them an opportunity to experience success in a situation where they are not in charge. The old (and incorrect) adage, "If you want something done right, do it yourself," needs to be *unlearned* by power-oriented teenagers.

4. Kindly point out the accomplishments and successes of others. Power-oriented teenagers tend to underestimate others' strengths. They see weakness and inadequacy in their peers and screen out any evidence of their competency. This unconscious choice to ignore reality helps these young people keep alive the myth of their own exaggerated strengths and abilities. In pointing out the capabilities of their peers, be sure no comparisons are made between power-oriented young persons and other successful individuals. If power-oriented teenagers feel threatened by such comments, they will strengthen their power defenses. Remember, that facade of power is intended to defend these young people's identities and preserve their self-esteem. Increasing their ability to see and value others' strengths without feeling demeaned is a sign of growth for these adolescents.

5. Supply opportunities and support these teenagers through their experiences of allowing others to lead. After power-oriented teenagers are able to recognize another's strength, their next step involves following the lead of someone who is superior in a certain skill or talent. These young people typically are threatened by others who appear more competent and stronger than they see themselves. They need support to maintain their stature when someone else enters and uses their position of dominance or leadership. Help power-oriented teenagers experiment with choosing to defer to their peers. They need to discover through personal experience that they can retain their respect and value, even after allowing another to lead.

Another factor which makes deference so difficult for power-oriented adolescents is their inability to accept anything less than perfection within themselves. Deferring to another can mean dependence on that person. Dependency is feared and avoided at all costs by the power-oriented young person. This is a delicate issue for these adolescents. They must receive sufficient support and trust as you help them gradually explore this area of growth.

6. *Help power-oriented adolescents recognize and accept their own areas of weakness and imperfection.* This central need for this type of teenager requires a safe and trusting relationship to support this most difficult task. Admitting to personal weakness requires a great amount of courage since these individuals view anything less than perfect as dangerous and unacceptable. A particularly loving and accepting youth sponsor or teacher may provide a safe and supportive relationship in which these young people can begin to take risks. (It would be wise to involve parents and family as an additional support system when you guide young people through this very difficult task.) This acceptance of imperfection is central and necessary to ensure the moderation of power-oriented teenagers' defenses. Future healthy functioning for this personality type requires this growth.

7. *Encourage these young people to value their own thinking.* Power-oriented teenagers need help to respond to internal reinforcement rather than praise from other people. Most dominant adolescents were either heavily praised for their strengths or discouraged for asserting themselves during their childhood. The Apostle Paul, in his letter to the Ephesian church, warned, "Fathers, do not exasperate your children . . . " (Ephesians 6:4). Frustrating or exasperating children's assertions of their identity causes difficulty with their attitudes about dominance and authority. Experiences of too much praise or excessive discouragement teach teenagers to be extremely sensitive to how others react to them.

You can use your position as an adult to help these young people accept their self-evaluation rather than depend on others. Encourage adolescents to trust and value their own thinking. When asked what you think, you might respond with something like: "I know you want me to tell you what I think, but I'll bet you have some good ideas. I'd like to hear what you've thought about first. Then if I have an additional idea, I'll share it with you."

8. Encourage and support new ventures.

Teenagers of this personality type tend to stay in their particular area of expertise. This is where they feel most confident and in control. An additional avenue of growth for these young people is to venture into another area of life. You might encourage the student body leader to learn to play a musical instrument. You might help the "brain" develop more of a social life. You might encourage the spiritual leader to participate in one or more sports activities. Understand that broadening personal interests represents taking a risk for power-oriented adolescents. To venture into something new means starting as a novice.

To go from expert to beginner takes real courage, especially if personal identity is associated with being perfect. So, be encouraging. Be supportive of new ventures. Help your power-oriented teenagers enjoy learning something new. Let them know the joy of adventuring into new expressions of their gifts, even if it means an imperfect performance. Support the higher value of enjoying their experience over the perfection of their performance. And be patient! Allow them to grow at their own pace with your support.

9. Help these young people understand and accept God's grace. Power-oriented teenagers usually have difficulty with the concept of grace. It is important to help these young people intellectually grasp and actively accept God's grace, for it can bring deep healing to them, both psychologically and spiritually. But these teenagers have a two-fold problem with this task:

● First, to rely on God's grace means to trust something other than their own expertise, strength and perfection.

● Second, to rely on God's grace also means to become dependent upon God and admit to the insufficiency of their own strength. They must admit they *need* God.

Both of these tasks are required if we are to accept the grace God offers so freely. Power-oriented adolescents have an especially difficult time overcoming their resistance to grace. In Paul's letter to the church at Philippi, he wrote, "I can do everything through him who gives me strength" (Philippians 4:13). The teenagers described in this chapter respond readily to the first part of this verse. However, they seem to overlook the last two phrases. "I can do everything . . . " becomes the ideal toward which they strive. But, ". . . through him who gives me strength" suggests they are not completely sufficient for the task. These phrases correctly suggest reliance upon a source of strength other than themselves.

Christ says, "Be perfect, therefore, as your heavenly Father is perfect" (Matthew 5:48). These young people respond readily to the call, but they seek perfection under the cruel illusion that they can reach this goal with their own strength. They honestly believe they can reach perfection within themselves. They don't know yet how to respond to Christ's invitation found later in Matthew. "Come to me, all you who are weary and burdened, and I will give you rest. Take my yoke upon you and learn from me, for I am gentle and humble in heart, and you will find rest for your souls. For my yoke is easy and my burden is light" (Matthew 11:28-30). As workers with youth, we can show them how to find the psychological and spiritual rest Christ promises by helping them understand and rely upon God's grace.

10. Recognize your own limits and refer teenagers to professional counseling when necessary. When teenagers exhibit extreme power-oriented defense mechanisms, consider referral to professional counseling. Strong, rigid defenses represent intense anxiety, pain, guilt or other internal conflicts against which people are defending themselves. These young people need help. Adolescents like Cynthia the "dictator" and Vincent the "perfectionist" require immediate professional help.

Young people like Stephanie the "brain" also need help but may gain enough understanding and support from parents and other adults to grow beyond their difficulties. Teenagers like Phillip the "leader" function very well. However, they too can benefit from your help and guidance, made even more valuable by your increased understanding of their personality type.

■ Guidelines for Parenting Power-Oriented Adolescents

Parents have a potentially greater impact on their children than anyone else. This is both a frightening and inspiring reality. We are unnerved as we observe our children emulating some of our less attractive personal traits. Yet, we are inspired to higher levels of personal responsibility by the challenge to "train up a child in the way he should go" (Proverbs 22:6). Each of the adolescent personality types discussed in this book provide unique parenting tasks and opportunities. Parents need to learn how to adapt their parenting styles to the personality needs of *each* of their children. This section offers suggestions specifically designed for parenting power-oriented adolescents.

1. Seek to look beyond your teenagers' actions to understand the meaning expressed in their behavior. It is dangerously easy during the pressures of everyday family living to react unthinkingly to our teenagers' behaviors. We must consciously ask ourselves, "What are they telling me by the way they act?" Remember, preadolescent children usually express their feelings and attitudes more freely through their actions than with their words. Though adolescents have developed a greater capacity for verbalizing their emotions and perceptions, they still act out their inner tensions and conflicts through behavior.

Become a careful observer of your children's behavior. Look for patterns and repetitive actions. Check with your teenagers about the accuracy of your thoughts concerning their actions. Realize their first responses may not be completely accurate or even honest. By using careful observation, patient listening and sensitive probing, you can gain a much clearer picture of what their behavior actually means.

Careful observation may indicate that your power-oriented young people demand perfection in almost everything they do. Note their patterns, and then gently check with your teenagers on what they mean by their behavior. Use these opportunities to help them deal with the underlying cause of their actions.

"Bill, I've noticed that when we have family discussions you usually speak not only for yourself but also for your brother and sister. I think they're getting upset about it. I wasn't sure if you were aware of what was happening. What does your 'taking over for them' do for you?"

Understand that one of the most important avenues through which teenagers express their developing identities is their behavior. By paying close attention to their actions, you can learn a tremendous amount about who they are.

2. Provide opportunities for your power-oriented teenagers to experience their strength in beneficial ways. God has blessed these young people with certain gifts and abilities. Help them find even more ways to develop their strength. Assist them in utilizing their gifts in ways that benefit others as well as themselves. Psychological research tells us that people are most likely to make positive personal changes when they feel positive about themselves. You can help your young people feel good about themselves by acknowledging their positive characteristics. As the value of their stock in themselves rises, power-oriented teenagers are more capable and willing to risk the hard work of making personal changes.

Provide opportunities for your teenagers to exercise strength and leadership at home with the family. Let them lead or moderate family discussions. Give them responsibilities like organizing and putting on Dad's 45th birthday party or planning part of the family's vacation this summer. Give them increasing responsibilities for younger children when appropriate. Gradually include them and their thoughts in making family financial decisions.

When your power-oriented teenagers assert strength and leadership, reinforce their positive efforts and behavior. Let them know you appreciate their decision-making abilities and their strength to take charge of a situation. Make sure they know you admire their persuasive skills and their ability to lead group activities.

3. Gently confront your power-oriented teenagers' excessive use of power. Young people don't automatically know how to use their strengths. They must learn the appropriate exercise of power. Teenagers need supportive correction rather than criticism. When parents misinterpret power-oriented teenagers' strengths to mean security and self-assurance, they have forgotten that their teenagers' presentations of power are defenses against their personal insecurity. Therefore, harsh, demeaning or critical correction can cause extensive psychological damage without the adolescents letting anyone know they are hurting. Remember, excessive use of power often suggests internal conflict, insecurity or low self-esteem.

Instead of confronting your power-oriented teenagers, help them recognize their excessive uses of power. You can guide your young people as they search for other ways to handle interpersonal situations.

"Bill, I've noticed that when you're with your friends you push extremely hard for what *you* want to do. I wonder how your friends would feel if you sometimes asked them what *they* would like to do?"

"Charlotte, at the party last night you didn't seem satisfied with how others wanted to decorate the room. I wonder if your friends get tired of always having to do things *your* way?"

As parents, you are in a critical position to gently guide your adolescents to recognize and alter their power-oriented ways of relating in social situations.

4. Help your power-oriented adolescents learn to work *with* others, not just control them. Power-oriented teenagers find a sense of security in social relationships when they operate within leadership roles or from positions of perfection. They feel safe in these roles because they feel competent and self-reliant. However, their own self-sufficiency insulates them from the social contact and interpersonal intimacy they really need. When you see your teenagers seeking positions of control, power and influence over others, help them balance these relationships. Encourage them to accept and recognize their friends and peers as equals. This recognition will help them develop a healthier balance in their own personality development.

These young people need to experience working *with* other family members to accomplish family goals. They need to know they can be treated like their brothers or sisters without losing their own personal value. They need to share a wide variety of family experiences like working in the yard or helping with housekeeping chores and in a capacity that does not make them special. Picking up dog droppings, pulling weeds and cleaning toilet bowls are unpleasant tasks, but they don't lessen the personal value of the teenagers who do them. On the contrary, willingness to participate in these jobs can indicate that adolescents are learning the art of serving others.

Structure chores and projects so that your power-oriented adolescents work equally *with* or serve *under* the supervision of another person. Follow these experiences with discussions about how they feel in those situations. Have the whole family share how they feel about working together. Mutual experiences and family sharing may open some doors for each person to recognize value within the other.

5. Encourage your power-oriented teenagers to recognize and value the strengths of other people. Often in their efforts to focus continually on their own sufficiency, perfection and strength, these young people either fail to see or actively avoid recognizing the strengths and leadership abilities of other family members. They may feel threatened and lose some of their self-esteem when a brother, sister or parent takes control of a situation. When another family member displays his or her expertise, power-oriented teenagers may withdraw or assert their strengths even more forcefully. Those who are better adapted socially feel less threatened when another family member takes charge. However, those who are less secure may need help to offer respect to others without losing their own self-respect.

You can help your power-oriented children see how they benefit from others' strengths. Point out how the athletic games in which they star would be less exciting without the musical abilities of the pep band. Help your strong academician appreciate the skills and talents of the mechanics who keep his or her car running. Use your own family as an illustration of the body of Christ presented in Romans 12:3-8. Celebrate each person's "different gifts" in a Bible study which focuses on these verses. Then have family members either write on a sheet of paper or verbally tell each other the strengths he or she benefits from or admires in the other. Recognizing and sharing appreciation for each other's value helps develop self-esteem for each individual without encouraging power or control over others.

6. Teach these young people the value of deferring to others' leadership. Power-oriented teenagers feel best about themselves when they are self-reliant. They feel most secure when they operate out of their own strength. They are accustomed to and even encourage others' dependency upon them because anothers' dependence makes them feel more valued and important.

Eldest brothers and sisters commonly and naturally experience positions where others depend upon them. Younger siblings may need guidance about school and social relationships. They may need an older sibling's protection against the neighborhood bully. They may seek their older brother's or sister's advice about how to dress and how to attract the opposite sex. Parents often rely on their power-oriented children's strengths to help them with parenting or household tasks.

Power-oriented teenagers need help learning how to depend comfortably upon others. Continually reassure these adolescents of your love and admiration for them even when you choose to depend on the skills of another family member. Arrange things so your power-oriented adolescents have to rely on another's leadership. Put someone else in charge of making party plans, directing the family meeting, driving the car or leading the way on a family hike. Reinforce your teenagers' dependency and any expression of a positive attitude when this response occurs.

"Sometimes it's nice *not* to be in charge, isn't it?"

"It's fun to let your little brother lead the way for a change, don't you think?"

"Sue, I really liked the way you let your younger sister design the menu for tonight's meal. I'll bet that was tough to sit back and let her take the lead!"

These young people gain the ability to balance their relationships as they learn to defer leadership to others.

7. Encourage these teenagers to accept their own weaknesses. We have already discussed how power-oriented adolescents feel more comfortable when they operate out of their own strength. We have also discovered that they feel uneasy about depending upon others. Therefore, it is not surprising that they are usually quite intolerant of any weaknesses they find within themselves. Their affinity to power is their primary defense against their feelings of humiliation when they encounter personal inadequacies. Their greatest fear is that others will also discover their weaknesses.

Effective parenting of these teenagers includes helping them accept their internal weaknesses. They need to know that weakness is an integral aspect of *every* human being. It is our inherent weakness that ultimately leads us to our greatest blessing, the love of God through Jesus Christ. Our weaknesses also lead us into interdependent relationships with others within the body of Christ.

Lead the way for your children to learn a healthy attitude toward their personal weaknesses. Accept your own inadequacies, and exercise patience as you seek to grow. Practice admitting to weaknesses and faults so your confessions can come with greater ease. Be willing to confess your own weaknesses to your adolescents and do so *without* a self-demeaning pretense.

When you observe a weakness or fault within your young people, express a non-judgmental spirit of acceptance.

"Jayne, that's okay. We've all broken crystal or china or something else of value."

"Hey pal, I know flunking your driving test really depressed you. Let's talk about it and see what you need to study. Then we can go out and get something to eat."

Acknowledge your teenagers' feelings. Let them know you think they're okay, even with their weaknesses. Then encourage them to move on.

8. Encourage your power-oriented teenagers to gradually expand their boundaries of comfort. Most of us tend to operate where we feel comfortable. We like the familiar. Situations and activities that previously offered feelings of success, accomplishment and acceptance are where we like to spend most of our time and effort. Power-oriented children like to stay with activities where they feel like an expert. They tend to focus most of their time and energy on a narrow band of activity. Concentrating on a particular area of academic study, playing a musical instrument, participating in one or more sports activities, working on cars, experiencing a hobby and developing an extensive social life are common areas of adolescent interest.

Encourage your teenagers' interests in their areas of strength. Then help them find and explore other avenues for self-expression. Point out that enjoyment and personal satisfaction are just as important, if not more so, than attaining a certain level of perfection. Call their attention to the pleasures they experience in *doing* something, whether or not they do it particularly well.

"Even though you're not a concert pianist, it's still fun to play."

"I guess your stamp collection is not an award-winner, but it sure is fun to see it grow."

"I know school is difficult for you, Bill. But how are you doing at making your studies more interesting?"

You will enrich the lives of your power-oriented children when you help them expand their horizons beyond activities where they experience control and perfection. Their insecurities may cause them to resist your efforts to help, but patiently and gently encourage and reinforce their efforts.

9. Let your teenagers know it's really okay to accept help and grace from others. Along with not accepting their own weaknesses, power-oriented teenagers do not easily accept help or assistance from others. To receive support from others, especially from peers, alerts these adolescents to their inadequacies. "If I accept help from you, then I admit I am incompetent." This dynamic also causes these adolescents to resist accepting God's grace. These young people *fear* dependency. They usually interpret accepting help as being dependent.

Parents frequently observe their power-oriented children resisting others' offers to help. "No, that's all right. I can handle it myself." "Gee, I really appreciate your offer, but I've got it under control."

Sometimes resistance becomes firmer. "No. It's not necessary for you to help." "I'm doing just fine, thank you."

When teenagers feel especially threatened, their resistance will sound and feel hostile or aggressive. "No, I don't need your help. If I need it, I'll ask for it." "I'm sorry you think I'm so stupid! Maybe if you just back off, you'll see I can handle things at least as well as you can."

One of the most effective ways you can help these young people is by modeling a gracious acceptance of help when it is offered. This is particularly powerful when power-oriented teenagers are the ones offering the assistance. "Alice, thank you so much. I can use all the help I can get." Point out to your power-oriented adolescents that everyone gains when someone helps another. Help them see that everyone needs to know that he or she can help somebody else. Let them know they don't lose any stature or personal significance because they periodically need assistance. Finally, help them recognize that as a part of Christ's body, they cannot be self-sufficient; they will *always* require the support of other believers.

These young people resist accepting help from others

because their needs make them feel more inadequate than others. They feel guilty about needing help. Your support and acceptance of their needs can make a significant difference in their ability to grow in accepting help and support from others.

10. If your power-oriented teenagers are extreme or excessively rigid in this defensive orientation, professional counseling may offer valuable help. Adolescent development brings significant stress to the emerging identities of young people. The conflict between psychological and sexual development, changes in social relationships, intensified family conflicts and increased challenges at school converge to bring mounting pressures on teenagers. These pressures create what therapists call psychological pain. When this pain reaches dangerous levels of intensity, adolescents resort to more extreme or rigid forms of their defensive orientation. Power-oriented young people may participate socially *only* when they control all activity. They may rigidly demand perfection from themselves. They may involve themselves in only those activities where they feel secure in their competence.

When you see these kinds of behaviors in your adolescents, consider seeking professional counseling for them. Ask your youth minister, pastor or priest for suggestions. Call your family physician for further advice. Taking your child to a therapist or psychologist may seem like drastic action, but failure to do so may cause even more devastating results.

You now have a basic understanding of power-oriented teenagers. You know more about what their behavior really says. And you are now equipped with specific strategies to help these young people express their personality style in a healthy manner. As parents and youth leaders, you can now choose to work as a team to help power-oriented adolescents accept their imperfections and grow to personal acceptance in a supportive environment.

■ C H A P T E R 5

The Competitive Personality

Competitiveness is characteristic of most adolescents. Teenagers constantly make personal comparisons between themselves and others because of their strong peer-orientation. Comparing and competing are essential to their identity formation process, for no one can determine who he or she is while living in a void.

Some teenagers become excessively competitive. Rather than compete normally as a part of their development, they choose competition as their primary way of relating to others. They also adopt this method as their main defense for warding off anxiety and feelings of insecurity.

Narcissism is another normal part of the adolescent personality. Psychologists say people are narcissistic when they:

● have a hard time seeing a perspective other than their own,

● are idealistic and exaggerate their evaluations of themselves,

- can love only themselves,
- perceive everything in light of what is good for them, and
- exert most of their efforts toward benefiting themselves.

We identify teenagers as having a competitive personality when their desire for competition and their narcissism become extreme. Located within the hostile-dominance quadrant, these young people's competitive defenses characterize the way they interact with everyone. Only when they see themselves as better than others do they feel comfortable with themselves. While power-oriented teenagers need to feel competent and in control, competitive teenagers must feel *superior* to others.

Competitive adolescents abhor dependency. Yet in a surprisingly ironic way, they are strongly dependent on other people. Without a standard for comparison, these teenagers have no way to establish their own self-esteem. They *depend* upon seeing others as inferior to themselves. What difficulty these young people have with Paul's admonition: "Let us not become conceited, provoking and envying each other. Each one should test his own actions. Then he can take pride in himself, without comparing himself to somebody else, for each one should carry his own load" (Galatians 5:26; 6:4-5).

Competitive teenagers engage in activities that reinforce their perception of themselves as better than those around them. They strive for perfection to further enhance their own sense of superiority. They seek dominance to gain power over others to make them feel inferior. They enhance their self-concept and security by reinforcing their own sense of superiority and drawing attention to others' inferiority. While the power-oriented teenager's motto is, "I need to be the best I can possibly be," the competitive teenager believes, "I need to be better than you."

■ Development of the Competitive Personality

Many factors that produce power-oriented personalities also help develop competitive personalities. Power is important to both types of young people. The *use* of that power differentiates these two types of teenagers. While power-oriented adolescents use their power to develop skills for their own maturation and growth, competitive adolescents employ their power *against others* to enhance themselves. Several factors influence development of the competitive personality.

First, since competition requires continuous striving, these adolescents require high levels of energy. To succeed with this defensive pattern, these young people must inherit a capacity for hard-driving power and vigorous action. Adequate nourishment and rest are essential. Physical weakness and low energy denote inadequacy, an unacceptable quality to the competitive teenager.

Second, many of these young people have grown up with adults who model the competitive style of relating to others. Children assume the same behaviors they see in their parents. Parents who regularly criticize the pastor, demean their neighbors or talk disparagingly about school and government officials are training their teenagers to do the same. These patterns assume particular significance when family members are also competitive with one another. These teenagers grow up believing this style of interaction is normal for relating within families and with other people.

Third, teenagers who compete well and succeed usually receive positive reinforcement. Whether the competition is in athletics, academics, popularity, wealth or even spirituality, our social system provides worthwhile rewards to the winners. Athletic success brings attention, respect and scholarships. Academic excellence earns adult approval and scholarships. Wealth attains power, prestige, possessions and attention from peers. Outstanding spiritual behavior elicits approval from adults and the Christian community. These desirable reinforcements increase teenagers' competitive behavior.

Fourth, many teenagers who develop a competitive personality have experienced pain and discomfort while under someone else's control. Severe or overly punitive parents have taught these young people the dangers of operating under another person's direction. Like power-oriented youth, competitive teenagers experience this hurt and decide they must maintain control of themselves and others. But competitive teenagers go beyond this decision. They use their power to deprive others of any vestige of strength and then employ this control to ensure their own supremacy.

Fifth, competitive young people learn to distrust others, especially others who have power. Unhappy or negative experiences with power figures have taught these young people not to get close to others. Since adolescence is also a time of high idealism and critical thinking, this combination of factors leads to self-righteousness and a strong critical attitude toward authority. Newspaper head-lines and television newsbreaks about dishonesty and cor-ruption in government, schools and churches merely reinforce adolescents' distrust of others. Competitive teenagers believe the only way to protect themselves is not only to prevent others from having power over them, but to possess power over others.

Sixth, competitive adolescents often distrust themselves as well as others. Some become aware of their own imper-fections and tendencies to mistreat other people. Others may recognize their misuse of power. Still others may lack trust in their abilities to maintain control. They feel driven to work harder and harder to keep the control they have. Compulsively, these teenagers seek more and more power, hoping to somehow find security and psychological comfort.

Most competitive teenagers have several of these six causative factors in their background. Identifying these conditions helps us understand the meaning of much of their behavior.

■ *Healthy Forms of the Competitive Personality*

Within our culture competition is highly valued and occurs in almost every interpersonal arena. Teenagers who develop a competitive personality can be very successful during their adolescent years. They can establish interpersonal habits that will serve them well through adulthood. The keys to a healthy adaptation through competition are moderation and balance. Let's take a look at some healthier forms of the competitive personality.

The Politician. Political activity is a socially approved avenue for expressing competition. It provides politicians with a chance to develop strategies, motivate people and gain in popularity. Politics provide adolescent competitors with immediate and tangible feedback. Politicians either win or lose. Those who win receive rewards of control, power and supremacy over others. Those who lose experience the pain of defeat and an unsettling reminder of their lack of power, loss of control and feelings of inferiority.

Randy is a junior in high school. He is deeply involved in his campaign for next year's student-body president of his school. If he wins, he will have accomplished one of his fondest dreams. This goal represents the culmination of his extracurricular activities since elementary school. Various kinds of political activities have been Randy's primary arenas for social involvement throughout school. He has helped friends run for election, competed in his own political races and campaigned for various social and humanitarian causes. Most of Randy's social interaction has been provided by these experiences.

As the fifth of six children in a home where both parents work, Randy learned early how to get his needs met. His four older sisters were delighted to have a younger brother. Each experimented with the role of "mommy," competing for his attention. He gladly entered the drama, intensifying their competition for his benefit. Randy quickly and happily became irretrievably spoiled.

Then along came baby brother. Randy lost his position at the center of his family's universe and was replaced by an unexpected and unwanted (at least not expected nor wanted by Randy!) baby boy. Suddenly, after 10 years of receiving everyone's special attention, Randy was expected to give. Randy had met his first competitor.

During his early childhood Randy learned how to pressure, entice and manipulate others into doing his bidding. During elementary school he extended his technique to include his classmates. He felt comfortable when he was controlling action on the playground. However, when he wasn't the team captain, he felt uneasy and awkward. Whatever the interpersonal setting, Randy needed to be in control.

Throughout his school years Randy's classmates respected and admired him. Gradually, he became selective of the activities he joined with his friends. He chose only those situations where he could quickly ascend to a position of leadership. In the process of gaining control, he caused others to feel inferior. He subtly manipulated them into believing he should be their leader. They accepted his efforts toward leadership as beneficial to their needs and gladly helped him attain that position.

As Randy progressed through junior high and into high school, he involved himself in other activist types of events. He organized and led student campaigns against poverty and social injustice. He coordinated students' efforts to pressure teachers and administrators to give them more benefits, like campus vending machines and longer lunch periods. He received much popularity, attention and respect from his peers and adults for his effective efforts. As effective as he was, he continually judged and criticized his peers' leadership efforts and put them down when they were not successful. He saw himself as superior, but soon learned he lost their respect and support if he allowed others to see his demeaning attitude toward them.

Randy opened many doors of opportunity for himself through his competitive political activities. He met and interacted with more people than he would have otherwise, but his competitive stance kept others at a distance. His automatic faultfinding and continual search for others' weaknesses made people around him feel uneasy. With each new meeting Randy worked to reaffirm his position of superiority.

The Jock. From the time he was born, Spence was a great delight to his father. As an outstanding high school athlete and an average college competitor, his dad had hoped for a position on a professional basketball team. But his height prevented his being a serious contender. Helping his son accomplish athletic goals he had failed to achieve became a driving force for this highly competitive father.

As Spence reached the middle of his elementary school years, his dad encouraged his participation in Little League baseball and soccer. When he was finally old enough, his father enrolled him in the community basketball league for children. Fortunately, Spence was naturally agile and had excellent eye-hand coordination. He quickly grasped the basic skills of the game and improved rapidly.

Spence's athletic activities were obviously valuable to his father. He was present at all of Spence's games and most of his practices. When he was with Spence in the car or at home, he centered their conversations on sports. Even his church attendance was regulated by "important" games in town or on television. He obviously avoided the open-house activities at school, board games and other non-sports activities, which let Spence know where his father placed his priorities.

As Spence grew up, he learned how to get his dad's attention and approval. Spence received positive reinforcement from his father for competing and succeeding in all sports activities. However, if Spence performed poorly, let his interest or intensity lag or chose to do something else instead of attending a sports function, his father made his disapproval obvious and at times even punished him. He was reprimanded when his performance did not meet his father's expectations and when he chose not to compete at all. In an important sense Spence had to vie for his father's attention and love. He learned that his dad's acceptance of him was conditional—conditional upon Spence's interest and active participation in sports (especially basketball) and upon his ability to win.

Spence's experience with his father taught him he had to compete for personal significance. After all, how much personal value could he have if he had to repeatedly earn his own father's respect and esteem? He believed the myth that his personal value was dependent upon his ability to compete with others on the playing field. Spence was not aware that he was having to compete with his father's needs to experience his own personal value.

Spence generalized what he had learned from his relationship with his father to other relationships. When he lost in any athletic competition, he felt a loss in self-esteem. Winning made his personal stock in himself go up in value. But there were always new competitions, and each one brought a new threat of losing personal worth.

Under the circumstances, Spence is now making a healthy adjustment to adolescence. His mother provides a stabilizing influence in his life. Her love and admiration are there for him whether he participates in a sport or not. And she accepts him, regardless of whether he wins or loses.

Spence's competitive stance toward his peers is primarily visible in his attitude about himself. Even though he is kind and friendly toward other people, there is an underlying, inner tension that prevents his relaxing and enjoying himself completely. A constant, though often unconscious, need to be better than those around him pervades his presentation of himself. He feels he *must* be superior to others, or he jeopardizes his personal value and lovableness.

The Entrepreneur. Everyone at church knows Marcus. He's delightful, mischievous, charming, and a bundle of energy! If you have a problem, Marcus has an angle. If you're down in the dumps, he makes you smile. He can talk you into anything. Everybody loves Marcus!

Nothing gets Marcus down. He is always happy and energetic. His obvious enthusiasm for life always surprises people when they hear about his background. Marcus was one of six children. His father was an alcoholic even before Marcus was born. The family never had enough money for food, let alone adequate clothing and household necessities. There was never money for entertainment. His dad was a good machinist, but because of his drinking he worked an average of only two days per week. When Marcus was nine years old, his father disappeared and was never heard from again. The family lived on welfare, plus whatever the children earned mowing lawns and baby-sitting and what their mother earned cleaning houses.

Throughout elementary school Marcus was quiet, shy and embarrassed about his appearance. Normally, he went unnoticed, except for some mild teasing about his clothes. He was a nice kid, but nobody paid much attention to him. During his junior high years, he became friends with members of a local church youth group. After attending several meetings, Marcus made a personal commitment to Christ. He felt accepted by this friendly group who cared about him. He lost his initial shyness and guarded attitude of mistrust. He excitedly joined in their activities and became a regular member of the group.

Even though he was accepted and enjoyed by the other kids, Marcus still felt different from them. He felt he must always strive for their acceptance. He continued to need reassurance that he really was a member and belonged. Since Marcus was and still is a very active boy, he didn't just wait for reassurances to come to him. Instead, he went out and earned them. Marcus carved out his own niche in the youth group. He became an idea man with enough energy to not only create schemes, but also put them into action.

Marcus developed into a whiz at dreaming up creative fund raisers. With his ability to advertise activities plus the active support of the kids in the group (along with their parents), he could make almost any project an outstanding success. With his enthusiasm and organizational skills, the youth group raised money for summer and winter camps, new Ping-Pong tables for the youth room and summer canoe trips. Other special projects produced Christmas gifts for orphanage children and elderly residents at a local convalescent home.

Marcus also earned a reputation for being an entrepreneur for his own sake. During the past year he gained control of six paper routes. He paid the younger children a percentage to deliver for him, and he made the collections. In addition, he hired himself out to school clubs as a fund raiser. He produced the ideas, directed the projects and pocketed 25 percent of the profits.

As an entrepreneur, Marcus has earned a popular and valuable place both at school and in his youth group. He receives reinforcement repeatedly for his creative and energetic efforts. But for Marcus, there is never enough affirmation. Each success is followed almost immediately by an empty feeling that drives him to devise new, more elaborate schemes to prove his worth and value to his group. When others come up with ideas, Marcus has to have a better one. When others work hard, Marcus puts out more effort. When others are charming, Marcus virtually oozes with social appeal.

Beneath his energetic, spontaneous and charming exterior, Marcus feels unsure of his social value. He questions how much people would like him if he didn't try so hard. When others begin doing what he does, he feels threatened. His competitive response reconfirms his position as *best* at what he does and provides Marcus with his only feeling of security.

Randy, Spence and Marcus are all competitive teen-agers. They depend upon seeing themselves as better than their peers for feelings of self-esteem and personal value. In their minds they secure their belonging by establishing their superiority over others. Even though all three believe dependence on others is an insecure and dangerous posi-tion, these competitive adolescents express their basic defense in a healthy, constructive manner to themselves and those around them.

■ Unhealthy Forms of the Competitive Personality

Some competitive teenagers who select the competitive defense mechanism are not as well-adjusted as Randy, Spence and Marcus. They compete with such strong feel-ings of insecurity that they are destructive to themselves and others. Their intense competitiveness ruins relation-ships, and they are unbearable to be around for more than a short period of time. Their movement toward supremacy is lined with those on whom they have stepped.

The Snob. Marsha obviously has a difficult time getting along with others. At 19, she never has had a good friendship for more than a few months. Few people can tolerate her self-centeredness. There is no room in her life for anyone but herself. Throughout her childhood Marsha was spoiled with excessive attention, immediate responses to her every whim and the fulfillment of most every material wish. Marsha was indeed spoiled . . . spoiled rotten!

Marsha's extravagant and indulgent upbringing also pro-tected her from experiencing almost every uncomfortable or threatening situation. She wasn't expected to go to parties, activities or other social events where she might feel awkward or uneasy. Her parents treated her as "special" and told her that she didn't have to mix with children who were "beneath" her. As a result, few social situations emerged where Marsha felt at ease. She knew few peers with whom she felt confident, and her interpersonal world became increasingly troubled.

Marsha went through high school feeling like an outcast among her peers. She never learned how to adapt to their needs and wishes. Furthermore, if they did not adjust to her demands, she withdrew from them, proudly pointing her nose in the air. Finally, she was forced to rely upon her superior collection of material possessions for comfort. She had to look to her endless array of dresses, designer jeans and shoes for her self-confidence.

Her life experiences were also different from those of most of her peers. Since her parents had plenty of money, they had taken her on many exotic vacations. By the time Marsha graduated from high school, she had visited Europe, Asia, Australia, the Caribbean and the Mediterranean. She still carries all of these vacation spots and other unique experiences in her collection of proofs that she is better than her peers.

Superiority became her only way to feel important. She earned the nickname "Princess" among her fellow students. Her freshman year in college was deeply disappointing. Hoping to find friends there, she instead found herself relating in the same distancing manner she did in high school. By boasting about herself, she automatically put people off. And whenever anyone tried to get close to her, she became arrogant and offensive.

Tragically, Marsha has become a social cripple. She desperately wants to be included by her peers. She yearns for a "best friend." And she can only imagine what it would be like to have a boyfriend. Her parents' lesson that she was "too special" to have to relate with other kids has limited her to the point she feels isolated and different. Her deepening depression, periodic anxiety attacks and deteriorating academic performance have caused her to leave college before the end of the semester. She has enlisted the help of a professional counselor. Their mutual task is to unravel the threads that bind her in her prison of social isolation. Her once lofty and secure place of superiority has become her desolate cell of alienation. Marsha is so good at competing she has now reached the top and has found just how lonely it can be.

The Macho Man. "Be tough, kid." "No son of mine is going to let himself be pushed around." "Make 'em respect you." "Don't take that kind of abuse from anybody." "Always treat girls with respect, but never let them forget who's boss." Herbert grew up enmeshed in his father's "wisdom." His dad's example and advice heavily impacted his view of himself, his world and other people. His father was dictator in their home, and his mother submitted to the role of faithful servant. Their children were to be "seen but not heard." The boys were taught to be "macho," which was their dad's interpretation of masculinity, while Herbert's sisters were instructed to be feminine and submissive.

Like most children, Herbert desperately wanted to please his father. He practiced the "tough kid" routine daily. He learned not only how to walk, but how to "move." He presented himself powerfully, using a few well-chosen words and an aloof, superior attitude. He observed most people through an expressionless, masklike face and half-glazed eyes, giving the overall impression of superior indifference.

Herbert looked down on outstanding students, serious athletes or students heavily involved in organized activities as people too weak to stand on their own. Underlying this critical attitude was Herbert's unrecognized self-rejection for his inability to succeed in a more productive manner. With no parental support for success in academic studies, involvement in sports or participation in other school activities, Herbert neglected these areas of his life. This neglect surfaced during junior high when he was held back a year. In an effort to please his father, Herbert sealed his own fate by emulating his dad's critical attitudes toward those who sought excellence in traditional avenues. He periodically experienced fear, anxiety and sometimes even panic that progress was leaving him behind. But these uncomfortable feelings quickly diminished when he renewed his efforts to prove himself the most macho guy around.

Herbert's style of competitiveness works well for him in his neighborhood and at school. But there is little payoff for his being macho at church. His mother attends church regularly and has always forced her children to attend with her. Upon reaching their teenage years, they were expected to become members of the youth group. Though their dad is an occasional visitor on Christmas and Easter, he enforces their mother's wish that they go to church regularly. Their youth group numbers about 20. Herbert is regularly invited to participate in discussions and special projects. Sometimes he overcomes his fears and apprehensions long enough to get involved. He allows himself a certain amount of enjoyment, but then withdraws when he feels his defenses dropping dangerously low.

Being a Christian poses some difficult problems for Herbert. It requires his being dependent on someone. It means he must express love and be vulnerable to others. These aspects of being Christian are in direct opposition to his defensive style. Herbert can relate to trying to survive in the wilderness for 40 days, but he struggles intensely with washing another's feet.

The Sexual Tease. Delores is the youngest of three children. Her brothers are two and five years older than she. During their early adolescent years, both boys engaged in sexual play with her. Threatened into secrecy, Delores never revealed these activities to either brother nor anyone else. Intercourse was never accomplished, but both boys fondled her breasts and genitals. They also required her to stimulate them and demanded that she allow them to lie on top of her while naked. When these activities first occurred, Delores was frightened. However, she soon learned her brothers would not hurt her, and gradually she began to experience pleasure, too. This was about the only time either brother gave her any positive attention.

By the time Delores was 14, these episodes had almost ceased. No one talked about them. Neither brother explained why they had occurred nor why he stopped. She merely assumed they had lost interest in her. The cessation of their attention was okay with her. With the onset of puberty, she had feared she might get pregnant. Plus, she became increasingly resentful about their using her. Although it had been pleasurable at times, she felt increasingly guilty and angry and vowed never to allow another boy to do those things to her.

These repeated molestations by her brothers deeply affected Delores. During a crucial time in her identity development, she mistakenly learned her primary value to boys was as a sex object. Because of the excessive stimulation and arousal she had experienced, she began relating to her body mainly in terms of sexual function and pleasure. She also learned that sex can produce guilt feelings; therefore, she felt a need to be secretive and deceitful.

Delores is now 16 and has had several short-term relationships with boys. She is quite seductive in her dress and movements. Boys stare and whistle. Behind her back girls talk with both envy and disdain. No one in the youth group really knows Delores. She pulls away as soon as someone starts to get close. She doesn't feel comfortable in close conversations and avoids them to subdue her rising anxiety level. She attracts boys with non-verbal suggestions that sexual activity is a good possibility. But she knows just when to cut them off. She has kept her personal vow to never again allow a boy to use her.

Her behavior pattern is circular. She needs affirmation and attention, so she presents a seductive come-on and attracts the attention she desires. The boy believes her message and responds sexually to her. Frightened and angry, Delores rejects him. With this rejection she reduces her anxiety level, reaffirms her belief that boys care only about sex and once again leaves herself alone and in need of attention. Delores' pattern is competitive in two ways.

First, she competes with other girls to be the sexiest in the group. Second, she competes and maneuvers to maintain constant control over boys.

These three case histories provide examples of unhealthy forms of the competitive personality during adolescence. All three depend upon some form of power over others. Each one is lonely, feels alienated from peers and expends great resources of energy to gain distance through some form of superiority over others. Each one feels little or no concern for others.

■ *Effects of Competitive Behavior on Other People*

Interacting with others makes all of us uncomfortable at times. Competition is used by a teenager to make him or her feel more comfortable, confident and secure. Let's look at the effects this defensive style is designed to have on others.

A competitive teenager who moderates this defense can be effective within relationships. Other people often respond with feelings of respect, admiration and even awe.

"I could never do that."

"I don't see how she can possibly accomplish so much."

"How can he keep coming up with all of those fantastic ideas?"

"I can't imagine being as good an athlete as he is."

Along with the high esteem other teenagers feel toward a competitive personality, they normally experience some degree of self-depreciation (inferiority). Different from the responses initiated by the power-oriented personality, a competitive teenager stimulates low self-evaluations in others. A competitive adolescent relies heavily on making comparisons between self and others and feels valuable only when he or she seems superior.

As a competitive teenager becomes less healthy and struggles with his or her personal adjustment, behavior becomes more and more destructive in its effect on others. Sometimes exposure to a competitive adolescent provokes extreme feelings of self-rejection within peers.

"I'm just not good enough."

"Next to him, I look really stupid."

"If she's the one I'm competing against, there's no reason for me to try. I'd just look foolish for even thinking I might win."

Strong feelings of resentment and distrust are aroused. Since negative self-concepts are difficult and painful for teenagers to live with, many times these bad feelings are projected back to the competitive young person whose relationship stimulated these negative feelings. Unconsciously, the injured teenagers are saying, "Since my bad feelings get worse when I'm around you, I am angry with you for making me feel so bad."

Not all teenagers respond to a competitive adolescent with submission; however, those who do often experience additional feelings of anger, hurt and resentment. Other teenagers may experience feelings of jealousy, envy and suspicion as common reactions to this personality type. Keep this fact in mind: The personality types of the *other* teenagers are also important factors in determining responses toward a competitive adolescent.

Depending upon his or her style, a "politician" like Randy often stimulates reactions of respect, suspicion or distrust in others. Typically, he or she can manipulate people into following or submitting. An adolescent "jock" like Spence usually draws feelings of awe, admiration and envy. An "entrepreneur" who operates like Marcus effectively elicits submission, agreement, following and trust from his or her peers.

Quite different reactions are expected to a "snob" like Marsha; he or she usually elicits envy, jealousy, resentment or anger from peers. A "macho man" like Herbert will gain envy and respect from some. Within others, he will stimulate feelings of anger, resentment and self-rejection. In addition to sexual attraction, the "sexual tease" like

Delores often elicits feelings of envy, jealousy, distrust and self-depreciation. Observing how other young people respond to a teenager will provide valuable clues for correctly identifying an adolescent's personality type. In addition, be aware of the response you and other adults have to a particular young person.

■ *Guidelines for Working with Competitive Adolescents*

Competitive teenagers use this defense to help them feel good and accepting of themselves. They feel most comfortable when they are "the best" and when they evoke feelings of weakness and self-depreciation from others. Their interpersonal problems arise from their misuse of power and from their relative inability to form close attachments with other people.

Our task as youth pastors, teachers and counselors is to help these teenagers accept themselves in non-competitive ways. By helping them better understand the root causes of their difficulties, we can encourage them to make significant changes in their attitudes, perceptions and behavior. As we understand more about the competitive personality, we have a clearer picture of what their behavior really says.

We need some specific ways to help these young people. Consider the following suggestions as necessary bridges between theory and application. Apply some of these ideas directly to your teenagers. Modify others to meet the specific needs of your group.

1. Accept and help these young people accept themselves just as they are. Let them know they don't have to earn your acceptance. Interaction between people creates anxiety for everyone. Each of us develops psychological maneuvers designed to lower this anxiety. Competitive teenagers develop their defense system because of an underlying lack of self-acceptance. These adolescents choose to use this defense destructively or inappropriately to reduce the value of others. Help these young people realize they can best find their personal value when they learn to recognize and appreciate themselves as purposeful creations of God. "Then God said, 'Let us make man in our image, in our likeness, and let them rule over the fish of the sea and the birds of the air, over the livestock, over all the earth, and over all the creatures that move along the ground.' So God created man in his own image, in the image of God he created him; male and female he created them" (Genesis 1:26-27).

Competitive teenagers need to know they have great value in just being who they are. Their competitive striving reflects their inability to accept their already-established personal value. Helping them understand and accept their inherent personal worth is essential to their future growth.

2. Help these young people find constructive ways to use their strength and energy. Competitive teenagers feel most comfortable when they operate out of their own strengths and when they perceive themselves as better than or ahead of everyone else. As with power-oriented adolescents, we do not take away their most natural way for feeling successful and good about themselves. Always begin with their strengths. Help these young people find constructive avenues to express their energies. Allow them to take leadership in the group. Give them responsibilities. Encourage them to exercise their gifts in the classroom. Then, help them develop their areas of weakness.

3. Offer opportunities for young people to work with a group, not just lead it. If these young people are always cast in leadership or power positions, it reinforces the myth that they really are better than everyone else. Therefore, as with the power-oriented youth, they need opportunities to learn how to work *with* and not just *over* their peers. Place them on committees where the whole group makes the decisions. Let them participate as a "worker" rather than "supervisor" at car washes, publicity parties and other activities. Be sure to compliment their contributions so they can see more easily the value of being a worker as well as being a boss.

4. Commend the success of followers as well as leaders. Dependency is as threatening for competitive teenagers as for power-oriented adolescents. To follow the leadership of another is an extremely uncertain position and requires great flexibility in these young people. In an attempt to help control and restrain their competitive reflex reactions, offer opportunities to experience "following" as beneficial to both them and the group. Guard them against loss of self-esteem. Applaud the successes of followers as well as the accomplishments of leaders. Help your young people recognize the dignity and productivity in following as well as leading.

5. Encourage competitive teenagers to accept and value others' strengths. Feeling threatened by another's strength makes it difficult for these teenagers to cooperate or follow others. Seeing someone else as capable presents an automatic threat to their self-esteem. Since being the best is essential, there is a constant guardedness about encountering someone better. Therefore, these young people must learn a new response. Cooperation and the ability to follow require acceptance and an ability to value others' strengths. These positive responses can occur only after adolescents recognize they are not risking or losing any of their personal worth. We must be gentle and supportive of these teenagers as they learn these difficult lessons.

6. Seek to affirm competitive teenagers' efforts with honest, caring feedback. Many times we don't know if our responses are appropriate to a situation.

Teenagers are even less sure of their actions. With a much shorter history in life experiences, teenagers are dependent upon honest feedback. They need to rely on us for the truth about themselves and their behavior.

We must commit ourselves to being gentle and non-critical. Remember, we are dealing with defense mechanisms. Whenever we confront competitive defenses, we must expect anger or resistance, especially from these adolescents. Be gentle with your confrontation. Offer genuine love and care with your feedback. This approach will affirm and not discredit these teenagers. Offer positive statements about what is right rather than listing what's wrong. Seek to build and help, not just to criticize and change.

7. *Help these young people empathize with others.* Competitive adolescents tend to be extremely narcissistic. These young people find it especially difficult to sense how others feel. They must struggle even to think about what is going on inside other people. Therefore, they have little concept about how their actions affect their friends. We need to help these young people "climb into the shoes of others." We need to help them understand how others might feel. Use television shows and movies for discussion material. Discuss with them how they think certain characters feel in response to various situations.

Help them consider how others feel in response to *their* behavior. Tell them honestly (in a loving way) how *you* respond to them. Offer them "I" messages.

"*I* like it when you allow David to lead the worship without interrupting."

"It bothers *me* when you have to interject some comment after each person shares in the group."

This kind of response offers teenagers a chance to respond and learn from a negative situation rather than thinking they are bad because they do something wrong.

Jesus told the believers: "If you hold to my teaching,

you are really my disciples. Then you will know the truth, and the truth will set you free" (John 8:31-32). The truth Jesus was talking about was the message of salvation. In a broad sense, all truth helps set us free—free from suspicion, fear, apprehension, guilt and shame. Truth also sets us free from excuses, rationalizations, denial and ignorance. Truth enables us to be responsible. As bearers of loving truth, we help our teenagers experience freedom to be the people God created them to be.

8. *Express your appreciation to these young people for who they are, *not* what they do.* Teenagers are very performance-oriented. This is especially true for power-oriented adolescents and competitive young people. They need our help to redirect their attention from external behavior to internal experience. We must encourage self-acceptance because of who they are as children of God.

Focus your comments on the pleasure of their presence, the enjoyment of their company, the good feeling of having them as members of your group. Do less praising of their performance, so they understand their value to you lies more within their person than in their actions. A pat on the back or an arm around the shoulders warms their hearts far more than saying, "You did a good job" over and over again.

9. *Help competitive teenagers learn to accept their weaknesses.* A major step toward moderating competitive defenses comes when teenagers accept their areas of weakness. This is the key to helping these young people get along better with others. They can't be perfect in everything they do, and it is impossible to be the best everywhere they go. Accepting their imperfections is closely tied to recognizing their acceptability for who they are, not what they do. All of us can accept our weaknesses more easily when we realize strength and perfection are not essential. Encourage your teenagers in attempting a difficult task. Let them know you value their effort more than the end result. Be consistently accepting of them in the midst of failure so they can learn by example that their weaknesses do not devalue them. As they grow in their self-acceptance, encourage them to attempt challenges they can't successfully or perfectly complete. Stretch them beyond their limits, but only a small amount at a time. Too much stretching leads to too much stress, which discourages them and causes even more sensitivity about their weaknesses.

10. Express *your feelings, and encourage these young people to examine and express* their *feelings.* Competitive teenagers need to continuously strive for superiority over others. Guardedness and emotional distancing are inherent aspects of this personality type. Tenderness, love and compassion cause an immediate rise in their anxiety, yet these qualities are exactly what they need. These adolescents benefit greatly from adults who can share their emotions with others. We need to be open with our feelings of love, affection and caring. Tender words and an affectionate touch soften the walls of these young people. However, we must remember caution. If we move too quickly, we frighten them and create the reverse effect. Competitive teenagers will reinforce their defenses if we express feelings that are too threatening for them.

As we openly express tenderness and positive feelings to these young people, we are modeling that behavior. Gradually they will realize that open expressions of positive emotion can occur without negative consequences. We can also encourage them to talk about their feelings with us and other group members.

Encourage a verbal experience with their feelings by discussing what they think people in Bible stories were feeling. For example, when you study accounts of Christ's healings, ask them how those who were healed probably felt. What emotional responses did the parents, children and best friends of the person healed experience? How do you think they expressed those feelings to those around them? This same process could be used when you discuss the feelings of characters in television shows, movies and books.

11. Encourage these teenagers to broaden their areas of interest. Like power-oriented teenagers, competitive adolescents develop rather narrow interests. They prefer only those activities where they feel competent. The more competence they feel, the more their sense of superiority is enhanced. To venture into activities where they are unskilled or awkward brings feelings of inadequacy. They experience a loss of self-respect and feel threatened, embarrassed or humiliated when they believe they have performed poorly. These feelings intensify when others see their inadequate performance.

Coaxing these young people into non-competitive activities can help. Board games focusing on communication rather than winning are an excellent resource. The Ungame, Social Security and Roll-A-Role are examples. Physical activities focusing on fun rather than competition are also appropriate for these teenagers. In addition, playing games that emphasize team cooperation rather than individual expertise offers another unique experience. For example, play volleyball with as many people as you can fit onto the court. Make it as fun as possible. Use no rules (e.g., hit the ball as many times as it takes to get it over, even on the serve). Use a beach ball instead of a volleyball. Change things around so that fun, not competition, is the obvious goal.

These teenagers need gentle encouragement to venture into new activities. Help "macho man" try his hand at writing poetry. His anxiety level probably will allow him to write only comical verse, but that's okay. He's doing something new and different. Let the "jock" lead some Bible studies. Encourage the "snob" to join the group in cleaning up the youth room. Be flexible and creative in your thinking. You can help your adolescents become more creative and flexible, too.

12. Offer opportunities for these teenagers to give or do for others. Competitive teenagers are particularly selfish and egocentric. They find giving and doing for others very difficult. Normally they are oblivious to opportunities for giving. The chances they do see are rejected as imposing on their own time or plans. As their youth sponsor or teacher, you are in an ideal position to help them experience giving and sharing themselves.

Thanksgiving, Christmas and Easter provide excellent opportunities to serve or give to others. Many youth groups visit convalescent hospitals, orphanages or poorer areas of their city during these holiday seasons. In one church the junior high group members "adopted" children from the local orphanage. On special occasions these young people took their adoptees out for a picnic or home for the weekend. Some young people selected senior citizens with no family as their "adopted grandparents." Sharing special moments and spending time with them offered opportunities for a deepening relationship for both seniors and adolescents alike.

13. Help these young people learn to accept God's grace and others' caring. Since competitive teenagers rely so heavily on their own competence, they struggle intensely with the concept of grace. Like power-oriented adolescents, these young people find it easier to rely on their own strength than accept God's grace. A merited reward is easier to understand and receive than unmerited favor. "What did I do to deserve that?" "I wonder why God would do this for me? The church is probably setting me up to go to the mission field." To accept God's grace means to rely upon him. It means to trust in a superior love and caring. It means depending upon a consistency, believing God will never let you down. All of these concepts are difficult for competitive young people to accept.

Sometimes it helps to point out to these teenagers that they rely on God's grace without knowing it. Their bodies continually fight off infection, bacteria and other microbes attempting to invade their bodies. Their parents and other responsible adults care for their personal needs. Their national, state and local governments adequately protect and provide for them. All of these are examples of grace they receive daily.

In addition, young people experience gifts of love and caring from each other. Support these competitive teenagers as they struggle to accept help. Work with them to understand that being served provides them an opportunity to grow rather than a challenge to their pride.

14. Refer those who need extensive help to a professional counselor, and support them in this experience. Sometimes competitive defenses become too deeply ingrained. When this occurs, teenagers' interpersonal relationships begin to deteriorate. As their defenses become stronger, their behavior becomes more inappropriate. These teenagers may withdraw into presumed superiority, lose touch with their peers and become a pain to have around. In these instances, consult with their family and refer them to a professional counselor.

Agreeing to see a counselor is usually extremely difficult for these young people. This step requires their recognition of a need for help and the decision to ask for it. Encourage them to take that step; sometimes you must insist on it. But remember, they will need continuous assurance that they are no less of a person for seeking help.

■ Guidelines for Parenting Competitive Adolescents

Many professional counselors would agree that parents are usually the most powerful influence in their teenagers' lives. Since a major part of helping adolescents is offering appropriate and meaningful assistance to parents, each chapter in Part Two presents a section just for you.

Competitive personalities present behavioral dynamics that run far deeper than normal adolescent competitiveness. These young people use brothers, sisters, and especially parents as common targets for their competitive attitudes and actions. To effectively parent these adolescents, you must develop a great amount of patience, special understanding and specific skills. By following the suggestions in this section, you can help your competitive teenagers mature through their adolescent years toward a healthier and more fulfilling adulthood.

1. *Learn to hear what your teenagers are saying about themselves through their behavior.* When parents ask their teenagers why they did something, they often reply, "I don't know." And most of the time, they're honest about their response. Your adolescents may be just as frustrated and confused about their behavior as you are. Many times they are not conscious of the motivations behind their actions, nor are they aware of the goals to which their behavior is directed. By becoming better *readers* of your children's behavior, you learn much more about how they think and feel about themselves, their family and their world.

Sometimes you may find it difficult to control your spontaneous reactions to your competitive children long enough to gain an accurate understanding of what they're feeling. Seek to understand what events and circumstances in their personal histories contributed to their developing a competitive personality orientation. Look for experiences that might have damaged their development of a healthy self-esteem. Consider times when they have been seriously demeaned or humiliated by important others. Take special note of rejections and losses they have experienced within personal and family relationships.

Recognizing patterns of recurrent behavior is always

more significant than noting individual incidents. Young people will naturally experiment with new roles and try various ways to interact with their friends. They *will* make mistakes, sometimes even serious errors that carry heavy consequences. However, you need to focus most of your attention on actions that continually repeat themselves.

2. Reinforce your competitive teenagers' personal strength and encourage their growth in this area. Much of your competitive teenagers' security and okayness depends upon their seeing themselves as not only strong, but stronger than others. Though this comparison is essentially unhealthy for building self-esteem, these adolescents must affirm their belief in their own adequacy before significant changes can occur. Let them know you recognize their talents and value their special abilities.

Show as well as tell your competitive teenagers that you appreciate their competency. Give them opportunities within your family and home to exercise their strengths. Place them in charge of certain household duties like planning the week's dinner menus or helping the younger children with their homework. Ask them to compose the family Christmas letter or coordinate and direct a younger sibling's birthday party. Perhaps they could be in charge of certain shopping and errands like delivering and picking up the dry cleaning. These are examples of tasks which may affirm your competitive teenagers' sense of adequacy if they accept and fulfill their responsibilities.

Helping your adolescents believe more fully in their strengths offers them a firm foundation on which to grow. When you recognize and value their strengths, these young people feel less insecure about themselves. With less insecurity and anxiety, they can more accurately assess their needs to make personal changes.

3. Help your young people applaud the strengths of others. Competitive teenagers' self-esteem is linked to their need to be on top. These young people struggle when their friends succeed and when others control situations in which they are involved. Their self-confidence receives a shock when they see others receive credit for a job well done. Their self-value is diminished when their friends are elected to positions of leadership. These same reactions occur when others make the first-string squad ahead of them, when another is selected as a girlfriend or boyfriend in place of them, when they think a brother or sister has received a better Christmas gift or when another person is selected as the lead in the senior play instead of them. Competitive adolescents experience these and other interpersonal situations as competitive events in which they either win or lose. If they see themselves losing, they usually feel angry or demeaning toward the other person.

Your children often learn their attitudes from watching you. Examine your own reactions to others' successes and ask yourself how *you* respond to others' accomplishments. Do your teenagers observe competitive attitudes from you? What kinds of reactions do they see when *your* friends and acquaintances make personal gains? Help your competitive teenagers by modeling a positive attitude toward others who succeed.

Affirm your teenagers' strengths, and guide them into positive responses toward others' successes. Encourage them to send a card, congratulating their friend. Suggest a phone call to express value for another's accomplishments. Or help them sponsor a party to celebrate the other person's achievement. No matter what response your teenagers choose, recognize their efforts to respond to the success of another. Once they realize others' accomplishments will not diminish their own value, they will develop the personal strength to initiate these positive responses on their own.

4. Help your teenagers accept their own weaknesses. Competitive teenagers develop their psychological defenses to protect themselves from the anxiety of feeling weak, incompetent or close to others. They develop their superior attitude to provide feelings of strength and distance themselves from others. These young people don't know they are okay without seeing themselves as *the best*. Their defensive needs cause them to constantly compare themselves with others. Then, they draw their self-esteem and feelings of okayness directly from these comparisons.

To overcome their maladaptive levels of competitive defensiveness, these teenagers need to develop the ability to accept their mistakes and their lack of certain talents. They will need your help to accomplish this goal. Gently encourage your youthful competitors to admit to their omissions, mistakes and inabilities. Model your own admissions of weakness. Let them see that you can maintain your self-respect. They need your example to know that recognizing and admitting to one's personal faults does not result in a loss of personal dignity.

In addition to sharing your own personal example with them, gently help these competitive adolescents recognize and admit to their own mistakes. Quickly assure them of your ongoing acceptance and esteem for them. Let them know you don't see them as a lesser person. Help them understand that their willingness to become vulnerable actually causes you to respect them more. As they give you opportunities to accept, affirm and encourage them, your love and sensitivity toward them increases. "Denise, since you have opened up about how bad you feel when you do poorly, my love and respect for you have grown even more. It's like you're letting me get to know you more deeply." Competitive teenagers need to learn they do not become less of a person when they recognize areas of personal inadequacy. By observing your modeling and hearing your affirmation, these teenagers gradually learn to do the same for themselves.

5. Help your teenagers know they belong in your family because of *who they are* rather than because they are *best* at something. One of the most fundamental psychological needs children have is to know they belong. The family unit is the ideal environment in which to nurture this sense of belonging. Since competitive young people seek to secure their belonging by being better than others, they will naturally compete with their brothers and sisters. Much of the sibling rivalry you have to deal with relates to this competitive approach to securing a position within the family unit. By understanding the relationship between your teenagers' competitiveness and their need to belong, you can respond in ways that meaningfully meet your children's needs.

Help your children recognize and experience your love for *who* they are rather than for *what* they do. Start simply by telling them that though their actions are important, you have grown to love them deeply, aside from what they do. Let them know that you love them as a gift from God. Even though your love cannot be as unconditional as God's love, share with your children the love you feel that is separate from considerations about their behavior. Tell them that you value them as individuals created in God's image. Help them understand that God has not *given* them to you, but rather he has *entrusted* them to you for your care and training during their childhood and adolescence.

Never put belonging in the family or your love for your children at risk during the process of discipline. Do *not* use these relationships as rewards or punishments. Do not threaten your children with statements like, "If you don't stop that, I'm not going to love you anymore." For the sake of your teenagers' security, they must recognize your love and being part of their family as givens, not to be withdrawn under any circumstances.

6. Help your competitive teenagers experience being equal within relationships. Competitive adolescents feel comfortable with other people *only* when they are in a superior position. Being in elevated roles that sufficiently remove them from others helps them feel secure. Relationships of equality typically produce anxiety within these teenagers. Equal relationships lack the superior-inferior role configuration which provides security for these young people. However, in order to function effectively in this world, these adolescents need to learn how to operate from equal and subordinate roles as well as from superior roles. You can help your teenagers experience and feel comfortable in all these roles.

These suggestions may help your competitive teenagers feel more secure in relationships of equality. Try using family meetings to make decisions and resolve conflicts within the home. Let each family member, including your competitive adolescents, have an equal say and vote in the final outcome. (As a general rule, only family members who are directly affected by the group's decision should be allowed to take part in the decision-making process. Also, in decisions where parental authority is an issue, a completely democratic approach may not be appropriate.) In most situations experiences as equal members with the rest of the family can benefit competitive adolescents. They may begin to feel closer to other family members and experience more connection with any final decisions.

Involve all of your family in non-competitive play activities, where no one wins or loses. Bicycling, body surfing, skiing, swimming, hiking, backpacking, watching television, going to the theater, listening to music, attending professional ballgames and even flying kites are examples of non-competitive recreational experiences. Playfulness usually relaxes individuals' defenses. When this relaxation occurs at home, competitive teenagers usually drop their defenses. Sharing equally in family responsibilities around the house or in the yard also provides these adolescents with opportunities for non-competitive family interaction.

The home environment is probably the safest place for competitive young people to explore equal relationships. As you present opportunities and involve them in these non-competitive family activities, ask them to share with you how they feel about these experiences. Remember to listen to their responses and guide them to understand and work with their reactions.

7. *Reinforce your competitive teenagers' understandings that dependence upon others is not only acceptable but a positive experience as well.* Competitive young people feel unsafe and vulnerable when depending upon a friend or even an adult. When these teenagers are not in a position of power or superiority, the close proximity of another person is unbearable to them. Dependency robs them of their superiority, which gives them their feelings of security.

Competitive teenagers often shun dependency because they feel a sense of failure. These adolescents prize their self-sufficiency so much that depending on another person indicates personal failure or inadequacy. Another implicit reason these young people seek to avoid dependency is their lack of trust in others. Many of them fear other people will use knowledge of their weaknesses and vulnerability against them.

The family is usually the best place to start helping competitive teenagers trust themselves and others more. Encourage your adolescents to begin taking risks by depending on other members of the family. You can take the first step by asking your teenagers for help. Depend upon their strengths and talents, when it is appropriate. Ask their advice, and then utilize their help. Ask for their suggestions when purchasing gifts for friends and relatives. Help them see you are depending on them when they help you carry in things from the car, when they help prepare meals, when they take over tasks in the yard and when they run errands for you. Express your sincere appreciation to them. Make sure they sense the relief and support you feel as a result of your depending on them. Explain to your competitive adolescents that everyone feels better when we mutually depend upon one another. It feels just as good to have a burden lifted from *our* shoulders as it does to be able to help *others*.

Provide opportunities for you to help and support your competitive adolescents. Then try to get them to tell you how they felt when they received your help. Build nurturing and affirmation into your conversation with them.

"Thanks for letting me help you with your homework. You sure catch on fast!"

"You did a good job on overhauling your carburetor, Son. I enjoyed helping."

These kinds of statements will help your young people not to feel demeaned or devalued by your assistance.

Remember to point out how you see their friends helping each other. And direct your teenagers' attention to the same types of mutually helping relationships you see together on television or in movies.

Depending on others is a frightening experience for these competitive adolescents. Helping them gradually experience relying on others is one more step toward a healthier interpersonal style of relating for these young competitors.

8. Encourage these teenagers to gradually explore and expand the activities in which they feel competent. Competitive teenagers consistently avoid the risk of being compared unfavorably to others. Since these young people need to feel superior to others, they usually restrict their activities to areas in which they feel competent. They focus only on activities in which they can specialize like sports, academics, auto mechanics, a particular hobby, socializing, playing a musical instrument, acting, singing or setting up and operating audio-visual equipment. Venturing into other activities in which they lack knowledge or experience brings instant anxiety and even panic, especially if others are observing.

This is just another example of competitive teenagers' excessive focus on performance. They miss most of the pleasures found in whatever they are doing. Their focus on the *quality* of their performance robs them of any personal or social enjoyment or pleasure in the experience itself. These young people need to build enough self-confidence to allow them to enjoy their activities without being intensely preoccupied with evaluating their performance. They need to get their eyes off themselves and onto what it is they are doing or the others who may be with them."

There are a number of things you can do to help your competitive teenagers grow out of this bind. Recognize that success, accomplishment and the attainment of perfection are extremely important to these adolescents. Take note of the areas in which your teenagers seem to have natural abilities. Are they skilled in music, sports, art, planning and organizing events or helping people who are sad? Select two or three of these areas in which your teenagers have yet to develop their talents and encourage their interests in these directions. Suggest ways to start and offer to participate with them. Take a flower-arranging class or rebuild an engine together. Play golf, tennis or some other leisure sport with each other. Encourage a total family activity that might stimulate your teenagers' interest in that activity. While your young people are trying something new, make comments that focus on enjoying the task rather than evaluating the quality of the performance. "It sure is fun trying something new!" "I'm sure others can tell we are beginners, but let's not let that get in the way of our having a good time."

Competitive teenagers will need support to try activities in which they do not feel competent. Helping them venture into new areas of interest will lend much creativity and stimulation to their lives.

9. Help your competitive adolescents gain a clearer understanding of how other people think. In an effort to preserve their own sense of security, competitive teenagers often shield themselves from knowing how other people perceive the world. They guard against knowing how other people think so they don't have to question their own perceptions, thoughts and attitudes. By isolating themselves from others' ways of thinking and perceiving, they maintain a comfortable void filled with only their own thoughts. Within this isolated sphere, only their own ways of perceiving the world and people exist.

The primary problem with this defensive structure is that it isolates the competitive type of adolescent from everyone else. These teenagers become quite rigid, casting aside everything that seems foreign to them. When confronted with a thought different from their own, they usually try to deny its validity, argue against it or otherwise discredit it.

You can help your competitive teenagers lessen their negative reactions to other viewpoints, positions and thoughts. Initiate discussions of issues which don't have a *right* or *wrong* answer. Deciding whether a particular painting is attractive or whether a Ford is better than a Chevrolet are issues that can't be resolved with absolute *yes* or *no* answers. Ask your young people to tell you what they think another person's statement means. "What are the strong and the weak points of Leslie's point of view?" "What did you understand Paul's point to be?" Reinforcing your teenagers for their creativity and thoughtfulness within their perceptions can build their confidence in themselves as thinking people. As their self-confidence increases, other points of view threaten them less and less.

For competitive teenagers to become more mature in their world-view, they need the ability to consider and evaluate others' perceptions and styles of thinking without feeling threatened. Your encouragement and affirmation as you participate with them in their struggle to understand others' thoughts and feelings can afford them invaluable help in this growth process.

10. Help your competitive teenagers open themselves to their loving and tender feelings. These adolescents protect themselves from emotional vulnerability with their competitive defensive structure. By comparing themselves with others and maintaining a self-perception of superiority, they establish distance between themselves and others. They also protect themselves from the vulnerability that comes from contact with their own soft and tender emotions. As this pattern continues, competitive individuals have an increasingly difficult time even knowing they have warm and sensitive feelings. This lack of awareness severely hampers their ability to form long-lasting, intimate relationships that require the capacity to give and receive love and tender feelings.

Competitive young people need patient help to risk opening themselves to their vulnerable emotions. Their personal vulnerability frightens these teenagers terribly because of their fear of losing control. Losing control of their emotions is even more threatening to them than not being in control of what is going on around them.

Effective modeling of emotional expressions is one of the most effective ways of helping competitive teenagers open themselves to their own tender emotions. Let your children see you cry. Be willing to express affection in front of them—to your spouse, your other children, your pets and your friends. Be sure to express ample affection and love directly to your competitive teenagers, and encourage them to do the same. Suggest ways for them to communicate from their hearts to others. Help them select cards, write notes, give hugs, do special chores to help others and put their special feelings into words. Many of their fears center in their expectations of humiliation if they expose these vulnerable emotions. Reassure them of their okayness and respond to them in ways that clearly show you accept and value them.

Competitive young people guard against experiencing tender emotions, especially their own. Help them gain an awareness of how they feel, and then encourage them to communicate their feelings to others. Learning to accept and share this tender part of their personality will help them grow toward wholeness.

***11. Encourage your competitive teenagers to
develop greater capacity to give to others.*** These
adolescents have a difficult time giving to others. These
young people perceive the act of giving as taking something away from themselves. Their competitive orientation
causes them to grasp all the power, attention, glory and
acclaim they can for themselves. Typically, the act of
giving places attention on the one receiving the gift. However, competitive young people handle their tension by
giving in a manner that focuses more attention on their
generosity or their self-sacrifice. Fear and personal insecurity normally motivate this kind of selfishness.

Help your teenagers by addressing the fears that block
their capacity to give. This task is difficult because these
young people are usually unaware of their insecurities.
Often they do not know why they resist giving. They only
know they don't like to give. Giving makes them feel
angry or uncomfortable even when they think about it.
Talk freely with your competitive adolescents about the
positive feelings you experience when you give to others.
Let your teenagers know how good it feels to give to
them. Be honest about any resistance you sometimes feel
so your teenagers can identify with those feelings, too.
You will have much more credibility with your children
when you are honest and open about your negative feelings as well as your positive attitudes.

Try to arrange situations where your young competitors can give more easily. Go shopping with them and
split the cost of gifts, especially those purchased for relatives. Give them numerous gift suggestions, and make a
fun outing of your shopping, offering them plenty of reinforcing personal contact. Suggest they do extra chores to
help those they care for. This physical act of giving provides these teenagers with an opportunity to get involved
in the actual process of putting others first. Participate
with them in a mission activity with the poor. Offer to
help them take an active role in food drives, toy collection
campaigns and work projects that minister to the needy.

Suggest mutually sponsoring a child in a famine-ridden country. These are just some of the many forms of giving that can help your adolescents experience some of the value inherent in the process of giving.

Competitive teenagers need your help to overcome some of their resistance to giving to others. The scriptural principles of dying to one's self and giving to others are difficult for these young people to embrace. Your assistance in this area of growth can effectively impact their social and spiritual development.

12. Consider professional counseling for competitive teenagers whose defenses are destructively affecting their personal and social lives. When teenagers become consistently and extremely competitive in their defensive orientation, they may need the help of a professional counselor or psychologist. Excessive needs to always be *the best* or *on top* plus an obvious void of warmth and giving indicate counseling is appropriate. When your efforts and the help offered by teachers and ministers fail to produce positive changes, professional help is needed. Ask your priest, pastor, youth minister, family physician or school officials for recommendations on which professional to call. Remember, seeking professional guidance is sometimes the best help you can provide for your competitive teenagers and yourself.

We are now more familiar with competitive teenagers and can identify them more easily within our group and in our homes. We understand more exactly what their competitive behavior says, and we are better equipped to help them meet their needs. We must work with these young people to moderate the intensity of their competitive defenses and support them if they need help beyond our own expertise.

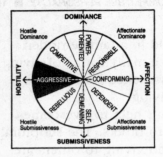

■ C H A P T E R   6

The Aggressive Personality

For some teenagers, power is not as important as aggression. Aggressive adolescents develop a very effective and impressive way of relating with others. Sometimes they threaten and openly attack. At other times they are more covert or subtle, but their intention is still the same. Positioning themselves against others is their primary goal. They feel most comfortable when they actively oppose their peers and adults. They feel most threatened when others expect cooperation and closeness. They *want* interpersonal distance, which they accomplish by being aggressive and threatening to those around them.

Most aggressive teenagers use hostility as their primary defense and do not relate well to others. On the surface, these adolescents do not want close friendships. People are useful to them only when they can be pushed against. They feel their best when they are punitive toward others. While competitive teenagers try to demean and put others down, aggressive adolescents genuinely seek to cause others pain and psychological injury. They highly prize their aggressive tendencies.

Aggression is easy to identify in young people unless it is well-controlled and moderated. Effects of aggressive behavior are usually dramatic and memorable. Adults often express their aggression through stern, critical leadership, like the Marine drill instructor. But during adolescence, few acceptable opportunities exist for expressing this personality type. During junior high and high school this style of leadership is intolerable both to other teenagers and the adults involved. Aggressive adolescents find it difficult to express the dynamics of their personality in appropriate, acceptable and constructive ways.

Aggressive adolescents make a statement to others. Essentially, they are saying: "I have been so wounded in life I can no longer trust or tolerate relationships with other people. Therefore, I will threaten everyone by showing them how aggressive and fearful I am. When anyone gets close to me, I will hurt them back in return for the pain I have felt."

■ Development of the *Aggressive Personality*

Although aggression is an issue for every adolescent, these teenagers have a difficult time controlling and moderating their aggressive impulses. Unlike power-oriented and competitive young people who attempt to control and dominate others, aggressive teenagers actively work to push others away. They learn to use their aggression as a defense to maintain a safe distance from others. A variety of dynamics in young people's lives influences their development of this particular defensive orientation.

First, all adolescents have been hurt during their childhood. In the case of aggressive teenagers, however, the injuries were significant enough to warrant developing hostilities toward other people. Most aggressive teenagers have had psychologically painful experiences early in life. Some have been abused either sexually, physically or emotionally. Others suffer from physical or emotional neglect. These teenagers have experienced other people as dangerous sources of pain. They have determined that their best approach to others is to keep them at a safe distance. And their most effective mechanism for accomplishing this task is presenting themselves as threatening and hostile so others will retreat.

God created us to need and enjoy contact with each other. His motivation for making Eve for Adam is found in the book of Genesis: "The Lord God said, 'It is not good for the man to be alone. I will make a helper suitable for him' " (Genesis 2:18). Each of the other defensive reactions we are studying in this book enables teenagers to make contact with others. Each personality type can find ways of overcoming interpersonal anxieties in order to build and maintain relationships. Even though excessive use of the other seven defensive styles can eventually destroy relationships, their primary purpose is to protect teenagers from anxiety when they enter a threatening situation. *Only* the aggressive personality type is designed to actually push people away.

Second, as with the other defensive styles, aggression reinforces itself each time it works. Whenever aggression pushes others away, the teenagers' levels of anxiety are reduced. Their feelings of security and comfort are enhanced as their anxiety levels go down. Thus, aggression succeeds; it accomplishes its purpose. And like the rest of us, aggressive adolescents continue to use what works for them.

Third, some aggressive adolescents learn their defensive operations from their parents or other adults. Sometimes children grow up in homes, neighborhoods or certain subcultures in which aggression is not only modeled by the adults, but also admired and praised. Aggressiveness is the way to get what you want. Most interpersonal interactions are seen as aggressive encounters in which the most aggressive wins.

Criminal and gang subcultures are typically aggressive

by nature. Aggression and intimidation rule. Young people from these subcultures use what they have learned in other settings, too. When these adolescents enter a new group, they will continue their attempt to lead with intimidation and toughness. They are similar to the "macho man," except their aggression is more overt. They openly display their bravado, which says: "I'm tougher and meaner than you. Don't mess with me, or you'll get hurt."

All children try to emulate their parents, believing that in doing so, they will please their parents. Unconsciously, aggressive adolescents also anticipate their adult role models will be proud of them and accept them as a result of their aggressive behavior.

Fourth, when young people express moderated aggression, it is often misinterpreted as strength or power. Subtle expressions of aggression can effectively get people to "back off" without appearing conspicuously hostile or sadistic. Teenagers who behave this way usually gain a great amount of respect from their peers. Only when others get to know the individual on a more personal level do they recognize their aggressiveness for what it is.

Girls are often attracted to aggressive boys because of their "strength." They soon find out that this "strength" quickly turns into aggression when they get too close. If the aggressiveness is masked well enough, a young woman may not discover the truth until after an ill-fated wedding.

Fifth, the adolescent community reinforces certain forms of aggressive behavior. Sarcasm and quick comebacks are signs of being "cool" and having it together. In moderation, these behaviors work well. They win respect and elevate individuals within the adolescent pecking order. However, when used as the primary way of interacting with others, aggressive young people severely limit their meaningful relationships. Other teenagers withdraw respect and interest as they recognize the aggressive adolescents' cloaked intimidation and become fearful.

Sixth, some teenagers can mask their aggressiveness well enough to draw the attention and praise of adults.

They emerge as leaders of the youth group or youth advisors to the church board. They win the admiration of unsuspecting adults through their super-spiritual feats. They rigidly hold to an approved lists of dos and don'ts. They have daily quiet times and avidly quote Bible verses. They express whatever is said and done in spiritual language. Within the Christian community these young people become excessively righteous and judgmental of others' sins. They view all of life through spiritual lenses.

The aggressiveness of this personality type is seen in the rigid judgmental attitude expressed toward others. Some direct their guilt-provoking moralizations primarily toward their peers. Others aggressively criticize the adult community. Unlike competitive teenagers whose criticisms are meant to put other people down, aggressive adolescents do not compete. They just want to make other people feel pain. They actually want to *hurt* others.

When you suspect a group member or your own child of displaying inappropriate aggression, examine these developmental issues. If you find several that fit, your suspicions are probably correct. We cannot list all of the possible reasons to explain an adolescent's aggressive personality. We can, however, offer many comon dynamics of the aggressive personality and list several ways to minister to this young person.

■ *Healthy Forms of the Aggressive Personality*

The aggressive personality style is essentially antisocial. Therefore, one could argue that there are no healthy forms of this defense. If aggression and hostility are essentially unhealthy or sinful, how can expressions of this personality style ever be constructive? Aggression within teenagers does indicate a problem in the young peoples' social adaptations. However, teenagers' abilities to moderate and control their aggression can indicate other personality strengths. With the help of God and a support-

ive community, all of us can control the negative or
destructive impulses within us. This control can strengthen
all who attain it, even aggressive teenagers. Here are examples of how some adolescents moderately express their
aggressiveness:

The Pious. As we discuss relatively healthy expressions of the aggressive personality, remember none of
these has a particularly positive impact, neither on the
individual nor on others in relationship to them. Piety, for
example, is an important virtue. Pious people have great
reverence for God and are deeply devoted to worshiping
the divine. Unfortunately, "pious" may also describe
individuals who are conspicuously religious and self-
conscious about their own virtue. In these cases, piety is
only one step away from hypocrisy.

Wanda is quite a contrast to her brother Steve, who is
three years older than she. (We'll meet him later in this
chapter.) Wanda watched her brother go through difficulties at home, church and school. She observed her
parents' reactions to his declining grades, poor choices for
friends, and periodic confrontations with the police. She
witnessed vicious verbal battles between her father and
brother. She not only *saw* the pain he experienced in his
life of rejection, withdrawal and revenge, but she also *felt*
the damage caused by his rage and hurtful behavior.

When Wanda was 7 and 8 years old, her brother
sexually molested her on numerous occasions. The rage
she felt was mixed with guilt because she enjoyed some of
the stimulation she had experienced. The intensity of her
feelings threatened her so much that she repressed her
memories and emotions associated with these experiences.
Now, as an adolescent, she does not recall what happened.
She doesn't realize why thinking of her brother makes her
so anxious. Nor does she comprehend the psychological
basis for her extreme piety.

Wanda saw commitment to God and a life of righteousness as the *only* way to be certain she would never experience what she saw her brother go through. Her rigid,

life-consuming religiosity also helped protect her from experiencing any sexual feelings normal for a girl her age. During her junior high years Wanda made a firm commitment to Christ. She had been a Christian for several years, but as a seventh-grader she decided to dedicate her life to being *absolutely* obedient to God. She read her Bible regularly, attended church and Sunday school weekly and sought to apply what she was reading and hearing to her life in every situation. Her religious commitment served as a protective wall. While presenting herself to others as the image of true spiritual devotion, this commitment also guarded her both from her brother's threat and her own sexual impulses.

Wanda is now 16 years old. She has been in the youth group for two years. Wanda's youth minister isn't sure whether he should be thankful or remorseful. Is she a blessing in disguise, or should he pray for the group's deliverance from her? When other kids are around Wanda in the youth group or at school, they feel uncomfortable. Although it's difficult for them to determine why, they usually feel criticized or condemned. The kids feel especially hurt by the things she says to or about them. Though she tries to involve others in regular Bible study and prayer, she ends up putting them down, criticizing them and pushing them away. As a result, her peers feel hurt, offended and alienated.

Wanda's earlier pain has caused her to defend herself against all relationships. She trusts no one. Her brother, whom she respected and looked up to, hurt her so deeply she unconsciously decided never to be close to anyone again. Her commitment to God represents a much safer relationship for her. For one reason, she never has to confront God physically. In addition, she relates with God in an environment that she controls. Wanda finds other people far more difficult to predict and control than her image of God.

Wanda's aggressive stance has obvious problems. She hurts and alienates others because of the pain she has

received and observed in her brother. But she has sought
a constructive path for expressing her aggression. Her own
devotion is certainly commendable, even with our deeper
understanding of its basis. And her desire to manipulate
her peers into an increasing spiritual commitment does
have a positive thrust, though it is largely ineffective.

The Drill Instructor. In his youth group Max is
another blessing with numerous blemishes. In many ways
he appears similar to Cynthia the "dictator," the power-
oriented personality we discussed in Chapter 4. But their
similarity ends not too far beneath the surface. To
Cynthia, the issues were power and dominance; Max's purposes are aggression and the ability to hurt or threaten
others. Let's examine how Max became the teenager he is
today.

Max has grown up in an extremely regimented home
environment. His parents love him, but they do not
express their love. Max has a sister four years older than
he. She is bright, assertive and self-sufficient. All of her life
she has been gregarious, but she was also hesitant to
express warmth or affection. During elementary and junior
high school, she has played sports actively, both in the
neighborhood and at school. She has always been tough
competition for Max. With only average intelligence and
less-than-average physical coordination, Max has never
been on an academic or athletic par with his older sister.
Plus, her minimal expressions of affection have left him
thinking she didn't love him.

Both of Max's parents have compounded his problems.
His dad is a career Marine who recently retired from active
duty. Max's father personifies the commonly accepted
image of the most rigid and authoritarian branch of the
military service. Everything is "spit-and-polish." He controls virtually every activity in the house. Standards are
high. He demands that his family meet his expectations
immediately and consistently. Punishments are swift and
severe.

Dad is even less emotionally responsive than Max's

sister. He demonstrates his love for Max through providing financial security, a well-ordered home and strong parental authority. When asked about his father's love for him, Max responds, "Yeah, I know my dad loves me, but I sure don't *feel* it."

His mother expresses her love for Max with more emotion. She hugs and kisses him and tells him how she feels about him. Max feels that his mother loves him, but in a curious way his knowledge of her feelings diminishes the value of her love. Her love is easy; it's always there. Therefore, his unconscious logic says her love can't be too valuable if it's so readily available. The difficulty of attaining his dad's and sister's love assures him that their love must have greater value.

When Max was in junior high, his parents had serious marital problems. They argued and fought, screaming at each other in front of the children. Max hated it. He feared they would divorce, and he didn't know what would happen to him. His sister was no source of comfort; her comments offered no support. "Oh, all parents fight. That's just the way it is. Don't be silly." He felt there was no one to whom he could turn for encouragement or understanding. He resented his parents for shaking his world and for not being there when he needed their reassurance.

Max's anger at both of his parents and his sister continued to deepen. Somehow he needed to express these bitter feelings. Since his home was too threatening for such venting, his peers at school and church became his targets. He masked his anger to make it look like power or control, but his intensity as well as the self-righteousness in his stern, demanding attitude revealed the aggression beneath his control. Max is the one who demands quiet and cooperation from other young people when it's time to listen. Max is the one who volunteers to enforce "lights out" at the winter retreat. And of course, it is Max who would volunteer to monitor and report others' regularity in their daily devotions, if he could only figure out a way to do so.

Max has been deeply hurt and discouraged by the insecurity of his father's and sister's love for him. He feels rage in what he perceives as rejection; he also feels guilty about that anger. So he expresses it in a masked form (aggressive controlling) which unconsciously threatens, demeans and hurts others. Depending upon how Max feels about himself, he can sometimes fulfill his "drill instructor" role in a relatively non-destructive manner. At times his aggression is well-hidden, but no mask can alter the presence of aggression within him.

These two forms of aggression, the "pious" and the "drill instructor," represent relatively healthy adaptations of the aggressive personality. But these forms are healthy only to the extent that they are not rigid or intense in their expression. With this personality type, however, the line of intensity is difficult to control. If crossed, aggression becomes evident, and others dramatically feel its destructive effects.

■ Unhealthy Forms of the *Aggressive* Personality

We have already suggested that the aggressive personality is at its core an unhealthy adaptation to life and its stresses. This personality style presents an antagonistic front to others, which is contrary to our basic need for intimate contact. God created human beings to draw naturally toward one another; aggression pushes people away. Aggressive teenagers are easy to identify because they leave such a negative impact on the people around them. In this section we will examine three adolescent expressions of the unhealthy aggressive personality.

The Bully. We have already drawn a comparison between the "dictator" and the "drill instructor." The "bully" can be compared to both of them. All three forms of social interaction involve exerting powerful influence on other people's actions. The "dictator" seeks control over others through power and influence. Like the "drill instructor," the "bully" stays in charge with intimidation and threat. But the actions of the "bully" are even more overt and intense. Remember, aggressive teenagers want to hurt or at least threaten to hurt others.

Brad illustrates many of the personal and social dynamics of the aggressive adolescent. By age 13, Brad had experienced more pain than many adults. Four years after his birth, Brad's parents divorced. He lived with his mother and saw his father only infrequently. During his elementary school years his mother invited nine different men to live with them. She married none of them, and most of those relationships lasted only a few months. She became pregnant several times and ended all but one pregnancy with abortions. Brad's little sister was born when he was 8 years old. He was expected to baby-sit his sister every weekday after school and during the evenings on most weekends. He was also given most of the household tasks as his chores.

Brad's mother was so immature she could attend to no one but herself. And the men with whom she lived had no interest in being a father figure to Brad. He was an unhappy boy. He found little in his life to make it worthwhile. His unhappiness turned into anger. He became sullen, withdrawn and sometimes openly belligerent and aggressive at school. He had never been popular with the other children or his teachers. Now he was gaining a reputation as a troublemaker. His downhill slide was gaining momentum, and there were no capable or concerned adults to stop or even slow his plunge.

Brad became discouraged. He knew he wasn't wanted at home. Although he used to have hope, he now knew he didn't belong at school or with the neighborhood kids either. He felt comfortable only when he was alone or when he was with a certain small group of boys who struggled to alienate themselves from everyone else. He discovered that his own pain subsided when he hurt others. Pushing other kids around, brazenly cutting into lunch lines and daring anyone to do anything about it, threatening to beat kids up if they didn't let him use their bikes and forcing them to give him money for snacks and drugs were common activities for Brad. Almost all of his social behavior was aggressive in some form.

By the time Brad reached his early adolescent years, he had experienced the world as a hurtful place in which to live. He felt people didn't care about anyone but themselves. He believed everyone would take advantage of him unless he could prevent it, and he learned he was on his own. He had already experienced getting close to someone as a dangerous thing to do. And he responded to his inner pain and experiences by adopting an aggressive orientation toward other people.

This aggression accomplished three tasks. First, it provided a release for the anger building within him throughout his childhood. Second, seeing himself as an initiator of pain caused him not to feel so victimized by life. And third, this aggressive behavior backed most people away, allowing him to keep others at a safe distance. In this way he protected himself from further potential harm. Accomplishing these tasks provided continual reinforcement for his aggressive behavior. At the insistence of school personnel and the county probation department, Brad finally entered counseling. Unfortunately, without parental or other support, it is doubtful much progress can be accomplished.

The Judge. Remember Wanda, the "pious" teenager we met earlier in this chapter? Wanda's piety served to reinforce her own feelings of okayness. She buried her painful, guilt-provoking memories beneath an exaggerated focus on God. She was aggressive in her efforts to *help* her friends become more spiritually devoted, but the intensity of her efforts put others down and alienated them.

The "judge" is much more aggressive than the "pious" adolescent. There is no doubt about judgment when it comes from this type of teenager. This young person not only makes a judgment, but also passes sentence on others!

Phyllis is a freshman in college. She comes from a loving home where both parents are involved with their children. Both of her parents are Christians, and she has learned to live her life according to scriptural principles. There has been adequate emphasis on family activities. Even annual vacations and periodic special occasions have been family-centered. Phyllis has grown up knowing she was loved and valued, so where did her problems develop? How did she adopt her aggressive interpersonal attitude if she had such a positive childhood family experience?

Her mother is a fearful, neurotic person. Coming from an unhealthy, unstable family, Phyllis' mother carries scars in her personality, expressed in her negative view of the world. Becoming a Christian helped her forgive her parents for their lack of loving. Her faith also helped her release her past and live more fully in the present. But she can't (or won't) shake her fears about the future, and she has passed these fears along to her daughter.

"You can't be too careful, honey."

"Don't believe what people tell you. They're not being completely honest. They probably want something from you."

"Be especially careful around boys, dear. Most of them only want sex, and they'll tell you anything to get it."

She has drilled these and many other precautions about life and other people into Phyllis since her early childhood.

As Phyllis grew older, her mother had less control. With less control, her mom's insecurity and fears increased. Consequently, the intensity and frequency of her warnings about life's dangers also increased.

Had things gone well for Phyllis in her relationships with friends, she might have been okay. However, that was not the case. Every time she had a scrap or hassle with a friend, her mother dwelled on it as further evi-

dence of how disappointing and unfulfilling relationships
are. Each spat or disagreement was another indication
people should be shunned or at least kept at a safe distance. Phyllis took these experiences as ongoing proof that
her mother was right.

Through early and mid-adolescence Phyllis became
increasingly angry at her peers when they failed to do as
she wished. When their actions hurt her, she became more
indignant and accusing. The more she responded as
"judge," the more her relationships deteriorated. She
became increasingly judgmental of her friends' wrongdo-
ings. She was verbal and confrontive. She took pride in
her honesty and courage to tell others exactly what she
thought. "You may not like what I say, but you will
always know what I think." She built a reputation for
utilizing her honesty to inflict pain on others.

Her self-righteous attitude promoted her boldness. Her
defense worked tragically well. No one wanted to tangle
with her. At the first sign of problems, her friends quickly
backed away. Few were willing to confront her about her
tendency to alienate so many friends. And when anyone
did confront her, she engaged in her notorious, air-tight
defense. First, she passed judgment. "You're being unlov-
ing (a lousy friend, unchristian, an uncaring person, etc.)."
Then, she delivered the sentence. "I'm not going to talk to
you anymore." "You're no longer welcome at our youth
group." "With your bad attitude you won't be heading
any committees this year." "Since you haven't done any
work this semester, you're off the leadership committee."

Phyllis goes way beyond Wanda in cruelty. Her goal is
to hurt others by judging them as bad and then to make
them suffer for their "sins." She enlists unsuspecting
friends to help carry out her sentences by gossiping and
turning them against each other. Those who trespass
against her are likely to be banished from her "kingdom"
or some other equally severe punishment.

Phyllis' self-esteem cannot rest upon being well-liked
and accepted. Rather, it depends upon how efficiently she

can hurt others through her judgments and severe punishments. Since she is a Christian, much of her defensive behavior is filled with judgmental thinking and morality. She believes this religious aspect adds even more credibility to what she is doing. Unhappily, the way she uses scripture and morality discourages, hurts and distances her Christian as well as her non-Christian friends. There is no ministry of reconciliation or healing in her actions.

The Sadist. Steve is now 19 years old. (He is "pious" Wanda's older brother.) Throughout his life Steve has enjoyed inflicting pain on animals and other people. In early elementary school he spent hours devising ways to torture bugs. As he moved through grade school, he began to torture neighborhood pets and any other animals he found. Sticking pins through goldfish, drowning cats, setting dogs on fire and wounding animals with his BB gun were common sadistic activities for him. He experienced excitement while watching them struggle and suffer. Sometimes he was remorseful when an animal died, but these feelings never lasted long. His need for renewed arousal drove him to devise new and more creative ways to inflict pain on animals.

Steve also included people among his victims. Usually the pain he inflicted on humans was emotional rather than physical. He delighted in playing practical jokes on his friends. The problem with most of Steve's practical jokes was that they left the victims open to embarrassment and ridicule. These experiences were quite different from laughing *with* a friend. His victims experienced cruel mocking and relentless public exposure of their weaknesses, awkwardness or vulnerability.

As Steve entered junior high school, he initiated physical abuse as well as emotional cruelty to those around him. Not only did he fight with smaller kids, but he tried specifically to cause others physical injury. He would trip people on stairways, push them over while they rode their bicycles, throw rocks at them from behind bushes and even place scorpions and tarantulas in his neighbors' mailboxes. These were just some of the ways Steve had been physically cruel to others.

During sixth-grade and junior high school, Steve also began molesting his younger sister. At first, he coaxed her with candy, money and other small payoffs for letting him do things to her and for her doing things to him. Soon the rewards ceased, and he began forcing his will. He threatened her with physical pain if she didn't submit to his wishes or if she told anyone what was happening. Their mutual fondling soon developed into his demands for intercourse and other bizarre sexual practices. During one of these sexual sessions, his sister screamed with pain and bled. He became frightened and never molested her again.

Steve did continue his aggressive sexual activity with other girls. He included elements of force, dominance, inducement of pain, entrapment and total disregard for the girls' feelings. His arousal and pleasure seemed related to his use of violence or force as much as the sexual nature of the experience. After he had taken what he wanted from a girl, he *always* dumped her. This sadistic act with each girl was his final way of hurting her and pushing her away, affording him the space he desired.

Steve fought viciously with his parents from his late elementary years until he moved out of their house at age 18. He resented their rules. He couldn't tolerate their authority over him. So he struck out against them, seeking to intimidate, threaten and hurt them so much they would back off. To some degree, his efforts paid off. They were unable to withstand the constant sting of his angry outbursts, the mocking or jeering when he succeeded in getting his way and the powerless feeling they experienced when he outmaneuvered them.

Steve's blatant aggression directed toward his parents was also expressed toward his teachers and other authority figures. Everyone received almost the same treatment. When individuals threatened to get close, Steve inflicted some pain to make them withdraw. Nothing was ever his

fault. Others were always to blame. Everything was externalized.

Steve is an angry young man who relates socially in
only one way—aggression. No one knows how this intense
anger first developed. However, it is painfully clear that it
has continued to intensify. Steve's aggression colors most
every action, word and decision regarding his social relationships. His primary goal is to hurt others. When successful, he experiences brief relief from his own internal
pain. And others instinctively back away, allowing him the
wider comfort zone he desires.

These teenagers present three unhealthy adaptations to
social living. All three are aggressive at their core and
express their hostility in different ways. The "bully" seeks
to push others away through the threat of causing pain.
The "judge" condemns and punishes others for their
transgressions. And the "sadist" enjoys inflicting pain and
experiencing pleasure as others wince from the physical
and (or) emotional discomfort he or she induces. All three
examples have successfully accomplished the goals of
aggressive teenagers—to hurt others and then push them
away.

■ Effects of Aggressive Behavior on Other People

Apprehension and fear are usually the first reactions
people have when they confront an aggressive teenager.
Even when aggression is moderated, other people back off
or take time to reflect on what is happening. These
responses are not surprising when we remember that the
intention of aggression is to push people away. The protective mechanism of aggression presents itself in such a
threatening manner that others retreat from the relationship. This distancing provides the adolescent with a
greater sense of security and protection.

People resent being threatened. This is an affront to
their dignity as well as to their own security. They distrust

the aggressive teenager's motives. And because of the threat or intimidation they experience, sometimes they distrust their own thinking and perceptions. An aggressive adolescent desires obedient submission as a response to his or her aggression. This type of submission is usually accompanied by the victims' resentments and desires to retaliate. A healthier form of the aggressive personality will draw less severe, negative reactions from others. Apprehension, fear, confusion and resentment are normally mild enough to allow others to maintain a relationship with this aggressive individual.

Another common response to aggressive behavior is guilt. This response normally occurs when confronted by a "pious" teenager. This aggressive youth flaunts his or her righteousness and morality, causing others to doubt their devotion, spirituality or okayness. This show of religious fervor is designed to stimulate feelings of inadequacy and self-depreciation in others.

The "drill instructor" often draws resentful compliance from others. People succumb to his or her pressure or threat of some aggressive attack if they do not submit. In certain situations, like a football game, this type of approach is useful. In most social circumstances, however, other interpersonal responses are preferred.

An extreme form of aggressive social behavior is always destructive. The levels of fear, resentment and guilt that victims of an aggressive adolescent experience can become damaging. The "bully" can create a deep sense of fear within other teenagers that causes them to give up possessions, do something for the aggressor or in some other way comply to his or her demands. Loss of self-respect, feelings of humiliation and self-doubt often follow victims of this form of aggression.

The "judge" is a master at motivating others through guilt. His or her condemnations and punishing actions draw rage from individuals who experience this unjust treatment. Their guilt and self-effacement turn into rebellious reactions to the judgment expressed by this aggressive teenager.

The "sadist" operates socially through the threat of physical or psychological harm. This is the most destructive and overtly aggressive form of the personality type described in this chapter. This young person feels best when he or she hurts others. The healthiest responses to sadistic behavior are fear and strong distrust, which lead the victims to withdrawal. Passivity, self-doubt and compliance to the "sadist" will only bring further pain.

As you evaluate the effect an aggressive teenager has on others, remember this personality type is always destructive to some degree. Other members of your youth group, class or family need protection from this type of young person. Adult intervention is not only appropriate, but sometimes necessary to minimize the negative effects of an aggressive adolescent.

■ Guidelines for Working with *Aggressive* Adolescents

These young people are among the most difficult to help. Instinctively, they push away anyone who attempts to get involved. Closeness and tender feelings are threatening emotions for these adolescents. Therefore, they will often reject caring adults who seek to help. But these teenagers need help as much as other young people. Our task is to learn to offer ourselves in a way they can accept, to minister in a manner they can receive. Here are some guidelines for us to follow:

1. Work to identify the basis for these teenagers' aggression. This understanding will motivate you to find a way to help. Within these examples of aggressive teenagers, we have discovered a variety of different sources for their aggression. Try to identify and understand the basis for adolescents' aggressiveness. This discovery can provide an important key in finding an approach to work with these young people. As

long as we do not understand the purpose or reason for
their aggression, we may not feel motivated to help. We
may find ourselves reacting to their defenses with anger,
hurt or just disinterest.

Only when we reach below the surface do we understand why their aggression exists. Only as we grasp the
meaning of their aggressive behavior can we begin to meet
the need it expresses. Phyllis' judgmental behavior is
somehow more tolerable when we recognize the destructive effect her mother's neurotic fears have had on her.
Brad's bullying will never be attractive nor even tolerable
to us. However, once we gain insight into his horribly
painful, rejecting past, we are more understanding. "With
a past like that, he has to release his troubled emotions in
some way."

**2. Help these teenagers learn to forgive those
who have hurt them.** Throughout the Bible God empha-
sizes the importance of forgiving each other. "Therefore,
as God's chosen people, holy and dearly loved, clothe
yourselves with compassion, kindness, humility, gentleness
and patience. Bear with each other and forgive whatever
grievances you may have against one another. Forgive as
the Lord forgave you. And over all these virtues put on
love, which binds them all together in perfect unity"
(Colossians 3:12-14).

Forgiveness is one of the primary processes through
which we release ourselves from the grasp of past hurts.
Aggressive young people struggle terribly with forgiving
others. They hang on to their pain, hurt and rage from
past injuries. They continue to draw energy from their
aggression which strengthens the grip their past has on
their present and future. Without forgiveness, they cannot
achieve God's admonition in the next verse from
Colossians: "Let the peace of Christ rule in your hearts,
since as members of one body you were called to peace.
And be thankful" (Colossians 3:15).

3. Support these teenagers and help them see themselves as valuable human beings. Aggressive teenagers almost always suffer from a severe lack of self-acceptance. Their life experiences have taught them they are of little value. They have come to the false conclusion that if others treat them in hurtful, disrespecting ways, they must be worth very little. The aggression they feel toward other people and their property is an outward expression of the internal anger and disappointment these young people feel toward themselves. They are angry at themselves for not being lovable, athletic, good-looking or talented enough for their parents, relatives and friends to treat them with more kindness and warmth. That level of anger and rage at themselves is too much to live with and is, therefore, externalized onto some other person or object.

One of our tasks when working with these adolescents is to help them correct their misperceptions of themselves. We need to help them separate their behavior from their person. Respond to these teenagers in loving, valuing and respecting ways. To the best of your ability, depersonalize their verbal attacks. Recognize these attacks are coming from their own inner turmoil. When aggressive teenagers attack caring adults, it usually indicates the adult is succeeding in getting close to them. Continue to love them. At the same time, make sure you have a strong and viable support system. Talk with your friends and colleagues about the pain and stress you are experiencing, being careful to respect the aggressive adolescents' confidentiality. Seek emotional support and other ideas to help you with your approach to these young people. Don't try to do it alone!

4. Learn to express your love and care in ways aggressive teenagers can accept. Be sure to check out their feelings and responses to your attempts to show you care. When working with these young people, try to understand how they perceive warmth and love. We may be trying to give them something we know is healing and nurturing. They may, however, be suspicious of the same behavior. We may offer what we know as positive, loving actions, but they may feel threatened by the hug, caring words or even the one-on-one attention we offer.

These teenagers may never have experienced accepting warmth and love. It is our task to gently provide them with that practice. Proceed at a pace that gradually stretches their ability to deal with love and gentleness. Going too fast may cause them to feel foolish and painfully self-conscious.

Keep track of how they feel. "When I give you a hug, I'm interested in how that feels to you." "I really enjoy the times when just the two of us get to talk together. I'm also interested in how you feel about it." Don't be afraid to ask. Check it out with them. Find out how they feel about their closeness with you.

5. Let these teenagers know you love and value them. The most powerful tool to help these teenagers is your own love. Express it to them. Let them know you value them as individual creations of God. Risk being tender with them. They need to know there are people who experience tender feelings and are not afraid to express them. "I really enjoy being around you." "I have some special warm and loving feelings for you." "Talking with you is one of the pleasures I really look forward to."

You can also express tenderness and love through your actions. The gift of your time may be the most powerful statement of your love for these teenagers. It doesn't matter whether you are a youth pastor, a counselor, a teacher or a youth group leader, when you set aside time to be with that one aggressive adolescent, he or she receives the message that you care.

Surprise them with phone calls that have no ulterior motive other than to check on how they are doing. Invite them to ride along when you run errands. One youth minister I know is almost never alone. Whether it's a trip

to the local hardware store or an out-of-state speaking
engagement, he's almost always got one of his difficult
kids along with him.

**6. Help these young people find opportunities
to express their caring in non-threatening situations.** In addition to receiving love and affection, these
aggressive young people need to develop their capacity for
expressing tender feelings. Often they have little opportunity within their own homes to say words or show
actions that express love.

Expressing love always leaves one vulnerable. Teenagers usually feel most threatened and vulnerable with
their peers. Arrange other opportunities for them to
express their caring in safer settings. Involve them in helping younger children or elderly people. Take them with
you when you visit newcomers or someone who is ill.
Encourage them to express their positive feelings in these
situations where there is little threat to their ego or self-
esteem.

As they grow in their ability and willingness to risk
tender expressions, give them new challenges. Ask them to
be a greeter at your youth meeting. They could make
phone calls or send cards to group members who are sick
or unable to attend meetings.

**7. Support these teenagers through the realiza-
tion that all love relationships involve some pain.**
Teenagers need to learn that pain is a normal part of the
process of loving. Young people don't automatically know
this. Most are highly idealistic about loving and relationships. Aggressive teenagers have already experienced
enough pain to cause them to give up.

We want to help these young people experience relationships that work. We want them to feel loved and
cared for. We also want them to experience the freedom
to love and care even though emotional rejection is a possibility. Our task is to help them increase their tolerance

for emotional pain so they can take the risks necessary for close relationships.

8. With these aggressive young people, continue to share your love, helping them recognize God as its source. Exposing aggressive young people to God's love helps them open themselves to receive and express love. John writes in his first Epistle: "Dear friends, let us love one another, for love comes from God. Everyone who loves has been born of God and knows God. Whoever does not love does not know God, because God is love. This is how God showed his love among us: He sent his one and only Son into the world that we might live through him. This is love: not that we loved God, but that he loved us and sent his Son as an atoning sacrifice for our sins. Dear friends, since God so loved us, we also ought to love one another" (1 John 4:7-11).

How do teenagers experience God's love? Usually through his children—you and me. In our ministry and counseling efforts with young people, we must never forget the source of love. As we are obedient to God in expressing love to these hurting teenagers, we expose them to God's love.

9. Offer these young people honest feedback about their behavior. Teenagers often do not understand how their behavior affects people. They are especially unaware of how their scowls, frowns, gloomy expressions, bored posturing, angry gestures and defiant stances influence others. They need to know how others see them. They need to recognize how their behavior affects other people's responses to them.

Honest feedback is a valuable gift to these teenagers. Let them know how they are seen by others. Tell them how you feel about their behavior. Don't mistake all of their actions as deliberate or even conscious. Tell them the truth gently and lovingly. Withholding the truth shows little respect for young people's abilities to handle reality.

It illustrates overprotection, not loving. In fact, it may belittle, for it certainly does not show respect or honor for the young people involved.

10. Help these teenagers utilize their high levels of energy for positive experiences within the group. Many aggressive teenagers are blessed (though it may not always seem like a blessing to you) with moderately high levels of energy. Try to tap into their energy. Enlist these young people's cooperation within their group or class. Help them find positive ways to interact with others. Encourage them to utilize their energies in helpful, positive directions rather than aggressive, destructive paths.

Enlist their help in car washes, pizza sales, publicity parties, planning sessions and other group efforts that require cooperative effort with their peers. As these teenagers learn to work with other young people, they begin to experience good feedback and positive feelings about themselves. These cooperative activities help young people see relationships as productive and worthwhile. These experiences can be a first step toward meaningful and emotionally close interaction with other people.

11. Guide aggressive teenagers' critical thinking skills into constructive channels where they can be accepted instead of challenged. As an important part of their intellectual development, all teenagers must develop the ability to think critically. Young people must broaden their thinking skills to find errors, see differences and make comparisons. During early and mid-adolescence, this newly developed critical nature may exasperate adults, but it is necessary for survival in this complex society.

Aggressive teenagers are also critical, but to an extreme. Their critical thinking often stimulates expression of their anger. In our efforts to help these young people reduce their aggression, it is important not to frustrate their natural, healthy tendency to be critical. Excessive suppression of adolescents' abilities to think critically often results in adults who will not think or make decisions on their own.

To reduce the negative and destructive aspects of these teenagers' critical nature, guide them toward constructive outlets. Let them chew on some tough theological, social and political issues. Compliment them on their ability to see inconsistencies. Encourage them to come up with several possibilities to resolve difficult situations and problems. Challenge their thinking without being defensive about some of their conclusions.

We don't have to feel pressured to answer all of their questions, for we certainly do not have all the answers. Paul assures us: "Now we see but a poor reflection; then we shall see face to face. Now I know in part; then I shall know fully, even as I am fully known" (1 Corinthians 13:12).

12. Recognize your limits, and know when to refer these teenagers to competent professional help. Continue to nurture these young people with your acceptance and support. Aggressive teenagers with a destructive or intense form of this orientation need professional help. Referral to a professional therapist or psychologist who specializes in treating adolescents is sometimes the most helpful thing you can do for these young people. Remember, making such a referral is not an admission of incompetence or inadequacy on your part. It is an act of love in helping teenagers get the specialized care they need.

After the referral is made, continue your relationships with these aggressive adolescents. They still need parents, teachers, youth sponsors and pastors. The professional therapist fulfills his or her function in Christ's body, and you must fulfill yours. As each of us expresses his or her gifts, we function cooperatively to encourage and support our teenagers' growth into the nature of Christ.

■ Guidelines for Parenting Aggressive Adolescents

Aggressive teenagers are among the most difficult young people to parent. Their defensive reactions, their style of relating socially and their ways of handling conflicts and interpersonal disagreements make living with them extremely difficult. Often they create turmoil, emotional pain and feelings of disruption within their families.

Offering love to aggressive teenagers who strike back in anger causes us to retreat because this rejection is painful. As a parent of aggressive adolescents, you will need a strong support system. Spouses need to talk with each other and reinforce mutual efforts. Single-parenting this kind of teenager is exceptionally difficult. Whether you are single or co-parenting, you will need the support of friends and relatives. You will need to share your pain and your parenting goals with your support system. Seek out other parents who are experiencing or have experienced similar parenting trials. Mutually supportive relationships are usually more successful than one-way support systems, but take advantage of what is available.

The purpose of this book is not to provide guidelines on discipline or behavioral control, but to help you and other adults understand and meet the needs of your teenagers. This section includes specific ways you can help your aggressive adolescents develop healthier and more adaptive personality orientations.

1. Work to understand the origins and meanings of the aggressive behaviors expressed by your teenagers. Aggressive behavior is essentially maladaptive, or unhealthy, in most situations. When aggression is a young person's predominant behavior pattern, there is some underlying, serious cause. All people begin their lives wanting acceptance; all individuals initially desire warm and tender contact with others. A severe trauma early in life or a history of painful interpersonal relationships are

the usual causes for development of aggressive interpersonal orientations. This social orientation suggests that
these young people have given up hope for loving and
positive relationships. They have succumbed to a lifestyle
that keeps others at a safe distance. "If I can push everyone far enough away, then I can at least prevent further
pain for myself." To aggressive adolescents, loneliness
seems a better option than risking more pain.

As you recognize these tendencies and struggles within
your aggressive teenagers, you are better prepared to
respond to these difficult young people in ways that can
help them heal. You can see and respond to their pain and
fear instead of their aggression. These young people must
learn to control their anger. Your primary thrust as a
parent, however, should be to bring love and healing to
your adolescents' injuries. Look for patterns in their anger.
When do they usually explode? Which types of people do
they push away? Look for clues to help you understand
what they are saying through their actions.

**2. Help your aggressive teenagers build a more
positive self-concept.** One characteristic common to
aggressive adolescents is negative or low self-concept.
These young people are usually just as angry at themselves
as they are at others. The anger they express toward
others often has its origins in self-directed rage. These
young people view themselves as people incapable of having meaningful or happy relationships. They may briefly
think something is wrong with them. However, because
that thought is terribly painful, they may project their
anger onto others, especially you as a parent. A central
part of your helping is to make healing contact with your
aggressive teenagers' hurting self-concepts.

Aggressive behavior is designed to keep others at safe
emotional distances. Therefore, your aggressive teenagers
may rebuff your efforts to understand and nourish their
self-esteem. Your task as a parent is to *keep trying*. You
need to be stronger and more tenacious than they. Take

inventory of the things you respect and enjoy about your teenagers. Focus on their good and lovable personal characteristics, and let them know that you see and appreciate these qualities.

"I really like your neatness and your ability to keep things organized."

"You have an amazing knack for getting things done on your own. You are so dependable in that way."

"Your sense of humor never ceases to surprise me! Your timing is fantastic, and you see things with just a little different slant that makes them seem so funny."

Focus more on your *young people* rather than their *actions*. By helping your aggressive teenagers develop healthy, positive self-concepts, you prepare them for altering their interpersonal relationship patterns. This is often difficult and discouraging work, but you can impact your children in this way.

3. Help your aggressive teenagers increase their capacity for receiving love. Aggressive adolescents push away people who try to get close to them. Their defenses subdue their anxiety, but keep them from receiving anything positive like warmth and love. Because of their restricted capacity for receiving affection from others, they may invalidate any tender responses you offer them. This restriction intensifies their isolation from others and reinforces their belief that they cannot gain from relationships. As long as they hold those perceptions, there is little chance these teenagers will alter their interpersonal responses. An important part of your parental task is to help your young people open themselves to accept the love you and others extend to them.

Try a variety of ways to offer love to your aggressive sons or daughters. Some will open themselves to receive one type of expression while others will respond better to other forms of loving. Try saying it with words.

"I sure do love you."

"We have our hard times, but I want you to know that

none of those experiences make me love you any less."

Many of these young people reject loving words, but they do receive loving actions. Surprise them with a plate of freshly baked chocolate chip cookies. Prepare their favorite meal, offer to run an errand for them, do their chores for a day, double their allowance for a week without having them do anything to earn it or let them stay home from school one day just to have fun. Be creative. Think about what your children really enjoy; then surprise them. Experiencing your warmth and caring will threaten these young people, but these expressions of your affection may gradually increase their capacity to receive love and help them make other important personality changes.

4. Encourage these teenagers to express their love to others. Aggressive young people react to *expressing* love and affection to others similarly to *receiving* love from other people. Both experiences leave them feeling vulnerable and out of control. They are too close to their own feelings and to other people to feel comfortable. Their most frequent recourse is to push others away with their anger to protect their bruised feelings and emotional sensitivity. Learning they can express love toward others without experiencing drastically negative effects is a major step toward their personal growth.

As a parent of aggressive adolescents, you need to use your family relationships to help these children develop their capacities for giving love. Birthdays, anniversaries, graduations, Christmas and other special events provide natural opportunities for these young people to practice giving to others. Encourage them to give gifts and offer different expressions of appreciation or thankfulness. Help them determine what they can do for others, and then support them as they decide how they can help or give to friends, loved ones or other people in need.

Encourage these aggressive adolescents to verbalize their feelings to others. This form of expressing love may be difficult for them. People often feel most vulnerable when they meet others face to face to tell them that they love them. Some do better by writing their feelings. Let them start the best way they can. It is important that these young people start expressing their love and affection to someone, rather than pushing everyone away.

5. Let your aggressive teenagers know that emotional pain is a normal aspect of loving relationships. Most aggressive teenagers develop this social orientation because they have experienced significant interpersonal pain in the past. Some of them come to the conclusion that other people are not worth the effort or the risk. Others believe there is something dreadfully wrong that causes their peers not to like or be attracted to them. The result is the same.

To prevent personal anxiety, these aggressive teenagers offend others or push them away with their anger, brashness or crudeness. Some of these teenagers, especially those who have experienced painful separations during their early years (such as their parents' divorce or the death of a loved one), believe they cannot survive another painful ending to an important relationship. They think they would be just as emotionally helpless as they were when they were young children.

You can help your teenagers know that choosing to love someone *always* involves a risk of getting hurt. Let them know some of your own history of pain within important relationships. Use good judgment and share personal stories about your own painful incidents with family, friends, girlfriends, boyfriends and even previous spouses. Be sure to include some of the positive experiences you have had within those loving relationships. These adolescents need to know that taking the risk to love can be worth it. They need to realize that allowing selected others to be emotionally close can add a new and vital dimension to their lives.

These young people also need to know they can survive and even grow from the pain they encounter within meaningful interpersonal relationships. They need assurance that everyone who risks loving periodically gets hurt emotionally. They need to know that emotional pain is not only normal and survivable, but a stimulating growth experience for most everyone involved.

6. Help your aggressive teenagers learn how to forgive others. The ability to forgive is fundamental to the process of loving. Without releasing our anger toward others, we can never move on in our relationships with them. Unresolved anger usually turns into bitterness, a desire for revenge or an intention to retaliate. Aggressive teenagers lack the ability to resolve their anger easily. Instead of forgiving others for their wrongdoing, they punish them with their intense feelings and cause them to withdraw. Therefore, aggressive adolescents seldom experience the pleasures of feeling forgiven by others, forgiving themselves or forgiving others.

You are in a strategic position to help your aggressive young people learn the value of forgiving. Observe your teenagers' interactions within the home. Daily encounters between family members provide perfect opportunities for practicing forgiveness. In teaching your young people how to forgive, remember that forgiving is a two-way process. If you want your teenagers to learn this art, you must actively forgive them. Let them hear your forgiveness in your voice and see it in your actions. Resolve your anger and your personal need to punish their behavior in some other way than directing it toward your aggressive adolescents. Help them feel a freedom from your anger. Tell them you forgive them. Give them tangible expressions of your forgiveness and evidence of God's forgiveness within your own role model.

When you see opportunities for your aggressive adolescents to forgive you or other family members, observe how they handle the situations. Let them know that forgiveness is appropriate under these circumstances. Ask your young people if they know *how* to forgive someone. Remember, forgiving does *not* come naturally; it has to be learned. Encourage them to ask questions. Remind them that forgiving requires making a conscious choice to let go of whatever they are holding against the other person. Let them know that they must express their forgiveness in both words and actions if it is to have its most powerful impact. Forgiveness is one of the most difficult interpersonal actions for aggressive teenagers to accomplish. As you enable them to give and receive forgiveness, you help provide the basis for their movement away from aggression as a personality orientation.

7. *Help your teenagers become more aware of the effects their behavior has on other people.* Many young people perceive themselves and their actions very differently from the way other people see them. They may not realize how their facial expressions, gestures, posture and body movements express emotions they think are well-hidden. Their body language often expresses feelings they have unconsciously repressed. Many times they fail to recognize how their actions might impact others. Aggressive adolescents often communicate their anger in subtle yet powerful ways, but continue to question why others back away from them.

"Why don't my friends like me for very long?"

"I don't get it. I guess there's something about me that turns people off."

Your adolescents need your loving but honest feedback. Even though they may not always welcome your insights, these young people need you to let them know when you see them do things that may offend or alienate others. You may see a sneer where they see a grin. You might hear sarcasm when they hear good humor. Their joke may sound to you more like making fun of someone. Often the most loving thing you can do for your teenagers is to tell them the truth. Make sure that when you share this honest feedback, you proceed in a loving and gentle way. "Sue, I'm sure you know that I don't want to hurt you, but there's something I think you're not aware of that I've seen you do with your friends." Be careful not to express your own anger indirectly in the *way* you tell them. "Sue, I don't think you have any reason to be surprised when your friends stop liking you. Look at what you are doing!"

Aggressive teenagers need honest, caring feedback from the people who love them. They need your loving confrontation with the truth. When they have been made aware of what they are doing, they are better prepared to make constructive changes in the way they approach others.

8. Help your aggressive young people direct their energies into constructive avenues. Aggressive teenagers often have high levels of energy. They are active, enthusiastic people who have a wide range of interests. They typically enjoy sports and other recreational activities that involve physical activity, surface-level communication and light interaction with others. Since it is always easier to give direction to a moving object, the high energy level of these adolescents provides an excellent opening when you seek to help. These teenagers are active and in motion, even though much of their energy comes from their anger. Realize you can help them direct much of this energy into constructive channels.

There are many ways to utilize these young people's energies to reach positive end results. Involve their help and participation whenever possible. Let them take leadership roles in planning family activities. Help them develop the resources for giving to others. Encourage them to participate in activities which help them experience love, warmth and caring.

Aggressive teenagers can use the energy that comes from their repressed anger to learn more positive ways of relating. When they complain about their younger sister's childish behavior, have them play with her more often so she will learn from their more mature ways. When they argue about how chores are assigned at home, place them in charge of designing an improved system and then presenting it to the rest of the family for their modification and approval. When they express judgmental and critical attitudes about another's behavior, request they make a serious proposal of changes they want the other person to make. Their proposal can then be discussed with just the other family member involved or with the entire family present. The primary task here is to direct these teenagers' negative energies into constructive lines of action that stimulate positive feelings about themselves, others and their world.

Aggressive adolescents need your help to open themselves to affection and love. Changing the direction of their energies is one good technique you can use to accomplish this goal.

9. Help your teenagers use good self-control while developing their critical thinking skills. A vital aspect of healthy adolescent growth is the development of critical thinking skills. Aside from the obvious physical and emotional changes occurring during the teenage years are the intellectual developments that dramatically alter the way adolescents view themselves, other people, their faith and their world. These changes in their thinking processes are also prerequisites to their maturation into adulthood. During adolescence young people begin to enlarge their ability to think abstractly. They formulate their thoughts in *"If . . ., then . . ."* patterns. They compare options and develop possible solutions to numerous situations. Developing skills in critical thinking is required for teenagers to succeed in their identity formation.

Early and mid-adolescents typically criticize their parents, the church, police and other authority figures. Often they are also extremely critical of their peers and even of themselves. This ability to think critically allows them to push far enough away from the beliefs, values and attitudes they have grown up with to develop their *own* thoughts and perceptions. Then, during late adolescence they usually begin to gravitate back toward the values with which they were raised.

As a parent of aggressive teenagers, you may find yourself in a particularly uncomfortable position with your own children. Being pushed away and rejected creates pain, and you will need to defend yourself against this intense upheaval. However, your children will still need your love, affection and acceptance. Offering them closeness that leaves you vulnerable to their criticism is particularly difficult when your children are aggressive adolescents who naturally overuse their critical defenses. As was mentioned earlier, it is extremely important for you to develop a good support system for yourself. You will need encouragement, nourishment and an active exchange of ideas for parenting these young people.

You need to encourage your aggressive teenagers to think critically while also teaching them self-control of their hostile impulses. You can benefit from recognizing God's plan for parents to be in authority within the home. "Honor your father and your mother . . ." (Exodus 20:12). Therefore, you do not need your children's approval or confirmation for your position; however, you do need to recognize a corollary to this commandment. As a parent, you must acknowledge the value of your children as ". . . created in his own image . . ." (Genesis 1:27). Use your authority in a way that encourages your teenagers' development toward positive, constructive expressions of their critical thinking abilities. When your teenagers express critical thoughts, respond with acceptance.

"That's an interesting point. Tell me more about your thoughts."

"Gosh, I've never looked at it that way. I like the way you come up with your own views."

Express neither agreement nor disagreement. These young people don't want your judgment as much as they want your acceptance.

As a parent, encourage your teenagers to develop their critical thinking skills as a normal part of their adolescence. Since most aggressive teenagers tend to exaggerate their use of criticism, you must help them develop positive, constructive expressions of this trait.

10. Consider professional counseling for your aggressive teenagers. Aggression is essentially an unhealthy form of adaptation toward other people. It reveals an extreme need to protect the self from others and the belief that relationships are dangerous. Though mild expressions of this orientation can be constructive, the underlying beliefs and defensive posture of these teenagers represents a worldview contrary to scriptural principles for human relationships.

Deep emotional pain and a history of disappointment within interpersonal relationships usually cause the development of this personality type. These young people can often benefit from professional counseling that helps them resolve the root causes leading to their aggressive orientation. Parental acceptance, faithful friends, loving relatives and care from other concerned adults are essential to the future maturation of these young people. Counselors and psychologists who are trained and experienced in helping aggressive teenagers can be a valuable addition to this team for ministering to these young people.

You now have more information and a better understanding of aggressive behavior and why some teenagers adopt this aggressive orientation toward the world. You are better equipped to identify, understand and help these adolescents. You may know a "drill instructor" or a "pious" adolescent. Possibly there is a "bully" in your group or a "judge" in your classroom. You may even recognize a young "sadist."

These aggressive teenagers are difficult to help. Growth comes slowly and with great difficulty. Realize you are not the only tool God can use as he continues his creative and healing work. Surround yourself with others who care about you and the teenagers with whom you work and live as you strive to maintain support for these young people.

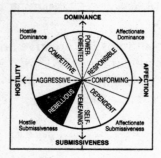

■CHAPTER 7

The Rebellious Personality

*R*ebellious adolescents have much in common with the aggressive teenagers discussed in the previous chapter. Closeness and intimacy threaten both personality types. These young people have suffered common experiences including histories of pain, embarrassment and humiliation. Both types of adolescents associate pain with any prolonged social contact or commitment to a personal relationship.

While aggressive personalities retaliate by inflicting pain on others, rebellious adolescents are less interested in revenge. They want only to push others away or withdraw from social experience. These young people are usually resentful, bitter and distrustful. Hurt or deprived during their early childhood, many of these rebellious teenagers never received the parental care and love essential to their early personality development. Many had parents who divorced during their preadolescent years. Others' parents both worked or for some other reason spent little time with them.

Usually these young people have also made poor social adjustments with their peers. They lack personal confidence because of inadequate training in social skills. They respond to their peers in awkward and displeasing ways. These experiences lead them into additional rejection and social alienation.

Rebellious teenagers typically internalize these experiences, blaming themselves for being unacceptable and unlovable to others. They are angry at themselves for not being more talented, attractive, intelligent or athletic. They are also angry at others. They experience bitterness and resentment about the rejection and alienation they receive from parents, siblings, friends or other adults.

The goal of rebellious adolescents is to protect themselves from further pain and emotional trauma by distancing themselves from others. Bitterness, resentment and fear influence their behavior. Located in the middle of the hostile-submissive quadrant, these young people struggle with mixed reactions. Those experiencing excessive resentment and bitterness *push* others away, while others who feel hopeless and afraid merely *withdraw* from social experiences.

Another difference between rebellious teenagers and aggressive adolescents is that aggressive adolescents have no intention of getting close to others. They are open and determined about their commitment to keep others away. Rebellious young people, however, are unhappy and frustrated with their social alienation. They *want* to be loved and even *admit* they want good relationships. Nevertheless, they experience deep conflict. When they begin reaching closeness or intimacy with someone, they sabotage the relationship. They destroy the very thing they say they want. They cannot tolerate the possibility of belonging, being part of a relationship, being included or being loved because it may bring too much painful anxiety or threat. So they deny themselves (and the other person) an experience they desperately need. Their behavior says: "I am hurt and angry. I do not fit in with the rest of you.

I cannot and will not trust other people again."

■ Development of the *Rebellious* Personality

Rebellion is a normal aspect of adolescent behavior. An important part of a teenager's identity formation is to push away from parents, teachers, church leaders and other adult authority figures. All young people need to see themselves as separate and different from their parents. They need to develop their own identities. This process usually involves rebellion of some intensity. Therefore, possessing some rebellious tendencies does not necessarily place teenagers in this category. Teenagers are described as rebellious types when their rebellion permeates and dominates most of their social behavior and their responses to others.

Rebellious teenagers have problems in two areas. First, they have difficulty controlling their aggression. Their reactions may include anger, bitterness, frustration and criticism. These young people also have serious problems with submission. Hopelessness, lack of power and dejection usually combine with their aggression to create these rebellious young people. Let's examine some of the factors that cause teenagers to develop a rebellious personality.

First, rebellious young people usually experience some significant pain, especially early in life. This emotional trauma normally occurs within a relationship, particularly one with parents. When children experience significant rejection or alienation during the first few years of their life, they will sometimes give up on trying to belong. The pain seems too great to risk again. In addition to this fear of pain, they become angry and direct their anger both *outward* toward the rejecting person and *inward* at themselves. This mixture of anger and giving up typifies rebellious teenagers.

Unhappy experiences with their peers are not uncommon for these young people as well. When they experience this further rejection in childhood, life's early lessons are compounded and reality becomes unclear. "I guess people really are dangerous." "I certainly cannot trust in any friendships."

Second, young people are often deprived of adequate affection, love or attention during their early childhood years. Through divorce, both parents working or incompetent parenting, these children fail to receive the parent contact essential for healthy psychological and social development. Alienation during these early years robs children of important social learning experiences. Plus, this deprivation provides a shaky foundation for developing their self-concept.

Third, rebellious teenagers have learned some of their negative perceptions from their parents. Children have *learned* to distrust others. They questioned others' actions and were suspicious of their motives. Throughout their impressionable childhood these young people listened, observed and learned from those around them. Perhaps they experienced negative conversation around the dinner table. Maybe they overheard the telephone gossip between Mom and her friends. They might have listened to Dad's constant complaining about his unreliable co-workers. All of these experiences could have contributed to their negative attitudes. Some of the things they experienced severely damaged their ability to relate positively with other people. With no concept of the impact they were making on their children, these parents were teaching cynical attitudes about relationships.

Fourth, like all defensive orientations, rebellion becomes a learned social reaction because it works. Pushing others away and withdrawal are rebellions that reduce anxiety. When people get too close, these teenagers experience threat and tension. Each time they react rebelliously, others respond. The rebellious teenagers reduce their anxiety level and increase the chances of reacting similarly in the future.

Fifth, other teenagers often value moderate rebellion in

their peers. Refusing to "go along with the crowd" makes young people appear strong. Questioning and holding back give the impression that these teenagers are particularly thoughtful and deliberate. Withholding themselves from others makes these adolescents appear superior and aloof. Standoffish social actions reinforce the impression that these teenagers are different. Unconsciously, this mildly rebellious behavior reconfirms their belief that they are special and shouldn't get too close or overly involved with others.

Sixth, mild critical rebellion can attract other adolescents, while hiding a multitude of fears and insecurities. Daring to criticize the establishment or defying the peer group's expectations appears courageous and powerful. Acting "cool," in control and daring promotes rebellious teenagers to hero status among their peers. These young people attract admiration and attention from other teenagers while simply defending against the inadequacies they believe are within them.

By understanding the developmental aspects of this interesting social orientation, you can better identify and help the rebellious teenagers with whom you live and work. Instead of reacting to their surface behavior, now you can understand more fully and respond to their deeper needs expressed by their actions.

■ Healthy Forms of the Rebellious Personality

Rebellion is not only healthy but necessary for effective identity formation during adolescence. Even when rebellion becomes the primary behavioral choice, it doesn't have to be destructive or vicious. When rebellion is neither rigid nor extreme, it can work constructively for teenagers. Adolescents can gain several positive interpersonal benefits from their successful use of this defensive orientation. To maintain a healthy form of this personality type, rebellion should not be used excessively or inappropriately.

The Individualist. The Robinson family came in
for professional counseling with their two teenage daughters—Brenda, 14, and Glenda, 13. Both girls provide
examples of healthy, adapted forms of the rebellious
personality.

The girls' parents married after discovering they were
pregnant with Brenda. Even though they were still in their
late teenage years, they loved each other and were determined to do what they believed God wanted. Abortion
was out of the question, and the young mother couldn't
tolerate the thought of another family adopting her baby.
In spite of their good intentions, they soon discovered
they were not yet mature enough to assume such adult
responsibilities.

After two and one-half years of marriage, their second
daughter, Glenda, was born. Financial pressures increased,
and the girls' father showed signs of strain. Increased frustration, growing intolerance and frequent displays of
temper accompanied his increasing use of alcohol and
decreased involvement in church. Finally, when the girls
were 3 and 4 years old, he left his family to live with
another woman.

After their parents' separation, the girls seldom saw or
heard from their father. His visits were few, and he never
acknowledged their birthdays or other special events.
Their mother worked at a low-paying job, and the girls
were cared for by a variety of friends and baby sitters.
There was little structure in their lives; their routine
changed almost daily.

Mom was still working when they started counseling.
There was money enough for only the necessities. Life
was rather mundane for the small family. Brenda and
Glenda had each other, but they had little contact with
their mother. Both girls were developing rebellious personality patterns, but both had maintained surprisingly healthy
levels of social adjustment.

Brenda, the oldest sister, had already become quite an

"individualist." She felt lost and rejected when her father left. She had also experienced a drastic change when her mother was forced to work. Her feelings of anger and pain combined to make these events traumatic to her childhood. She felt lonely and empty. Though most of her caretakers were kind, life seemed unfriendly to her. Peer relationships never worked out well either. Feelings of distance usually prevailed, and Brenda felt that few of her friends ever really liked her.

Brenda's rebellious response was to withdraw, and hers was a strong withdrawal. She didn't push others away; instead she actually pushed herself to a safe distance where she felt protected from interpersonal pain. She emphasized her individuality. She joined no clubs. She never played team sports. And she successfully resisted temptations to conform to current fads in fashion, speech, interests and activities.

Brenda's limited money shaped part of her individuality. Her dress consisted of only jeans and assorted tops. Popular fashions changed around her, but she still wore her jeans. Rock stars came and went on the popularity charts, but Brenda remained faithful to *one* musical group. She collected their albums, covered her bedroom walls with their posters, wore their T-shirts and displayed their buttons.

Everything Brenda did proclaimed her individuality. She wasn't militant about it, just consistent and assertive. She showed no interest in football, basketball, baseball or track; however, she did enjoy speech. And her speeches provided her with a constructive way to make strong proclamations about her beliefs and principles. Her speeches, her interests and her activities all seemed to shout the same message: "I am different from all of you. I am an individual!"

Brenda was a loner. Even in her small, church youth group, she stood apart. Again, she used her dress, taste in music and many of her ideas to establish her individuality. The intensity with which she expressed her identity ensured her recognition as different, and she wanted it that way.

The Antagonist. Glenda's early life experience was much like that of Brenda's, her older sister. She too lost contact with her father at an early age, and she felt both confused and rejected when he left. She also experienced sadness, pain and anger about her mother's lengthy absences every day.

Glenda was more successful than Brenda, however, in developing relationships with her peers. She wasn't afraid to let friends get emotionally close to her. During elementary school she had several long-term friendships. At church she also developed several meaningful relationships.

Adults were the primary target of Glenda's anger, distrust and suspicion. Adults had caused her pain and confusion; they had removed themselves from her. So she chose to differentiate between how she responded to adults and how she responded to other children. Closeness with peers proved to be safe and rewarding, but intimacy with adults was painful and frustrating.

Glenda became a hero among her friends. She did not fear confronting adults with whom she disagreed. Nothing was sacred. School rules, standards for dress, behavior at church and family expectations were all targets for her verbal attacks. She wrote letters to the school board, met with the principal, spoke out during congregational meetings and argued endlessly with her mother. Virtually all her contacts with adults were antagonistic. She was consistently critical, always finding something wrong with what adults either said or did. If she could find no fault with their actions, then their motives were at fault.

Glenda continued to kindle her anger and bitterness about her father's departure and her mother's absence. She felt powerless to change the situation, so she redirected her antagonism onto the whole adult community. This response kept all adults away from her. She was unconsciously protecting herself from being hurt again. If she could keep adults far enough away, she would be safe.

Brenda and Glenda were both relatively well-adjusted rebellious teenagers. Both found constructive ways to live out their social orientation. Through individualism, Brenda found ways to gain respect from her peers, even though she still struggled with feelings of alienation and loneliness. Through her antagonism, Glenda gained a reputation both with adults and with her adolescent community. She operated as a thorn or a gadfly with adults, but she was a hero to her peers. Although she didn't relate in a healthy manner with adults, she did experience closeness with her peers.

■ Unhealthy Forms of the *Rebellious* Personality

Some degree of rebellion can be a healthy part of adolescent development, and rebellion is an essential element in identity formation for most teenagers. The "individualist" and the "antagonist" take rebellion beyond its normal function during adolescence. These styles represent a well-adjusted degree of rebellion, excessive enough to warrant the label "rebellious personality," but adapted well enough to be healthy. We will now meet two examples of teenagers whose rigidity and intensity make their rebellious responses clearly unhealthy.

The Complainer. John is a 13-year-old junior higher. He is the third of four children in an upper-middle class family. They live in a good suburban community and attend a well-established, traditional church. John's other family members are recognized achievers. His father is a successful executive in a nationwide corporation. His mother is active on several church committees, is involved with two parent-teacher organizations and chairs a local community fund-raising group. John's brother and two sisters are also high achievers. They are usually A students. His brother and one sister are good athletes, and his other sister is active in student government. All three are fully involved in their active youth group at church.

John differs from most rebels because he did not suffer from early-life rejection within his family or his most intimate relationships. His family is reasonably close, warm and mutually supportive. His parents encourage each of their children within activities where they seem most interested and talented. John hasn't found a lasting interest in much of anything, nor has he developed any particular abilities either. He's just *average*; and average can be a miserable state when one lives among exceptional achievers.

When John began preschool, it was soon obvious he didn't fit in nor was he comfortable with the other children. He was never an outcast, and he never experienced actual rejection by others. But he never felt his peers accepted him either. He felt the same at church, too. In reality, most everyone accepted John, but they did not include him nor seek his involvement in what they were doing.

The one enduring social characteristic that describes John in any group is his *complaining*. He whines. He has gained the nickname, "Wimp," which certainly doesn't give his ego a big boost! The origins of his whining and complaining are difficult to trace. His parents say his complaining began during his preschool years and has worsened throughout his childhood and early adolescence. Our best understanding of John's behavior indicates that during his early years he saw himself as inferior to everyone else in his family. His negative self-perception led him to feel insecure in this family of achievers. This feeling was accentuated when he entered preschool and again found himself performing less adequately than his peers. His self-doubts deepened, and his self-rejection intensified as he progressed through elementary school into junior high.

John's self-image as inadequate became well-entrenched, and he gave up trying to better himself. He is angry, frustrated and feels hopeless about his situation.

Complaining seems to be his only outlet. When things don't go his way, he whines. His low self-esteem doesn't allow him to express himself in a more direct fashion. He has only enough inner strength to release his bitterness through complaining. His behavior accurately expresses the weakness within his personality.

John's complaining also accomplishes his rebellious defense in another way. He soon becomes unbearable for most adults and peers. People avoid him. At the first sounds of his complaining, people withdraw. His defense works. As others withdraw, his level of anxiety is reduced. He withdraws into his own weakness and pushes others away with his obnoxious behavior. Of course, John then complains because no one wants to be his friend.

When asked, John replies that he does want friends. He also admits he wants adults' approval. But he takes no responsibility for his negative interpersonal relationships. John's behavior illustrates the typical internal conflict of rebellious adolescents. They want relationships, but closeness creates such strong anxiety that they sabotage the specific goal they wish to attain.

The Delinquent. Charlotte's life provides a clear, unmistakable example of unhealthy adolescent rebellion. When referred to counseling, Charlotte was 16 years old, living in a group home as a ward of the court. Her parents never married and lived together only a few months after her birth. She lived with her mother and two older sisters in a series of small apartments.

She attended several elementary schools, but she was truant almost as often as she was in class. She had average intelligence, but could read at only a third-grade level when she was a sophomore in high school. Her writing and grammar skills also fell far below expectations for her grade level. School made her feel uncomfortable and inadequate. Without parental support and because of limited teacher involvement, Charlotte's learning disabilities were never diagnosed. She falsely learned through her failures in school that she was dumb. Discouraged and bitter, she felt forced to compete in an environment in which she knew only failure.

Charlotte received little attention from her mother. She was raised primarily by her sisters and grandmother. During her elementary school years, neighborhood boys sexually molested her on several occasions. But she never told anyone because the boys threatened to kill her if she did tell. These sexual encounters taught her she had something boys liked.

She also discovered she had something her girlfriends liked; she had the nerve to steal things for them. At first she stole candy bars, pop and toys. Later she took clothes, shoes, jewelry and radios at her friends' request. She kept a few items for herself, but most were "commissioned" by others or given as gifts.

Store owners caught her several times during her grade school years. However, she usually charmed her way out of any serious consequences until she was caught during sixth-grade. At the end of a 10-minute chase through a shopping-mall parking lot, Charlotte was apprehended with three bottles of perfume, two blouses, four swimsuits and one makeup kit. Charges were filed, and she was placed on probation. Three months later a similar incident occurred; and one week after that, she was caught stealing again. Because of her quickly growing police record and the lack of adequate adult supervision, she remained in juvenile hall for four months. She was made a ward of the court and placed in a foster home where she stayed two weeks. The foster parents brought her back to juvenile hall because they couldn't prevent her stealing food, clothing, jewelry and money from their home.

Her second stay in juvenile hall was for eight months. The court attempted another foster-home placement. This one lasted almost one year. Everything appeared to progress satisfactorily until authorities discovered her foster father was having sexual intercourse with her on a regular basis. She was transferred back to juvenile hall once more and finally was moved into the group home where she was living when she initiated counseling.

Charlotte had little in her life to feel good about. The only security she had experienced came from her own efforts, and those moments of apparent safety passed quickly. She honestly believed only those adults who wanted something from her would try to get close to her. Charlotte learned how to "out-use" them. She believed her friends would remain only as long as she could get something or provide something for them. Therefore, the items she stole, the drugs she procured and the sex she provided were the commodities she traded for acceptance.

Charlotte had a brief experience with church when she was 13 years old. At the invitation of a friend, she attended a small church and its youth group for a few months. But she felt so different from the other "church kids" that she stopped attending. Unhappily, her church attendance became just another experience in failure, alienation and perceived rejection.

Charlotte began learning her rebellious lifestyle at an early age. Her adaptation to her world had resulted in an obviously unhealthy and unacceptable social orientation. To Charlotte, people became objects to outwit, "out-use" or avoid. Social rules were for bending, interpreting or breaking for her benefit. The basis for her morality narrowed to, "Whatever helps me get by is good, and whatever blocks me from getting what I want is bad." Her delinquency succeeded in keeping people at a safe emotional distance. And she effectively alienated others by repeatedly offending them with her behavior.

We have met two unique examples of unhealthy rebellious teenagers. Both expressions effectively accomplish the purposes of their rebellion. The "complainer" *withdraws* into unattractive whining and refuses to accept personal responsibility for his or her behavior. The "delinquent" actively *pushes others away*, using them as objects to protect himself or herself from the threats and anxieties associated with intimate social contact.

■ Effects of Rebellious Behavior on Other People

A rebellious adolescent has an overwhelmingly negative effect on other people. This teenager directs much of his or her underlying hostility and bitterness toward adults. Peers are attractive as long as there is mutual need-fulfillment. As soon as the rebellious adolescent fails to gain from this exchange, the apparent closeness ends. This individual deliberately sabotages any relationship when closeness or intimacy with others results in anxiety.

When confronted with rebellion, most people are confused and upset. "Why is he doing that?" "I can't believe she is acting this way." "It's hard to guess what's coming next!" This type of teenager exposes underlying bitterness and distrust for others through his or her rebellious behavior. Unsure of what these actions mean, other people feel vulnerable and uncertain. Their spontaneous reaction is to back off with sufficient space to think through the situation objectively.

As people continue experiencing this rebellious behavior, they typically react with irritation or anger. Helping adults eventually lose their patience. They become angry when their best efforts to nurture and support are degraded or rebuffed. They withdraw from the rebellious teenager to protect themselves from the pain of personal rejection.

A rebellious teenager commonly provokes other people's rejection. Healthy, loving people don't enjoy a bitter, distrustful or sullen individual. This type of teenager has a toxic effect on others. When the level of toxicity reaches a certain point, other people have to protect themselves by rejecting or pushing the young person away. (Try to identify a rebellious personality within your group, class or family. Have you found yourself withdrawing or pushing him or her away from you? Then you can recognize the need to protect yourself from this type of teenager.)

Another common response to a rebellious adolescent is

to retaliate by putting him or her down. Competitive individuals usually use this natural defense to protect themselves from the pain or feelings of inadequacy a rebellious adolescent fosters. Some adults exert their position, their dominant power or their greater strength in a way that enhances their own sense of superiority over this personality type.

Most reactions to a rebellious teenager's behavior are punitive in nature. Angry shouting, criticism or rejection operate as effective methods of punishment for this type of individual. But by the time many adults begin working with one of these adolescents, their natural reactions to the young person's rebellious behavior have temporarily sabotaged their ability to help.

Overt rebellion pushes others into anger or withdrawal. These negative reactions confirm a rebellious adolescent's distrust of others. This lack of trust increases underlying bitterness and resentment toward other people so that the individual can defend himself or herself by rebelling again. Within this negative cycle, this personality type keeps creating and re-creating his or her own world of alienation and isolation.

A rebellious adolescent will remove himself or herself from relationships in numerous ways. The "individualist" finds security by using constructive avenues for being alone and self-reliant. The "antagonist" keeps others at a distance through continually criticizing those who might attempt intimacy. The "complainer" repulses others with constant whining about life and its unfairness. And finally, the "delinquent" actively pushes others away through illegal and antisocial behavior. Each of these teenagers uses a type of rebellion for protection from anxiety related to feelings and a need for interpersonal relationships.

■ Guidelines for Working with Rebellious Adolescents

When trying to help rebellious young people, we

encounter many of the same difficulties we experience when working with aggressive teenagers. The purpose of rebellion is to protect these teenagers from their anxiety which arises from close interpersonal contact. Some rebellious behavior pushes other people away. Other forms of this defense may cause individuals to withdraw from threatening situations. Pushing others away and withdrawal protect these young people from their fears of leadership or responsibility. These teenagers also feel threatened when someone offers help or expresses concern for them; therefore, they usually resist any care that parents, teachers, counselors and youth workers express toward them. But we can help these rebellious young people in numerous ways; let's examine some of these suggestions now:

1. Seek to understand the origin of each rebellious teenager's behavior. Seek to understand how your particular teenager's rebellious personality pattern began. Discover the forces which helped mold this manner of relating to other people. The more you understand this teenager's development, the more effectively you can help him or her resolve underlying conflicts and adopt more effective social behavior.

Knowledge about how each adolescent's behavior patterns began will help you assess the specific meanings of his or her particular rebellion. Was the pattern learned from mom or dad? Did it develop early in childhood, or is it a more recent change? What significant experiences led to this particular personality development? Finding the answers to these and similar questions provides you with a good start in understanding how best to help your rebellious teenager.

2. Help these young people resolve their pain and anger from the past in order to live fully in the present. Rebellious adolescents must work through their painful experiences from the past before they can begin to move into their future. As you understand the sources of their hurt, fears and anger, work with them to recognize the origins of their difficulties. Encourage them to talk about their past interpersonal histories. Help them discuss their childhood experiences with their parents, brothers, sisters, friends and other adults. As they talk with you, look for non-verbal cues suggesting areas of particular importance. Notice what makes them nervous, angry or sad. Let them know which issues seem to have special significance for them.

As you help these rebellious teenagers discuss their formative experiences, they come closer to resolving their inner conflicts and emotional pain. These young people need our help to successfully let go of emotional hurts and release themselves from past anger and conflicts. They can learn from you how forgiveness sets them free to live fully in the present and the future.

3. Encourage these adolescents to forgive themselves in order to increase their self-esteem. Many young people have negative feelings about themselves as well as other people. They are sometimes angry at themselves for not being more successful. They feel guilty about their lack of emotional or moral strength. "If I were only smarter . . . If I were only more attractive . . . If I could just have more willpower . . . If only I had made better decisions earlier . . ." Their list of "If onlys" is endless. Many teenagers enmesh themselves in this kind of wishful thinking, but it leads them nowhere. This negative thought process only worsens their situation. By focusing on their faults, weaknesses and failures, they entrap themselves in deep, self-directed anger and entrenched guilt feelings.

Our task is to help these teenagers forgive themselves. Encourage them to believe they did the best they could at the time. If they know we value them, we can help their progress toward increased self-esteem. Our expressions of respect and trust help them value, respect and eventually trust themselves more fully. As they progress through this healing process, they should discover the self-esteem necessary to reduce their self-directed anger and unfounded guilt feelings.

4. Determine how rebellious adolescents view your efforts to help and alter your responses to each young person's understanding and needs. Discovering how each rebellious adolescent perceives warmth and loving is important to your helping strategy. His or her views on caring, intimacy and closeness will impact the way he or she responds to your help.

Many rebellious young people are suspicious of any kind of caring approach. They usually distrust tender or gentle feelings. They are quite successful at discouraging adults who seek to help. Find out how young people view you and the help you offer. Try to understand what they distrust or why they are suspicious. What do you do or say that raises their anxiety level? When do they push you away or withdraw from you? Seek a sensitive understanding about their individual defenses so you can find ways to move closer without triggering rebellious reactions.

5. Support these young people through their painful interpersonal experiences. Help them realize pain and rejection are normal, survivable parts of life. When teenagers experience pain and personal rejection, they need support and help. They need to know they aren't always the cause of their social problems. They require reassurance that pain is a normal part of growing up. Let them know that adults also feel rejection, have friendship problems and experience interpersonal pain. Spend some one-on-one time with these rebellious young people and help them work through these tough issues.

Sometimes these young people hurt so badly they don't know if they will survive the experience. For some, suicide is their final, ultimate rebellion against an unfair and difficult world. Others simply withdraw into deeper isolation to avoid further pain. Within your youth ministry programming include some sessions on adolescent relationships. Make sure your teenagers realize that everyone experiences intense relationships and breakups. And more importantly, stress the fact that these people survive and go on to risk again.

6. Recognize the tendency of rebellious personalities to reject those who try to help, and keep trying other strategies. A common reaction to confrontation with rebellious adolescents is to think: "If we can just give her enough love, she'll turn around. After all, that's what she's really wanting." This approach causes a problem. Many rebellious adolescents really *don't* want love, affection or friendship. Some can no longer accept human relationships as pleasurable, meaningful or fulfilling. To confront these teenagers with the very thing they fear and seek to avoid forces them to push away more vigorously. This rejection of close relationships is a primary difference between rebellious young people and other teenagers. When people offer or force love and close relationships to rebellious adolescents, the situation worsens. This well-intentioned affection intensifies rebellion and creates negative reactions.

We do not advocate withholding ourselves from these rebellious young people; they *do* need our love. We must realize, however, that their rebellious defenses may actually *increase* when we try to help. Cast out the naive thought that love and attention are sufficient to meet these teenagers' needs, and follow the other helpful ideas presented in this section.

7. Accept these young people for who they are, not *what they do.* To outmaneuver these teenagers' rebellious defenses, make sure you clearly accept them for *who they are.* When they realize you are not so interested in approving of *what they do*, they are much less defensive. Acceptance always focuses on the individual as a person. Acceptance communicates our recognition of each teenager as worthy and valuable. Christ would certainly have us express this view of others. And Paul reminds us: "Do nothing out of selfish ambition or vain conceit, but in humility consider others better than yourselves. Each of you should look not only to your own interests, but also to the interests of others" (Philippians 2:3-4). When your actions consistently express this acceptance, you will win openings in rebellious teenagers' defense systems.

With these teenagers, not focusing on their behavior is essential. When we play the approval-disapproval game, we make it easy for these young people to keep us at a safe, ineffective distance. Avoid their attempts to trap you into judging their dress, music, social alienation and delinquent behavior. Focus on the *person* as quickly and as much as possible. "Well, I must admit you have some interesting insights for someone with blue-spiked hair, but I really like talking with you." "You already know what I think about your language and use of drugs. What you may not realize is how much I still like having you in our group. You have a lot to share, and we appreciate your willingness to do so."

Rebellious teenagers appreciate acceptance much more than gushy affection. They may suspect your actions and intentions at first, but expressing love through your acceptance makes rebellious teenagers far less defensive than displays of affection, loving words or patronizing approval.

8. Provide for and encourage rebellious teenagers' gentle growth into accepting and experiencing tender feelings. Rebellious teenagers fear and distrust any tenderness and warmth. Part of their healing and growth, however, involves enhancing their capacity for receiving and expressing these "soft" emotions. Since these young people have experienced their own personal and social pain, they may identify with the pain others experience. Identifying with another's pain can soften the hearts of these adolescents.

Softness and tenderness expose these rebellious youth to vulnerability, an extremely frightening emotion for these young people. Therefore, sensitizing these young people to others' feelings must be a gradual process. First, provide opportunities for them to experience tenderness toward younger children, orphans or other people who clearly represent no threat to their own sense of security. Then help them identify with the pain of weaker, younger or less capable members of their group, class or neighborhood. They will need some success to continue this threatening process of growth and healing. Try to develop their awareness of world hunger. Offer opportunities for them to experience the specific pains and needs of people in their own community, like the homeless, the elderly or the handicapped. Remember, these young people must progress at their own pace. Gently encourage their growth. If you push for too much too soon, you will lose them.

9. Help these young people develop their capacity for giving. In addition to developing their capacity for tenderness and warmth, rebellious teenagers also need to learn how to help others. For these young people offering help is generally as difficult as receiving it. When these teenagers offer assistance, they place themselves in close contact with other people. This vulnerable position affords them opportunities to receive natural expressions of appreciation, gratitude and even help in return. These types of social situations are healthy to experience, but they are also extremely threatening. Rebellious young people resist helping others both because of their fear of intimate relationships and their normal adolescent narcissism.

Breaking down these barriers to helping others is similar to increasing their capacity for giving love and tenderness. Start with opportunities offering the least amount of possible threat. Ensure early success by protecting these young people from high-risk situations. Involve them with helping younger children. They might volunteer to help in a primary Sunday school class for one week or one month. Maybe they could serve as playground aides at a local elementary school. Enlist their cooperation in teaching young children how to care for pets, how to put puzzles together or how to tell time. Gradually encourage their assistance with children closer to their own age.

Involvement in helping ministries to the poor or the elderly might also increase their capacity for giving. Perhaps some poor or elderly parishioners could benefit from help with their yard work, housecleaning or even weekly visits.

What a joy it is when alienated young people experience personal growth and rewards resulting from their giving. "Remember this: Whoever sows sparingly will also reap sparingly, and whoever sows generously will also reap generously. Each man should give what he has decided in his heart to give, not reluctantly or under compulsion, for God loves a cheerful giver" (2 Corinthians 9:6-7). Leading these adolescents into rewarding giving experiences can open the door to many other growth opportunities.

10. Help these young people discover, develop and use their internal strengths to direct their own lives. Most rebellious teenagers have little confidence in their own personal strengths. They do not see themselves as individuals who positively influence others nor direct the course of their own lives. Growth and healing come to these young people as they begin to believe in their own strengths. Significant personal growth occurs when these adolescents perceive themselves as active participants and directors of their own lives rather than as helpless victims.

Rebellious teenagers need help to take more personal responsibility for their lives. Instead of blaming authority figures, the "system" or their friends, they need to recognize and admit the part their own decisions and actions

played in getting them where they are. Recognizing how
their own actions led to negative consequences makes it
more believable that their actions also could have positive
outcomes in their own lives. As their self-confidence
develops and grows, these young people express less fear
in social situations. What others say and do becomes less
threatening. As their internal strength builds, the power
others have over them diminishes.

Part of our task is to help these rebellious teenagers
find strength within themselves. Developing strength is a
personal growth experience. Encourage each teenager to
recognize and celebrate his or her own rate of development and growth.

A sure sign of increasing personal growth is the ability
to function comfortably in a leadership position. Don't
define leadership too rigidly. It doesn't have to be president of the group. Leadership might mean chairing the
social committee. Or it might manifest itself more infor-
mally like having a positive influence over other kids
within the group. Help rebellious adolescents assess their
personal talents and interests to ascertain their most
appropriate styles of leadership.

***11. Share God's love and healing power with
these young people in ways they can bear and
accept it.*** There is no love more healing than God's love.
These teenagers desperately need love even though they
strongly reject it. We know that all love comes from God.
We also know that God regularly expresses his love for us
through other people. As members of the body of Christ,
we have the same privilege of generously offering his love
to others. Unfortunately, rebellious teenagers suspect and
reject people who approach them with expressions of
love.

Sometimes these young people find it easier to accept
God's love through his written Word. "Consequently, faith
comes from hearing the message, and the message is heard
through the word of Christ" (Romans 10:17). These

teenagers need faith in themselves, faith in others, faith in their futures and, of course, faith in God. In our psychologically oriented world, we mistakenly discount the direct healing power within God's written Word. Expose these withdrawn, alienated and angry adolescents to this vital power through Bible readings, Sunday school experiences, group Bible studies, biblically based teaching and one-on-one disciplining. Let them read and hear over and over again the stories of God's consistent, active reaching-out to heal and help his children.

Be prepared for your rebellious teenagers to reject God's love the same way they discounted your love and the love of others. To cover their insecurities, these young people may encourage disruptive behavior and negative responses within their small groups. This behavior may aggravate some of their classmates. Help their peers recognize the disruptive behavior of these adolescents as their rebellious defense; help them understand rebellious teenagers' struggles for acceptance. Your continued risking and reassurance for both groups of young people are essential for presenting the consistency of God's love.

12. Pray for patience and sensitivity for yourself, and then use these Christlike qualities to work with these rebellious young people. This section has stressed the principle of patience, allowing rebellious adolescents to grow at their own pace. Concerned but non-demanding encouragement toward positive change is especially pertinent when working with these young people. They cannot be rushed into giving up their defensive withdrawal too soon. They cannot be shoved prematurely into accepting closeness with others. Neither can they be prodded into giving or receiving help before they are ready.

Remind yourself of Christ's patience in waiting for us. Waiting for our response while gently drawing us to him models the patience we must have as we work with these young people. We must recognize and incorporate his

tolerance in our own lives. We must move at a pace determined by each teenager's own inner time clock. And we
must practice sensitivity to accurately read and respond to
their timing instead of our own.

When you sense growth and development, suggest a
new step or offer another opportunity. Make sure your
quiet urgings always supply a way out for them. Accept
the fact that it really is okay for these teenagers not to
follow through. They must not lose your respect or their
personal dignity by not completing a task or refusing to
accept a particular challenge.

**13. Respect rebellious teenagers' critical-
thinking skills, and encourage the positive use of
those skills.** Critical-thinking skills play an important role
for rebellious adolescents. These teenagers rely heavily
upon their ability to hold thoughts, feelings, people and
other influences at a safe distance. One way they manage
this distancing is through their critical evaluation of
everything. These young people use a basically healthy
intellectual function to such an excess that it limits their
personal and social effectiveness.

Our task with these teenagers is to genuinely respect
their critical abilities. We want them to discern right from
wrong. We wish for them the ability to distinguish wisdom from foolishness. These intellectual tasks require
adequate development of their critical thinking skills.

Try to provide avenues that allow for positive expressions of their critical nature. Encourage them to participate
on debate teams. Be willing to discuss difficult political,
religious and social issues with them. Model a willingness
not to have everything concrete. Help them realize that no
one person has all the answers. They also need to recognize that being right isn't always the highest good.

Accept their critical nature. Don't let these rebellious
teenagers "hook" your defenses. Guard against retaliating
with your own criticisms of their way of thinking. When
that happens, both of you lose; but theirs is the greater

loss. Instead of criticizing, encourage. "Gee, I don't think I've ever looked at it quite like that." "You have some of the most interesting ways of figuring things out." "I like the way you're able to plow through difficult problems."

14. When rebellious young people manifest unhealthy adaptations of this personality type, refer them to a qualified professional counselor. Consider referring rebellious adolescents for professional counseling when these young people present unhealthy forms of this personality style. Often, these teenagers will heavily resist your attempts to refer them to a counselor. To them, any new relationship represents a new possibility for failure. They may also construe your referral as a sign of rejection, rather than an opportunity for growth. Encourage, clarify and reassert your caring, but don't back down when you know this is the appropriate course of action. You're the adult, and the decision to refer or not to refer belongs to you. You cannot force the teenager to cooperate with the referral process, but you can decide when to do your part.

■ Guidelines for Parenting Rebellious Adolescents

Like the aggressive young people in Chapter 6, rebellious teenagers create significant challenges for you as a parent. The behavior of these teenagers is not only trying but wearing. Their hostile and submissive characteristics often cause family disruptions and make it difficult to resolve conflicts. Remember to rely upon your spouse, other family members, friends and parents of other teenagers for support. A good support system provides a "listening ear" for your frustrations and problems. It also offers opportunities for input from others on how to work with these difficult young people. Since rebellious teenagers are among the most difficult adolescents to parent, this section is designed to offer help and support in understanding and responding to the needs of your young people.

1. *Work to understand the meaning of your rebellious teenagers' behavior.* Rebellious teenagers act out their feelings in ways that get adults to react strongly to them. Their rebellious behavior often threatens and angers authority figures. Then, acting directly out of their own emotions, adults respond defensively or angrily in ways that intensify the unhealthy dynamics within these adolescents. Instead of reacting to your own emotional impulses, you need to understand and respond effectively to what your rebellious teenagers' behavior actually says.

Rebellious teenagers have usually experienced emotional pain, especially in early-life relationships. As with the aggressive adolescents we met in the previous chapter, these young people are angry. They lack the self-confidence aggressive young people have; therefore, they handle their anger through either active or passive rebellion. Usually, they pull away from others, but it is an angry pulling-away. Rebellious behavior essentially says: "I have been hurt and disillusioned within relationships. Therefore, I will withdraw and discourage you from trying to help me."

Your parenting task is to *listen* effectively for the needs your rebellious teenagers' behavior expresses, rather than just react to their behavior itself. Try to hear their pain, their anger and their fears. Listen for *their* understanding of what they feel has happened to them.

2. *Help these young people find release from their past emotional injuries.* Teenagers usually select rebellion as a personality orientation because of past emotional pain or some form of deprivation in earlier childhood. Many of these young people have been rejected, left (as in a divorce or a parental separation) or abused. Others have had extremely difficult or unsuccessful experiences at trying to fit in with other children in their neighborhoods and at school. They have learned that interaction with people brings pain and disappointment. They have also lost confidence in themselves as individuals who can succeed in relating to others.

You can help your rebellious teenagers work through and let go of their emotional hurts from the past. Encourage them to gradually talk out their feelings. *Listen quietly* to them when they tell you about their painful experiences. A significant number of these experiences will probably include you since parents are usually the most important people to young children. Listening and encouraging them to talk will require a great amount of patience and selfless love on your part. This does not mean that you should allow your adolescents to verbally abuse you. Let them know when their conversations become destructive. Encourage them to talk honestly about their pain without condemning others.

Rebellious teenagers need to release their emotional pain and anger before they can successfully grow into healthy adults. You can be your children's best source of love and care through your patient listening.

3. Help your aggressive teenagers become less angry with themselves. By experiencing your acceptance and support, they can let go of their personal guilt and anger and accept themselves as they are. Associated with aggressive adolescents' pain are feelings of anger and guilt. These young people are angry at *others* for not providing love and fulfilling relationships with them. And they are also angry at *themselves* because they are unable to attract and interact with other people. Being angry both at others and themselves, they feel a deep sense of guilt. They perceive themselves as too weak, ineffective and unattractive to succeed within their relationships. Judging themselves as failures, they rebelliously set themselves apart from others out of their fear, anger and guilt.

Your expressions of love and acceptance are probably the most effective source of healing for your rebellious teenagers. Their self-doubts and tendencies to demean themselves express their deep needs to be cared for. Be sure to include them in special activities. Provide one-on-one activities that offer opportunities for dialogue and building relationships. Invite them to help you with projects. Assure them of your appreciation while you work together. Involving your children in your life is one of the most effective ways of saying: "I value and highly respect you. You are worthy of my love and relationship." As they experience your respect, they can begin to value themselves more highly.

Reassure your rebellious adolescents that *all* of us have made serious mistakes in our pasts. Get personal. Let your sons and daughters know about some of the errors and failures that lurk in *your* childhood or adolescence. Help them understand they too can have major problems in their past and even their present and still have successful, constructive lives as adults. Teach them about redemption and the life-changing power God extends to all people. Guide them in learning how to apply his grace to themselves through confession, repentance, obedience and seeking ways of extending love toward others.

Rebellious adolescents desperately need to let go of the anger and guilt they feel about themselves. Your support and acceptance can have a major impact in releasing your children from these crippling forces.

4. Help your rebellious teenagers reduce their levels of distrust for others by being a trustworthy parent. Teach your adolescents how to recognize others they can trust. One of the hallmark responses of rebellious adolescents is a strong distrust of people. Because these young people suspect others' motives, their lack of trust pours out in angry sarcasm or demeaning attacks on the values, intents and actions of other people. By considering other people unworthy of their interaction or involvement, these adolescents effectively distance themselves from others and protect themselves from the possibility of further pain. The intensity of their distrust is particularly dangerous because it may result in a life-long perceptual bias. Distrust can become an ingrained part of their attitude that severely restricts their desire and ability to form meaningful relationships.

The quality of your relationships with your sons or daughters can either help or hinder their ability to trust others. One of the greatest gifts you can give your teenagers is your own trustworthiness.

Are you dependable?

Do you follow through on what you promise?

How consistent are you?

Do your actions fit with what you say?

Can your children accurately predict how you will respond to various situations?

Can they trust you to keep their confidences?

Do they believe you will act on what you think is best for them?

Your answers to these questions will give you an indication of your trustworthiness from their point of view.

When critical thinking reaches the extreme proportions common to rebellious teenagers, it may lead to intense distrust for almost everyone. You can help your children accept others' failures and imperfections. Point out the presence of good and bad in everyone, including themselves. Let them know that choosing to trust or distrust is not an all-or-none proposition. Everyone can be trusted for some things, but a few can be trusted for almost nothing. Encourage balance in their perceptions of others.

Rebellious teenagers tend to distrust others. Encourage them to risk trusting others to help them remove one major block that impairs their ability and freedom to form fulfilling and intimate relationships.

5. Help your rebellious young people realize that emotional pain is a normal part of being involved in interpersonal relationships. Rebellion is designed as a defense to protect adolescents from emotional pain and a sense of weakness. Often these threatening feelings arise from unhappy and injurious interpersonal relationships. Many young people don't realize that *everyone* experiences occasional emotional pain while building relationships with others. Friendships, romantic relationships, work relationships and family relationships are all vulnerable to the imperfections of the people involved.

Just knowing, "I'm not the only one," can mean relief to someone who is hurting. Gently reassure your daughter when her boyfriend doesn't ask her out. Comfort your son when his girlfriend breaks off their relationship. As part of their consolation, help them realize painful experiences are a normal part of adolescence. Reassure them that just because others have had similar experiences, you are not saying their pain shouldn't be taken seriously. Recognize their hurt and let them talk with you about their feelings. Also let them know that almost everyone survives this type of experience. They need to know that life won't always look as hopeless and depressing as it does at that moment. These young people need to know they aren't weird or flawed because they have experienced painful relationships. You can play a major role in offering them reassurance.

6. Realize that some rebellious adolescents really don't want to experience expressions of love. These young people have been injured seriously enough to convince them that nothing can be gained from loving relationships. They have assumed the position of not wanting love. Remember, this is not an all-or-none trait; not all rebellious teenagers are extreme in their personality dynamics. While some adamantly reject love, others are just mildly resistant. Nevertheless, all rebellious adolescents distrust and avoid loving relationships to some degree.

When you force your expressions of love on rebellious teenagers, they may react in one of two ways. First, they may become aggressive. They may act out their anger toward you or displace their aggression onto safer individuals like a younger brother or sister. These young people may also respond by internalizing their anger toward you. With this response they become more self-depreciating and guilt-ridden because of their inability to accept or respond to love. When you fail to recognize or respect the resistance your adolescents put up against you, you are forcing love on your children. Hugging, kissing, gift-giving, doing activities with them, making them be with you and excessive verbal expressions of "I love you" are all ways you can unwisely force love on your rebellious young people.

As a parent, it is a difficult struggle when your children reject the love you offer them. When your love is effectively blocked, you aren't sure what else you can do. Here are some helpful suggestions:

● Respect your teenagers' defenses. When they feel a need for space away from you, allow it.

● Don't try to overpower them. If they resist your hugs and kisses, don't force them. Listen when they say: "Please stop. I feel uncomfortable with this."

● Offer *your* need for love and allow them freedom to respond when *they* feel comfortable. Comments like "I need a hug. Do you have one to spare?" give your child the chance to say "Yes," "No" or "Not right now." If they see they can control and limit these expressions of affection, they may feel more willing to risk. Remember, responding to another's request is a powerful way of communicating love for both you and your children.

Another important skill for parenting rebellious teenagers is your flexibility. When one expression of love is rejected, try another. When a verbal "I love you" is pushed away, try doing something special for your children. Bake their favorite cookies, fill up their gas tank, buy them cut flowers or a plant for their room, surprise them by doing their chores or leave a special "I'm thinking of you today" card on their breakfast plate. Be creative. Brainstorm new ideas with your spouse or with friends.

When one thing doesn't work, that's okay. Just try something else.

Rebellious teenagers will characteristically reject your attempts to express love. That means you will need flexibility and creativity to communicate your love in ways your children can accept. This patient process will help your adolescents gradually open themselves to accept love and affirmation from other important people in their lives.

7. Focus your attention on accepting your rebellious teenagers rather than approving their behavior. *Acceptance* focuses on people while *approval* focuses on their behavior. These teenagers desperately need affirmation that they are accepted. They are filled with self-doubts about their inadequacies. Approval of their performances in statements like "You did a great job," "I'm amazed at how well you handle those situations" and "I'm extremely pleased with how well you're doing" have little influence on helping rebellious teenagers improve their self-concepts. It's okay to offer those kinds of affirmations, but realize that these responses to their behavior will have less of a positive impact than responses that focus on the individual. Here are some examples of appropriate accepting responses:

"Shirley, I'm not sure you realize just how much I enjoy having you in our family."

"Bill, your sense of humor adds so much to our family. I really like it that you're here."

"There is just so much that I like about you, Mark. I'm really going to miss you when you go off to school."

Each of these responses focuses more on teenagers' personal characteristics than on their behavior.

Rebellious teenagers may easily argue that their performances or skills really aren't that good. They are quick to refute your positive appraisal of their competencies. It is much harder for them to counter statements that you enjoy or value them. Your messages of personal acceptance will gradually accumulate within them and powerfully impact their capacity to develop a higher level of self-esteem.

8. Encourage your rebellious teenagers to express more tenderness toward others. Expressing soft and tender emotions frightens rebellious young people because they feel vulnerable, and vulnerability is exactly what their rebellious orientation is designed to protect against. Because these teenagers lack self-confidence, they withdraw from close contact with other people. Experiencing warm feelings threatens these young people in two ways. First, it frightens them by bringing them closer to others in an affectionate and caring manner. Second, rebellious young people usually misinterpret their own warm and soft feelings to mean personal weakness and incompetency. This misunderstanding verifies their self-condemning beliefs about themselves.

Expressing tenderness toward others is extremely threatening for rebellious young people; however, it is important for them to develop this capacity. Adult relationships will require their commitment and intimacy with important others. Dealing effectively with tenderness and warmth is an important part of developing their relationship skills. Help your adolescents increase their capacity to deal with tender feelings. Model expressions of these feelings in your own actions and words, both toward your family members and your friends. Let your young people see how these emotions can benefit you and those to whom you express them. Point out situations in which risking your own vulnerability by expressing your feelings was rewarded with love from another.

Rebellious young people often find it less threatening to expose their vulnerability to younger children than to peers or adults. Encourage their tenderness toward younger brothers and sisters. Set up opportunities for them to play with younger cousins, nieces, nephews and small children of your friends. When sensitive emotions and tender interpersonal issues are presented on television

238 ■ *WHY TEENAGERS ACT THE WAY THEY DO*

or in the movies, try to elicit your teenagers' responses to
that material. See if they can express how they feel while
watching those situations. Get them to talk about how
they might have felt if they were in similar circumstances.

Rebellious teenagers resist warm and tender situations
with other people. Help them adjust to their emotional
vulnerability as they prepare for healthy adult relationships.

**9. *Help your rebellious teenagers involve them-
selves in assisting other people.*** Rebellious teenagers
often avoid helping other people because they lack self-
confidence and fear emotional vulnerability. Offering help
places people at risk; their help may be rejected or
ridiculed. Others may look at their offers of assistance as
inappropriate or weird. These young people are acutely
aware of the personal risks they take when offering help.
Their lack of confidence actually sabotages their capacity
to help others. Offering assistance presupposes belief in
one's personal skills and values as potentially beneficial to
other people. Low self-esteem characteristically causes
these teenagers to disclaim any positive belief in themselves and underestimate their abilities to help others.

Helping has a central value in Christ's teachings. It also
plays a significant role in developing healthy interpersonal
relationships. Therefore, as a part of teenagers' spiritual
and psychological growth, these young people need to
develop their abilities to help others. You can assist your
rebellious young people by maximizing their chances for
success in helping ventures. Structure situations that don't
seem dangerous or threatening to them. For instance, helping younger children is usually less threatening than
working with their peers or adults. Request your teenagers' help with younger brothers and sisters. They might
set up and run birthday parties. Perhaps they could teach
their younger siblings how to play games or work with
them to develop new skills like riding a bike. They could
also help them with their homework or babysit.

As your rebellious teenagers gradually gain confidence in their abilities to give, encourage them to offer help to their peers or adults. Suggest ways likely to produce success and good feelings so they will gain confidence in themselves and their abilities. Building their capacity to help can provide another way for these young people to develop healthier relationships with others.

10. Help these young people develop greater trust in their own strengths. One of the differences between rebellious and aggressive teenagers is rebellious teenagers' lack of confidence in their inner strengths. Initially, they withdraw from others and internalize their anger. They often blame themselves for their perceived inadequacies and then live with long-term guilt. This insecurity in their abilities then produces even more anger and guilt within them.

You can be a vital support as rebellious adolescents seek to build confidence in their inner strengths. Think about tasks they can do that will expand their confidence in their abilities. Are there specific chores that would help them see themselves as responsible people? Try placing them in charge of meal preparation for one or two nights per week. Offer them responsibility for washing and waxing the cars or changing the oil. Perhaps they could do the laundry or help with the ironing. Suggest they take care of the rose bushes and the fruit trees or make them responsible for the special plants in your house. Give your teenagers tasks that require developing special abilities and learning new skills. These tasks should have more meaning than just taking out the trash or picking up in their room.

Encourage your teenagers to tackle new tasks. Start with easier ones first to maximize their chances for success. Help your young people develop self-concepts that say, "I can learn to do important and valuable things."

Interpersonal relationships also present opportunities for your rebellious adolescents to gain confidence in their strengths. Developing social skills, gaining ease in relating to a wide variety of people and assuming leadership responsibilities will encourage them to believe in their own strengths. Rebellious teenagers need to find *good* reasons to trust their own worth, value and strengths. You can help your teenagers prove to themselves that they *do* possess trustworthy inner strengths.

11. Encourage your rebellious adolescents toward more positive expressions of their critical thinking skills. Without the ability to think critically, teenagers cannot adequately evaluate ideas, values, thoughts and attitudes. They must learn to analyze their thoughts to develop their own faith, beliefs, attitudes, value systems, preferences, likes and dislikes. Failure to develop critical thinking skills produces adults incapable of thinking for themselves. Rather, they will align themselves with people they respect and then copy or assimilate their beliefs, attitudes and values as their own.

Rebellious teenagers often exercise their critical thinking skills in only negative or destructive ways. They may criticize their parents, teachers, police, Sunday school teachers, pastors and even their friends. They also become exceedingly critical of themselves. You can help your rebellious young people exercise their critical thinking skills to think positively as well as negatively. Help your teenagers sort out the good from the bad when discussing a person's character. When they criticize a teacher's action, ask them if they see anything positive in what their teacher did. As they speak critically about one of their friends, see if they can balance their view with some positive observations. When they make disparaging remarks about themselves, encourage them to list their beneficial characteristics also.

Rebellious teenagers can be excessively negative in exercising their critical thinking skills. You can help them temper their views with positive evaluations. This guidance can help your rebellious adolescents reach a healthier balance in the way they view the world and themselves.

12. Work patiently with rebellious teenagers as they try to grow. Remember, individuals grow at different paces. You cannot demand your adolescents change their behavior just when you think they should. They are their own persons; and though they sometimes need encouragement, reminders or prodding, you must respect their own internal time clock. Self-concepts, defense mechanisms, emotional blocks, repressed pain and anger, fears and insecurities and their ways of perceiving reality affect the rate at which they will accomplish certain changes. It is helpful for us to remember the patience that God and others, even our *own* parents, had with us!

You express great respect and love for your teenagers when you are patient with them. This message of caring and valuing can have an additional positive impact on your adolescents as they continue to mature.

13. Consider professional counseling for rebellious teenagers when they seem unable to move to a positive adaptation of their personality type. The anger and self-depreciation that rebellious teenagers harbor within themselves can cause significant problems. When angry withdrawal becomes common behavior, these young people probably need help from people specifically trained to work with adolescents. An authority figure, a friend or third party who is not a family member is sometimes easier for these young people to trust. Remember, making sure your teenagers receive the help they need may be the most loving thing you can do for them. No sense of failure should be implied when your children need counseling, any more than when they need medical attention. Seek referral to appropriate sources of counseling from your pediatrician, pastor, youth minister, teacher or friends who have had good experiences with particular counselors.

You now have a deeper understanding of rebellion as

an adolescent defensive orientation. You are better equipped to differentiate between normal teenage rebellion and rebellion which dominates the personality style. You are aware there are both healthy and unhealthy forms of this interpersonal orientation. You have also been exposed to active types, like the "antagonist" and the "delinquent," as well as passive types, like the "individualist" and the "complainer." Though rebellious teenagers are difficult to help, you now have some tools that can help you work successfully with these teenagers in their movement toward growth and healing.

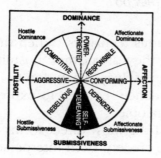

■ CHAPTER 8

The Self-Demeaning Personality

Self-demeaning young people are the least likely to be noticed as having problems or as people who need help because of their ability to retreat into the background. They purposefully avoid attention and are quick to shun responsibility. Perhaps their strongest psychological feature is their lack of belief in themselves. They see themselves as inferior and incompetent. These adolescents are located in the most submissive position of all personality types.

Self-demeaning adolescents are the opposite of the power-oriented young people discussed in Chapter 4. Instead of finding security in strength, these teenagers emphasize their own weaknesses. Positions of leadership and vulnerability to others' expectations create strong anxiety within these young people. They do not possess the aggressiveness of competitive, aggressive or rebellious teenagers. They withdraw passively rather than angrily withhold themselves like rebellious teenagers. When they do become angry or frustrated, they direct their hostility and negative feelings toward themselves. They don't possess the energy or self-confidence required to express anger effectively toward other people.

Demeaning the self is one of the most direct forms of self-protection against excessive anxiety from interpersonal contact. These young people actually hide from others. They conceal themselves from possible failure while they hide from others' expectations, judgments and rejections. Success even brings increased anxiety; these young people fear that when they publicly succeed, people will expect more, increasing their chances for failure in the future. Self-demeaning behavior essentially says, "I want you to believe I am a weak, incompetent person so you will expect nothing from me."

■ *Development of the Self-Demeaning Personality*

Most adolescents experience periods when they need increased quiet and privacy. During these times they spend hours in their bedrooms, listening to their stereos, drifting in fantasies. This withdrawal is common during early and mid-adolescence. It accompanies the task of identity formation that consumes so much of teenagers' psychological energy.

By themselves, these behaviors do not suggest the presence of self-demeaning personalities. When teenagers withdraw and express self-depreciating behavior over a long period of time, however, we should be alert. If these behaviors continue and then link themselves to our teenagers' inadequate self-concepts, we must assume that our young people are developing self-demeaning personality patterns. Several common causes often emerge in the personal histories of self-demeaning adolescents. Let's identify some of these important causes and understand how they contribute to the formation of this personality type.

First, some of these teenagers lack sufficient training in their homes. When parents are inadequate socially, mentally or otherwise, they have difficulty providing their children with instruction and experience in the interpersonal skills required to live effective lives. Other parents consciously withhold their love, affection and important teachings in response to the resentment they feel for their children.

Some young people are raised in homes where both parents work; others are raised by a single parent. Within these busy families, managing a schedule plus numerous jobs, household tasks and social obligations leave little time for the demanding requirements of effective parenting. In these situations young people miss important training which leaves them inadequate in many social arenas. They may not know nor have much experience in building relationships. They may feel uncertain about communicating their feelings or accurately understanding the behavior of their peers. These deficiencies typically lead to interpersonal awkwardness, social rejection and further belief in their own inadequacy.

Second, many of these young people lack adequate nurturing and encouragement from their parents. What happens during early childhood dramatically impacts young people's later psychological development. Young children desperately need their parents' affection. Infants know they are loved when their parents hold them, talk to them and attend to their basic needs. When parents deprive their children of adequate love, the children develop intense feelings of insecurity and strong self-doubts.

Negative or neglectful early-life experiences falsely teach young people they are neither valuable nor important enough to warrant the interest of others. When young people have no personal support, they typically accept this devastating, false conclusion. These teenagers, then, continue actions that reflect their negative beliefs about themselves. The self-demeaning patterns of behavior you observe in adolescents may reflect this deprivation of parental nurturing and support.

Third, some young people are criticized for their strengths. Most parents are well-equipped to love and care for *young* children. However, many parents reach their limits when these same children reach their adolescent years, develop more personal strength and begin to assert themselves as individuals. Teenagers easily challenge insecure adults. Parents who question their own identities and sexuality are threatened by aggressive adolescents. Parents struggling within their own careers are intimidated by young people who idealistically forecast great successes for themselves. Other adults believe any boasting is sinful and resent these young people for their bad taste and inappropriate behavior.

When parents, teachers and other adults struggle with their own identity or resent teenagers for their efforts toward maturation, they often criticize young people and discourage their independence. In many cases these adults project their personal anger on relatively defenseless young people. The adolescents then blame themselves for not pleasing adults. By internalizing the anger of adults, these young people chastise themselves for their pride. They also battle the guilt feelings that arise each time they experience personal strength, independence or other steps toward maturity.

Fourth, some adolescents take on excessive guilt with little encouragement from adults. This is particularly true of self-demeaning teenagers. These sensitive young people often misinterpret scripture and pulpit messages to mean that *all* positive thoughts about themselves and *all* positive actions on their own behalf are wrong. They mistake their personal recognition of maturity for pride. They view healthy self-concern as selfishness. These teenagers become their own most severe critic. They judge themselves harshly for personal confidence and strength, qualities essential for continued growth and maturity. Unfortunately, churches and youth groups sometimes reinforce this self-punitive thinking, forgetting that *all* of us are God's valuable creations.

Fifth, during childhood and early adolescence, peers sometimes misinterpret passivity and withdrawal as strength. The defenses of self-demeaning young people work so well they can fool even their closest friends. Adults make this same miscalculation. Consider how often women choose men who are the "strong silent type," only to discover their dreams of masculinity are really passive and insecure boys. Masks of quiet strength and superior "cool" effectively hide withdrawal and passive personalities. In addition, when friends and buddies reinforce these self-demeaning skills with fear and respect, teenagers will probably use these psychological defenses more and more.

Sixth, teenagers who successfully learn how to express self-demeaning defenses reinforce their self-depreciation. The effectiveness of their defense leads to a reduction in their personal anxiety. Their coping methods lessen their fears and insecure feelings about their interactions with other people. Remember, these young people fully believe in their inadequacy. They are convinced they are somehow insufficient and undeserving. They *expect* rejection, ridicule and negative judgment from other teenagers and adults. Therefore, when their levels of fear and anxiety are reduced by these negative experiences, they will seek to reinforce these feelings by seeking more of the same. After several years of this pattern, altering their behavior becomes difficult. To change, they must challenge the beliefs upon which they have built their defenses—they must begin to believe they are okay. This change in attitude automatically creates more anxiety which discourages growth.

As we live and work with young people, it is important that we increase our knowledge and awareness of their personal histories. How have they become who they are today? Which forces have impacted their personality development? What experiences have helped shape their behavior, thought and emotional patterns? Our awareness of their background and how they view it increases our understanding of their present behavior.

■ Healthy Forms of the Self-Demeaning Personality

As we continue our study of adolescent personality orientations, we must remind ourselves each personality type has its healthy, adaptive forms of expression. Within our complex culture, avenues of social interaction vary. Opportunities for the healthy interaction of virtually all personality types are available. Demeaning one's self is certainly not a healthy dynamic at its core; however, the young people described in this chapter can find adaptive, constructive ways of interacting with other people. There is one crucial element—their interpersonal behavior patterns cannot be excessively rigid or intense. They must develop the ability to moderate and adapt their interpersonal style to fit with different people in different social situations. The following two case studies present examples of self-demeaning teenagers who made healthy adjustments within their personality orientation.

The Modest. Jill is kind and considerate to everyone she knows. Adults especially enjoy her. From her teachers and Girl Scout leaders to her youth minister and her mother's friends—all adults find Jill respectful and considerate. Jill finds adults less threatening than her peers. She notices that most adults don't talk to her or other high school kids much; and when they do, they are usually satisfied with a smile and a polite response. Then they leave her alone.

Jill's peers also like her, but they have a hard time getting to know her. Although self-consciousness is normal for most teenagers, Jill is extreme. Any attention goes beyond discomfort; it is actually unbearable. To avoid these unpleasant situations, Jill seeks anonymity. She operates as an average student in an attempt to repel any attention, whether negative or complimentary.

Jill's personal history helps explain her modest behavior. When she was 4 years old, her father was killed in an industrial accident. Shortly after his death, Jill and her mother moved to another city to be close to relatives. Once they had arrived and settled into the community, they joined the local church, and Jill was enrolled in violin lessons.

When Jill's mother was finally forced to work, she began to expect more of Jill. Her mother relied heavily on her for housework, cooking and other household chores. Just before Jill's 11th birthday, her mother met a special man in their church and began to consider remarriage. Jill's mother encouraged her to attend a few brief sessions with a professional therapist to help her adjust to the possibility of a change in their family life. Then when Jill was 12, her mother did remarry and quit working outside the home. By this time Jill had so incorporated the values her mother had taught, she altered her lifestyle very little, even though less was required of her.

Jill is now a junior in high school and is an excellent musician. She has continued her violin lessons up to the present time and thoroughly enjoys playing her instrument at home when she is alone. She struggles terribly with public performances. When she has to play at school concerts or during church programs, she panics. She is just as uncomfortable *after* her presentations as she is before and during them. Because she is so talented, everyone wants to congratulate her and express their appreciation. But the awkwardness and embarrassment she experiences from this extra attention is more than she can handle.

Nothing is wrong with Jill, except for her excessive modesty. She is managing her life very well, but why is she so modest and shy? When compliments are directed toward her, why does she respond with comments like, "No, not really; it was nothing," "Anybody could have done as well" or "It was really God, not me"? Her self-consciousness goes beyond uncomfortable. And the intensity of her discomfort doesn't appear to diminish.

Throughout her childhood Jill heard her mother stress the value of modesty. She was disciplined *not* to be proud. Her mother also emphasized the importance of considering others before herself and of giving God credit for *all* the good she accomplished. With her mother's emphasis on these modest values and extensive responsibilities, Jill learned to think of her own needs and wants as unimportant. She also believed she was secondary in comparison to others. She felt most comfortable when she was last in line or when she got the smallest piece of cake. She continually struggled with guilt feelings both before and after purchasing nice clothes for herself. Asking for something from her parents or becoming assertive with her friends about something she wanted to do was difficult for her. Her modesty permeated every area of her life. Even though Jill is a self-demeaning teenager, she is essentially a psychologically healthy adolescent. She relates well with her peers and exceptionally well with adults.

The Servant. The youth leader had known Walter since he was 6 years old, when he first came to the church with his family. Now in the eighth-grade, 13-year-old Walter has been part of the junior high group for two years. His personal history provides an interesting example of factors which can lead to the development of an adolescent self-demeaning personality pattern.

Until he was 6 years old, Walter's life seemed completely normal. He lived in a loving family atmosphere, the youngest of three children. Though he was small for his age, he adapted well during preschool and kindergarten. Other children liked him, and his teachers reported good progress in school.

Shortly after entering first-grade, Walter complained of pains in his hip. His parents noticed a slight limp and took him to his pediatrician. Further consultations with an orthopedic surgeon revealed a congenital problem in the development of his right hip socket. During the next six years, Walter had four surgeries and spent 54 months in the hospital. During this important part of his childhood, his whole life was focused on his physical problem and its correction. Because of his traction, casts, braces and physical therapy, he was unable to attend school for months at a time; so he was tutored at home.

To fulfill his need for social contact, he depended upon friends who came to visit him. His church youth group also supported him. Their periodic visits and special arrangements included Walter in as many activities as possible and helped him maintain his feeling that he was still part of the group. Fortunately, his family was loving and supportive. They did their best to attend to his needs without spoiling him.

During the months following his rehabilitation, Walter returned to his school, friendships and youth group activities with full intensity. But the way in which he became reinvolved was particularly interesting. At school he became a towel-boy in the boys' gym, helped his English teacher after school and served as the manager's helper for his school's baseball team. His friends recognized him as an excellent choice to ask for help with homework or other projects. Walter arrived early for every youth meeting and helped set up chairs. He spent extra hours preparing papers, organizing handouts and helping his youth leader with anything else that was needed. He also remained after each event to help with cleanup. At home he faithfully completed his chores and sometimes volunteered to help his older brother and sister with theirs.

Walter made sure he was always involved and available to help, but he *never* took any leadership position or role of authority. He declined every invitation to lead in prayer, give announcements or organize activities. He seemed to avoid being noticed. He felt socially comfortable only when he helped or served others. Receiving from friends, relatives and family members without any opportunities to reciprocate during his rehabilitation had made him feel uncomfortable. He *had* to be doing something for others. Yet his self-confidence was not developed to the point he could function well in any leadership capacity.

Walter's physical difficulties severely hampered his social development. By resisting the dependent type of contact he had from age 6 to 12, he became a "servant" to others' needs to allay his own feelings of uselessness. It was the one social role he felt comfortable and confident enough to fulfill. Walter had done a marvelous job of adapting and recovering from a difficult life experience. His level of social involvement was remarkable, but it was also seriously limited. Walter would need encouragement and guidance to help him relate to other people in more ways than just as their servant.

Jill and Walter are two examples of healthy social adaptations of the self-demeaning personality style. Jill models excessive modesty, and Walter relates to others *only* as their servant. Both young people, however, capably interact with others in positive ways that meet both their own needs and the needs of others.

■ Unhealthy Forms of the Self-Demeaning Personality

All of the personality types examined in this book can be expressed in healthy, adaptive forms during adolescence, but each one can take on unhealthy, maladaptive forms when teenagers become too rigid or intense in their behavior patterns. While most personality types strive to develop positive experiences to fulfill their needs, the self-demeaning personality strives to feel better by experiencing pain. This personality pattern is one of the most difficult to break because it thrives on negative feelings that normally deter behavior. Like the child who playfully places his finger on the stove to get his mother to notice him, these young people willingly stick their hands in the flame just to receive a scream of attention. We will look at three unhealthy patterns of self-demeaning behavior in this section.

The Recluse. At her mother's insistence, Shana initiated professional counseling when she was 19 years old. She was about 5 feet 11 inches tall and weighed over 200 pounds. In her first session she had little to say. Angry at being forced into counseling, Shana used her silence as a weapon to preserve her sense of dignity. To talk freely with the counselor would have meant losing the power struggle with her mother. Although this reaction is common for a teenager forced into counseling by parental pressure, there was something more involved in Shana's silence. Three times she told her therapist, "If I can't even talk with my mother, how can I talk with someone I don't know?" Something inside blocked her from releasing her thoughts and feelings to others. Something inside kept her from making contact with people who cared about her.

Therapy progressed slowly at first. Shana had difficulty developing trust in her counselor's care. Finally, the invitation to open up to her inner pain and turmoil within the safe environment of her counseling sessions proved too much for her defenses. Gradually, mixed with many tears, her story emerged.

Until her sophomore year in high school, Shana had enjoyed life. Her family provided adequate, though not outstanding, love and support for her and her younger brother. She was an avid athlete, playing soccer and softball on community teams since she was 6 years old. She went through school with her best girlfriend from early elementary to high school. She was a strong-B student and was reasonably popular, both in her neighborhood and at school.

Shana's psychological development progressed well, and her future looked promising. Then in her sophomore year, everything seemed to go wrong. Within a few months, her life crumbled. And during the past five years, she has unsuccessfully attempted to pull herself back together. Let's examine the combination of losses, pressures and feelings of rejection that overwhelmed Shana. They are the same forces that seriously affect many teenagers.

First, Shana broke off her friendship with her best girlfriend. Inseparable for 11 years, both girls desperately wanted to date the same boy, and Shana lost.

Losing the boyfriend she liked was the second event that contributed to Shana's devastating sophomore year. This young man and her girlfriend dated steadily until a few months before Shana initiated counseling. Thus, between the ages of 15 and 19, Shana was not only without a best girlfriend, but she had never experienced a positive relationship with a boy.

The third negative event of Shana's 10th grade year came during a volleyball practice at school. Diving to return a difficult ball before it hit the floor, Shana severely damaged her knee. Her injury forced her out of volleyball for the rest of the school and community league seasons. Since volleyball was her best sport, Shana's outstanding performances had become a primary source for her affirmation and ego support. Now that was gone for the rest of the year.

Shana's fourth major blow was also related to her injured knee. She was one of the leading players on her school's softball team. When she sustained her injury, the coach removed her from her regular first-base position and allowed her to participate only as a designated hitter. The coach's decision was appropriate, but Shana viewed it as another rejection. She had lost one more valuable source of affirmation for her personal value and identity.

During this pivotal school year Shana experienced her fifth trauma. As Shana's school work deteriorated while she struggled with everything that was happening in her life, her English teacher remained cold, demanding and emotionally aloof. Instead of expressing concern and finding out *why* Shana's work was declining, her teacher criticized her and openly shamed her in front of the class for not working up to her potential. That day was a turning point for Shana. She gave up; she broke. Now she was in therapy, desperately trying to regain the developmental losses she had accumulated during the past five years.

At age 15 Shana gave up and withdrew from those around her. It wasn't a violent withdrawal, like the rebellious adolescent. She merely retired into passive hopelessness and gave up on life. Her pain was too great. Too many of her supports had been knocked out from under her. Trying to succeed in athletics, academics and relationships had led to pain, rejection and failure. Shana became a "recluse." She avoided all contact with people, unless absolutely necessary. She walked alone to and from school and spoke to as few people as possible while she was there. She did only minimum school work, passing her classes with a C or a D. Shana even withdrew from her family, forcing them to initiate interaction if they hoped to converse with her.

On many occasions Shana had felt suicidal, but told no one she was in such danger. The intensity of her withdrawal and the depth of her hopelessness had become a pattern. Her interactions with others were self-destructive and self-demeaning. She felt she had no value. She chose to believe she could never succeed. Her negative self-image was the *only* way she could feel okay about not trying to succeed in any area of her life.

The Martyr. Beverly is a 16-year-old high school junior in her youth group. Her behavior reminds us of Walter, the servant teenager we met in the previous section. Beverly also does things for other people. She, too, is helpful in her youth group. She does the tasks most kids neglect. When volunteers are requested and few respond, Beverly is almost always available. Since she got her drivers license, she provides regular transportation for other group members to meetings and other activities. She runs errands, moves equipment and is generally available to do whatever task needs to be done.

Beverly is similar to Walter in another way. She feels comfortable relating to her peers and adults *only* when she is helping or providing for someone. Her youth minister, who has known her for six years, says Beverly has operated with this behavior pattern since he has known her. Each year she assumes more responsibility in doing things for other people.

There is one aspect of Beverly's behavior that differs from Walter's servant pattern. Even though Walter limits the way he relates to other people, he *enjoys* serving others. Beverly, however, *resents* her social position. She readily volunteers to do a task and then completes it with an air of self-righteousness: "I am more willing than you to work hard. I always pick up where you fail. Therefore, I am an exceptional person."

In much of Beverly's attitude toward others, there is implied anger mixed with her self-righteousness. Like most martyrs, Beverly is angry that others make demands upon her. Like most good martyrs, she fails to accept any responsibility for choosing her role. She feels victimized, and in subtle ways she projects her anger at those around her. She always makes others pay in some manner for the work she chooses to do for them.

Beverly's youth minister shared some significant personal history explaining why she might have developed into an adolescent martyr. Beverly was the eldest daughter in a family of three children. Her father was an alcoholic who became a binge drinker when Beverly was about 4 years old. About five times a month, he would drink every day until he passed out on the family room couch. These binges would last up to three or four days. Other times he would leave one evening for his favorite bar and not return until the end of his binge several days later. Many times he would come home in a drunken stupor. Sometimes he would be belligerent and angry, and other times he would be remorseful and apologetic. But Beverly's mom always calmed him down and cleaned him up when necessary. Finally, Beverly's mother was forced to take a full-time office job because of her family's decreasing income and the increasing costs of her husband's addiction. In addition, she took a part-time waitressing job, which necessitated her working numerous evenings and weekends.

As the eldest daughter, Beverly was required to take over many household duties like cooking, doing the laundry, ironing and watching her younger brother and sister. Beverly was destined to become a martyr. Her mother was the perfect teacher, and her childhood home was the perfect breeding ground for developing a self-demeaning personality. Her mother spent many hours complaining about how hard she had to work, how unfair it was that her husband was an alcoholic and how she would surely leave him if it weren't her "Christian duty" to care for him. "After all," she would remind Beverly, "it's not every woman who could put up with what *I* do day after day."

By the time Beverly entered her teenage years, she had mistakenly learned that her only value was to meet others' needs. She felt guilty when she received anything positive for herself. Although she was angry about not having her needs met, she felt she had no right to her own happiness or personal fulfillment. She avoided friendships with peers. Even though she attended all youth meetings at church, she never found the time nor the opportunity to go to their socials. Her self-demeaning pattern became self-limiting and destructive, and she desperately needed professional help.

The Masochist. One of the most tragic forms of the self-demeaning orientation is the masochist. Teenagers who develop this pattern learn to associate pain and personal loss with pleasure. They usually have destructive personal histories. Leon's case history helps us see how this unhealthy personality pattern can develop.

Leon initiated professional therapy when he was 17 years old at the insistence of his physician. Within nine months after getting his drivers license, he had been involved in seven automobile accidents. Five were minor and were never reported to either his insurance company or to the police. In four of these minor accidents, Leon was driving the only moving car. In one instance he scraped a parked car while trying to parallel park. On another occasion he hit a tree while backing out of a friend's driveway. On two other occasions he hit parked cars, one while he was trying to enter a diagonal parking space and the other while he was driving down a residential street. His fifth minor accident took place in the school parking lot and resulted in crumpled bumpers on his and another student's car.

His two serious accidents occurred within the short span of three weeks. On both occasions he collided with cars that had come to a full stop in front of him. Mild injuries and several thousand dollars in car damages were sustained in both accidents. Leon rapidly gained the nickname "Crash" with his friends. He personified the phrase "an accident waiting to happen." Few of his friends' parents would allow their children to ride with him. And after his second serious accident Leon's physician advised his parents to take him to a professional therapist.

As counseling progressed, Leon's background and the reasons for his frequent accidents were revealed and more clearly understood by his therapist. Leon was born into his family as the younger of two children. His sister was seven years older, and he was the unexpected and unwanted "surprise" that arrived when his parents were in their early 40s. Leon's father was gruff, stern and sorely lacking in communication and parenting skills. His responses to any misbehavior consisted of yelling, cursing, hitting and any number of belittling put-downs. Raised in an abusive home, Leon's father never learned how to express or receive physical affection. Leon couldn't remember his father ever telling him he loved him or giving him a hug.

Leon's mother wasn't a big improvement. Her relationship with Leon's father was her third marriage. During her childhood and in both of her earlier marriages, she had been the victim of physical violence. She received financial support and companionship from her marriage, but had no expectation of a positive or fulfilling relationship, especially with men. She had thought she wanted to be a

THE SELF-DEMEANING PERSONALITY ■ 259

mother. But shortly after her daughter's arrival, she realized she resented the intrusion this baby made in her life. Therefore, Leon's accidental conception and unwanted birth seven years later stimulated a return of her anger and rejection. She resented the physical discomfort and pain associated with his pregnancy. And she immediately withdrew from him after his birth, punishing him with her rejection.

Leon's sister also resented him. Forced to assume much of his parenting and caretaking throughout his infancy and childhood, she became bossy, cruel and punitive within their relationship. She teased him incessantly and ridiculed him in front of her friends.

Leon's childhood was miserable. Tragically, his family taught him that he was unwanted, unlovable and inadequate. He felt he had no personal value and didn't belong in his home. During early childhood he expressed rage at his mistreatment. However, the physical and psychological pain of his family's cruel and abusive punishments taught him to internalize those strong emotions. He soon learned it was safer to blame and hate himself than express his anger toward anyone else.

Leon grew into adolescence with no confidence in himself as being socially acceptable. He had no self-esteem, and his bag of social skills and other resources for meeting life was empty. Desperate for attention, he had to gain some type of acknowledgment. Anything was better than nothing! So Leon picked up where his sister and parents left off. He learned to make fun of himself. He gained skill as the "straight man" who was always the butt of his own joke. He finally had learned how to gain attention, and *any* type of attention felt like acceptance. He became a buffoon, a clown.

He began to associate the *pleasure* of being noticed with the *pain* of being laughed at by others. At least being laughed at offered some form of attention. His search for acceptance became a continual reaching out for new ways to experience social derision and humiliation. His physical clumsiness, social awkwardness and even serious accidents became sources for his pain/pleasure connection. By the time he initiated therapy, Leon was a severely disturbed boy. His self-concept and his way of interacting with others contained little that was healthy. Leon's rigid, intense masochism combined with limited support from his social environment had produced a guarded and doubtful picture for his future.

Within this section we have met three young people who developed unhealthy, maladaptive forms of the self-demeaning social orientation. As a "recluse," Shana has given up trying to become part of the social world around her. Beverly the "martyr" has found self-demeaning and self-denying servitude an effective way of trying to be part of other people's lives. And Leon has tried to find pleasure in the social, emotional and physical pain he has developed as a "masochist." All three young people illustrate the rigid, unyielding characteristics of self-demeaning behavior.

■ *Effects of Self-Demeaning Behavior on Other People*

At first glance self-demeaning behavior benefits only the young person exhibiting the behavior. Like all interpersonal actions, however, this type of behavior is directed at others and serves to draw certain responses from them. The responses most commonly received correlate with the kinds of people with whom the adolescent feels most comfortable.

A self-demeaning teenager prefers people who will reinforce self-depreciating feelings. As he or she assumes the role of clown or buffoon, others respond with laughter and demeaning responses. These reactions are particularly intense when others are convinced this adolescent really *is* inept, foolish, clumsy and inferior.

Initially, a self-demeaning young person will elicit feelings of sympathy and caring from others who are concerned and want to help. But when others' responses bring closeness, warmth and intimacy, their positive and helpful efforts threaten the self-demeaning teenager to the point he or she pushes them away. Caring people are soon discouraged and give up trying to help. Their positive efforts give way to irritation and frustration. Repetitive self-depreciating acts eventually draw anger from these people whose helping has been thoroughly discouraged.

A self-demeaning teenager often gravitates toward young people who act arrogant and superior. He or she may choose to spend time with power-oriented and competitive youth because these teenagers naturally behave in ways that feel comfortable to the self-demeaning adolescent. These teenagers disapprove of, laugh at and put down others who appear inadequate and foolish. This type of mutually unhealthy relationship brings out the worst in both personalities.

A self-demeaning teenager also assumes roles that have no dignity. He or she subjects himself or herself to others to be used in self-derogatory ways. This experience of being used enhances a self-perception of worthlessness.

■ Guidelines for Working With Self-Demeaning Adolescents

These young people push away or withdraw from people who wish to help them. They avoid intimacy with anyone who promotes their feelings of strength or enhances their feelings of self-worth. Their social orientation is designed to protect them from the anxiety which arises when they are cared for by teachers, ministers, counselors and youth leaders. These people want to help, but self-demeaning teenagers view their help as threatening. Therefore, any assistance is sabotaged by these adolescents' defense mechanisms. Let's look at ways we can work successfully with these self-demeaning teenagers.

1. Seek to understand what factors caused these self-demeaning behavior patterns to develop. An important key to helping teenagers is to understand what events and forces brought them into being who they are. Through the case studies presented earlier, we could see how childhood experiences lead to the development of self-demeaning defenses. When you see this personality pattern, find out what caused its development. Gain knowledge of early childhood experiences, school adjustments, family dynamics, physical health and the history of interpersonal relationships. The more you understand about the teenagers in your group or class, the more effective your helping efforts will be.

2. Self-demeaning teenagers need your help to critically examine and re-evaluate their past experiences with growing maturity. Self-demeaning teenagers often have extremely painful experiences in their pasts. The path to healthy adulthood often requires personal re-evaluation of these injuries and pain as these young people mature. Adolescents need to understand how past events have affected their lives and the way they respond to the world and people around them. They need to learn how to forgive and let go of things they cannot change. They need to be reminded of God's power to bring good from every evil and destructive experience they have had.

In faith we can help these young people look for benefits within themselves. Resolving past injuries doesn't mean repressing them or pretending they never happened. It means reframing them or seeing them in a different context. We can help these adolescents choose a perspective on their past that allows anger at injustices done to them and expression of their pain. We can help them mourn their losses and still provide for a healthy passage to the present and their future.

3. Observe teenagers' behaviors as indicators of their feelings. Don't assume, but check out your understandings of adolescents' behavior. Teenagers, like young children, often express their thoughts and feelings more through actions than words. They may destroy property rather than tell you they are angry. Instead of telling you they're depressed, they may relax their efforts and get lower grades in school. Or they may clean their room rather than express their relief or happiness in words. "Listen" carefully to the meaning expressed in self-demeaning teenagers' behavior. What are they "saying" to you?

A sudden run to the bedroom accompanied by a slammed door may indicate, "I'm feeling too embarrassed and ashamed to be around anyone right now."

The silent smile with the ready dish towel may be saying, "Being helpful and doing what you want me to do is the only way I can feel secure in our relationship."

The rude bump in the hall followed by angry eye contact tends to push others away and can relay the distinct message: "My relationships in the past have been too painful for me to ever hope for good friendships. I'm going to avoid contact with people at any cost."

A resigned sigh uttered while cleaning up the mess at a party may evidence feelings like: "People never care about meeting *my* needs. I'm angry. But I need to be with people, so I'll do what they want me to do. Don't ask me to like it though."

Bizarre self-punitive behavior that keeps young people at the center of attention screams out their inner fears: "The only way I can feel I belong is to make jokes about myself, get people to feel sorry for me or put me down. When I experience those responses, at least I know I'm important for something."

Once we discover what teenagers' behaviors are saying, we have a clearer picture of where their pain lies and how to initiate their healing.

4. Help your self-demeaning young people understand their reality, including what was and was not their responsibility. As we gain deeper under-standings of these teenagers' past histories and present psychological conditions, we can also improve the accuracy of *their* understandings. Many times children incorrectly perceive what is happening around them. They usually feel guilty when their parents divorce, thinking they are somehow responsible for their parents' relation-ship. Physically and psychologically abused children usually feel responsible for what has happened to them. We must help these teenagers correct their misperceptions and resolve the strong emotions they have attached to these past experiences. They need our clear and accurate view of what really happened. They need our strong asser-tions about what was and was not their responsibility. Encourage them to rely upon you as a trustworthy source for truth while they sort out reality from fantasy.

5. Work with self-demeaning teenagers to take control of their own lives. Self-demeaning teenagers have little confidence in their personal power and control. Other people and circumstances typically dictate their behavior. One of our tasks is to encourage these teenagers to use their own strength. Help them make decisions, choose options and take control. Start slowly with easy tasks at first. Remember, acting from their personal strength produces anxiety for these teenagers.

Help self-demeaning adolescents identify their areas of greatest expertise, and then guide them in ways to use their skills. They may have some artistic ability. If so, let them make decisions about the group's publicity posters. They might coordinate the colors and graphics for the group's calendar or design a youth group emblem. If they write well, perhaps you could enlist their help in preparing newsletters or writing skits. Our goal is to help these adolescents begin to believe in themselves.

As they begin to experience their own strengths, they

will take that first step toward accepting responsibility for their own actions and their own lives. Normally, adolescence is the developmental phase when people start taking control of and assuming responsibility for what happens to them. "The devil made me do it" is no longer an acceptable reason for doing wrong. Paul writes: "When I was a child, I talked like a child, I thought like a child, I reasoned like a child. When I became a man, I put childish ways behind me" (1 Corinthians 13:11). Self-demeaning adolescents have great difficulty moving from the childish rejection of personal responsibility to a mature acceptance of responsibility for their own lives.

6. Be alert to self-demeaning teenagers' needs to belong. Reinforce their strengths, not their weaknesses. Self-demeaning teenagers want to belong. They desperately long to feel valued as a member of their family, their class, their youth group, their neighborhood buddies or any group that will recognize their presence. Their self-demeaning social orientation provides the only behavior they recognize as acceptable. Receiving social attention reinforces this behavior, even if the attention is negative or punitive. It's still attention, and attention says to these young people, "You are noticed; therefore, you have some value here."

As involved adults we can use our knowledge of social reinforcement to help. Do *not* respond to their self-demeaning behavior. Don't reinforce self-demeaning patterns, even with negative attention. Discuss something else they are interested in or have recently done. Initiate positive conversations. Reinforce their strengths, not their weaknesses.

7. Help young people identify the source of their anger, express it appropriately and then release it. Self-demeaning adolescents usually have some anger directed primarily at themselves. Often this anger is masked behind other attitudes and feelings. If it is too threatening or feels frighteningly intense, it may be deeply repressed. Remember, the essence of self-depreciation is giving up one's self and giving in to the world. This action represents a loss of hope and belief in the self. Something or some series of events has caused these young people to turn their backs on their own dignity.

Anger is almost always a part of any loss of dignity. At first, the anger is directed at the people, organizations and events associated with challenging these teenagers' identity or dignity. When adolescents become too discouraged or frustrated, they may internalize this anger and redirect it toward themselves. At this point they repress their self-directed anger because it is too painful to live with at a conscious level. Even though their feelings may be suppressed, they may evidence themselves in some passive-aggressive behavior or some other disguised form.

If left unresolved, this debilitating anger can prevent these teenagers from maturing into healthy adults. This intense feeling sabotages personal growth and causes further alienation from others. We can help self-demeaning teenagers identify the sources of their anger. Encourage them to talk about their feelings. As they share freely within a trusting relationship, they can grow to accept their anger and be less afraid of it. They will need our guidance to discover healthy, constructive ways to express their anger and then let it go.

8. Work with these teenagers to recognize, reject and resolve the self-blaming typical of their personality type. At the heart of self-demeaning personality types is the tendency to internalize anger and blame themselves when something goes wrong. These teenagers focus all negative experiences and feelings back on themselves because projecting those feelings onto others would produce even more anxiety. They also withdraw from any interpersonal contact, especially when that contact requires assertiveness, strength and energy.

Help these young people decrease the frequency and

intensity of their self-blaming reactions. Just telling them not to blame themselves won't work. And giving them reasons why they shouldn't feel guilty will probably provide little impact. Their self-blaming comes from unconscious self-rejection which needs to be brought to the conscious level and resolved.

Help them understand *why* they began to depreciate themselves. Encourage them to work through their earlier rejections, injustices and other injuries so they can release these hurts and be free. As they gain freedom from their past anger and guilt, they will be less likely to automatically blame themselves when something goes wrong.

9. Help self-demeaning young people question, recognize and establish peer relationships that build up their self-esteem, rather than tear it down. Observe the peers with whom your teenagers associate. Many times self-demeaning teenagers choose people who reinforce and intensify their guilt, withdrawal and self-depreciating reactions. Try to discourage these teenagers' involvements with power-oriented and competitive youth. These personality types are the ones most likely to capitalize on the weaknesses of self-demeaning adolescents.

Seek to move these young people toward adolescents who can have a positive influence on their lives and allow them space for developing their strengths. Remember, self-demeaning adolescents avoid warm and kind people who respect others. Healthy relationships threaten these young people because they offer friendships based on equality and mutual respect. When self-demeaning teenagers perceive themselves as less than others and undeserving of their respect, they experience anxiety and reject these mutually beneficial types of friendships. In many cases their anxiety actually causes them to sabotage potentially constructive social relationships.

Obviously, directing or guiding adolescents' personal relationships is "easier said than done." Teenagers do not relish adults tampering with their friendships. Be respectful of their choices and their right to choose their own friends. Rely on your influence as their counselor, teacher, youth leader or minister, and arrange opportunities for these young people to work and spend time with other types of teenagers. Guide them to carefully question how they feel when they are around their different friends.

● "Do you feel good about yourself when you are around him or her?"

● "How do you like the way you act when you are with those people?"

● "Do you feel up and elated or down and flat after being with these friends?"

Use questions like these to stimulate their thinking about how their relationships operate within both healthy and unhealthy friendships. Through your questions, observations and support, you can help self-demeaning young people recognize the positive or negative impact others have on their lives.

10. Continue to offer your love and attention even when your efforts are rejected. Your perseverance will enhance their self-esteem along with fulfilling their most basic needs. While rebellious youth reject love, self-demeaning young people are desperate for attention, love and affection. They are hungry for these positive experiences, but believe they are too inferior or too inadequate to deserve them. To open themselves to receive love and then lose it or experience rejection would bring even more failure and self-derision. Therefore, self-demeaning teenagers both avoid and seek to sabotage caring and mutually respecting relationships. They are afraid to risk themselves because of their painful experiences in the past.

Because these young people are so effective in destroying healthy social contact, most caring people become discouraged and give up on trying to reach these teenagers. As adults, our job is not to give in; we must refuse to give up. They need us to ignore their efforts to make us believe they don't want love or acceptance. It is our task to persevere beyond their defenses, to offer them respect and the gift of affirming love.

11. Be conscious of self-demeaning teenagers' sensitivity to criticism. Self-demeaning teenagers are extremely sensitive to criticism, judgment and negative reactions. They have learned to defend themselves against others' criticisms by being the *first* to judge themselves. In this way they steal their enemy's ammunition and then use it on themselves. In their mind they magnify any negative hint in what is said to them. For example, a teacher's encouraging statement, "Maybe next time you will do better" might be heard as, "You did so poorly this time that you sure better improve next time."

Our consciousness of their extreme sensitivity to rejection and criticism can help us avoid making comments they may easily misinterpret. We cannot, of course, monitor each word we say, but some precautions may help. When you notice these teenagers withdrawing or growing quiet, check with them about what they think or feel. Encourage them to tell you when they are hurt by something you or someone else has said. Help them take part in clarifying what is said to them. Teach them relationship skills that make them more responsible in their social interactions and more objective in their evaluations of themselves and others.

12. Help self-demeaning teenagers understand the nature of Jesus' love as a model for their own behavior. Self-demeaning teenagers misunderstand the personal nature of Jesus Christ. They stress his loving nature, but do not perceive what his love was really like. They picture Jesus' love as always soft, supportive and kind. They incorrectly associate "love" with "nice" and assume that these two concepts are the same.

Jesus' life is the truest, most complete picture of love we have. But there is no way to describe all of his actions as nice. "Nice" people do not tell others they are "hypo-crites, sons of hell, blind guides, blind fools, blind men, whitewashed tombs, snakes and a brood of vipers" (see Matthew 23). Just being "nice" requires no courage nor personal strength. Loving someone means taking action on that person's behalf. It also requires the courage to con-front people when you realize they are in error. Help these self-demeaning adolescents differentiate between love and being "nice."

Describing Jesus as "meek" also confuses these young people. Images of timidity, fearfulness and cowering are often associated with this spiritual characteristic. A well-respected Biblical dictionary helps us understand this term more fully.

> *(Meek) consists not in a person's outward behavior only; nor . . . in his relations to his fellow-men. . . .Rather it is an inwrought grace of the soul; and the exercises of it are first and chiefly towards God. It is that temper of spirit in which we accept His dealings with us as good, and therefore (we respond) without disputing or resisting; . . . It must be clearly understood, therefore, that the meekness manifested by the Lord and commended to the believer is the fruit of power. The common assumption is that when a man is meek it is because he cannot help him-self; but the Lord was "meek" because he had the infinite resources of God at his command.*[1]

More simply put, "meek" does not mean weak! It implies identity with an inner core of strength that finds its security and meaning in relationship with God. With such a core of strength so centered and grounded in the nature of God, there is no need to assert, defend or demean the self. Helping these teenagers develop this "meekness" or inner strength in their identity will assist them in becoming less demeaning of themselves.

13. Help these teenagers understand and accept God's unconditional love. Another valuable key for self-demeaning adolescents is to help them understand and accept God's love for them just the way they are. God's love is unconditional. God offers each of us an intimate relationship within which we can change and grow. "You see, at just the right time, when we were still powerless, Christ died for the ungodly. Very rarely will anyone die for a righteous man, though for a good man someone might possibly dare to die. But God demonstrates his own love for us in this: While we were still sinners, Christ died for us" (Romans 5:6-8).

This unconditional aspect of God's love is essential to each of us. It is of particular importance to self-demeaning individuals who have such strong doubts about their personal worth or value. They can be greatly encouraged by exposure to God's love which is given freely without consideration for behavior. Realizing they cannot *earn* God's love helps them realize they also can do nothing to discourage it.

14. Be patient. Allow teenagers to change behavior on *their schedule, not* yours. Frustration is common when working with teenagers. We often mistakenly think their troublesome behavior is fully under their conscious control. We impatiently decide they could change the way they act if they really wanted to or would just try. Remember how frustrating it is when you ask teenagers why they act the way they do, and you get the shoulder-shrugging response, "I don't know."

As youth workers, we need to remind ourselves that much human behavior comes from unconscious motivation. This means that individuals really don't know the reasons underlying their behavior. Therefore, since adolescent behavior is typically more unconscious than adult behavior, we can expect teenagers to be far less certain about reasons for their actions.

Changing our behavior usually requires conscious control over our actions. Therefore, when we seek to help self-demeaning teenagers change their destructive patterns, we need to make them conscious of *why* they depreciate themselves. This process takes time. It is also difficult and threatening because gaining awareness goes directly against their defenses.

Self-demeaning adolescents need our patience. They need us to respect their difficulty in altering their self-demeaning behavior. They need us to respond to *their* timing rather than ours. As we patiently love them and extend ourselves to them, we create a safe relationship in which they can grow and alter their attitudes, perceptions, thoughts and defenses.

15. Be willing to accept and support your self-demeaning teenagers, but refer them to professional help, if necessary. Not all self-demeaning teenagers need counseling. Not all of them are in pain or doing poorly in their social relationships. Earlier in this chapter, we saw case studies of two healthier self-demeaning young people. However, many adolescents of this personality type do need help. Some may need encouragement and emotional support, while others might need to learn appropriate social skills. Still others may require professional therapy to release them from the pain and deprivation that stunted their self-concept and restricted development of their relationships with others. For these teenagers, referral to a qualified psychologist or therapist who specializes in the treatment of adolescents may be the most appropriate and loving gift you can give.

■ Guidelines for Parenting Self-Demeaning Adolescents

Self-demeaning young people often experience significant psychological pain, but most people don't realize these teenagers are hurting. Other people not only fail to recognize self-demeaning teenagers' pain, but are also oblivious to their presence. The self-demeaning social orientation enables these teenagers to go through interpersonal situations virtually unnoticed. Even those who care for them often miss these adolescents' painful struggles. In this section we will look at many ways you, as a parent, can help your self-demeaning teenagers.

1. Seek to understand the origins and meanings of your self-demeaning teenagers' behaviors. You are in a unique position to understand how your adolescents feel about themselves and how well they are doing with their lives. You gain your understanding not only from what your teenagers say, but even more from how they behave. You are aware of your children's personal histories better than any teacher, minister or counselor. As you observe your young people's behaviors, think about what has happened to them in the past. Notice behavior patterns that help you understand their present actions.

While some teenagers feel awkward when receiving *any* kind of attention, others are uncomfortable with only *positive* attention. Many teenagers strive to help others, but teenagers with histories of physical abuse may seek to help in different ways from adolescents who were nurtured in their early childhood. Your teenage son's shy and withdrawn behavior around *girls* means something different from his shy and retiring behavior around *everyone*. Observe your young people's actions carefully and then seek to understand the meaning of their behavior in relation to their past.

2. Help your self-demeaning teenagers understand the meaning of their behavior. Understanding why we act as we do is often the first step toward making desired changes. Insight alone rarely causes us to change our behavior, but it does help. Teenagers usually need guidance to understand the meaning of their behavior. They are not aware of the reasons or motives underneath their actions. Their typical response to "Why did you do that?" is "I don't know." Even though this response may frustrate you, it is usually honest. Children consistently express their emotions through their behavior, while adults verbalize their feelings. Teenagers operate somewhere in between. Even though they talk about their feelings and thoughts more than younger children, they still function with less consciousness than their adult counterparts.

With your own teenagers, gently suggest possibilities about why they act as they do. Use extreme caution. Recognize that humans defend against self-awareness for a good reason—there are truths within us that would upset us if we suddenly became aware of them. So suggest the least-threatening possibilities first. Then, as your teenagers accept their inner feelings and motivations, gradually suggest more potentially threatening possibilities.

As an example, your 17-year-old daughter may be shy and especially withdrawn around boys. She claims she has no idea why she avoids boys her own age. Initially, you might suggest she lacks experience with her peers, especially boys, and therefore feels uncomfortable.

In later conversations you might point out that since she has never dated, she might be afraid no one will ask her out. She may be avoiding this possible "failure" by staying away from boys. If she accepts this possibility, you might imply that she could be scared of not knowing how to act if a boy *did* ask her for a date.

At a still deeper level, you might help her recall a negative experience that may be affecting her behavior. Perhaps she was sexually molested by a relative or a baby sitter during her early childhood. She may unconsciously fear that something similar might happen on a date. Only when she recognizes and accepts this possibility can you ask if she is afraid of controlling her sexual impulses and those of others.

Helping your teenagers understand why they act as they do can help them gain a feeling of control over their behavior. This awareness will help them feel more comfortable with themselves and more secure about their own development.

3. Help your self-demeaning teenagers correct their negative self-perceptions. These young people characteristically have negative self-images. Their family, social and school histories have probably assured them they are of little value or worth. They mistakenly assume they are also unworthy of meaningful relationships. Their self-concepts focus on the negative aspects of their bodies, intellect, feelings and behavior. Some of these young people can see only their negative traits. When asked, they are incapable of reporting good things about themselves.

These teenagers need positive feedback from people they trust. And contradictory to popular opinion, your adolescents *can* develop trust in you as their parent. One way you can earn your teenagers' trust is by your honesty in what you say. When you share your negative thoughts and opinions with your teenagers, your children have more reason to trust you when you are positive. Develop a believable balance between your negative and positive observations. One 14-year-old girl told her counselor: "Of course my mother told me she thinks I'm attractive. How is she going to say I'm ugly? She's my mother!"

Build trust within your adolescents that you will always tell them the truth. Remember, honesty can be kind and gentle or harsh and uncaring, depending on the *way* you offer it. Parental love necessitates sharing the truth in healing and uplifting ways. Telling your self-demeaning teenagers the truth can help them correct their unrealistic negative perceptions about themselves.

4. Listen to your teenagers and assist them in their efforts to let go and resolve past injuries. Most self-demeaning teenagers have histories of significantly painful experiences or long-term hurtful relationships or events. These unhappy histories have taught these young people not to believe in themselves. To build positive self-concepts, teenagers must release and resolve their painful pasts. They cannot accomplish these tasks alone. Even if you are centrally involved in some of their pain, there *are* past hurts where you can help your teenagers release their pain and resolve their injuries.

One of the most important ways you can help your self-demeaning adolescents is by encouraging them to talk about their feelings. Spend time with them. Arrange one-on-one opportunities conducive to sharing feelings. Go to dinner together. Take a walk, or work on a quiet task together. Have a regular Bible study time and pray with one another. There are numerous ways of helping your young people begin to talk with you about their pain.

When they *do* share some of these past hurts, listen and let them know you hear them. Give them verbal responses that indicate you understand. For example, your youngest daughter may complain: "You always listen to Karen first. She always gets her way." Acknowledge what she has said. Calmly repeat her thoughts back to her in your own words. "I can hear your concern about your oldest sister. It sounds like you feel we put Karen's needs and wants before yours." This rewording type of response allows adolescents to correct any of your misunderstandings before resolution can take place.

Help your young people realize that past experiences may affect their lives, but do not have to control them. Remind them that accepting God's grace can help release them from their pasts. They need to know how to forgive those who have hurt them. They need your support and care. Releasing hurts and emotional injuries from their pasts is necessary for adolescents' personal growth. You can play a major role in this part of your teenagers' psychological development.

5. Help your teenagers reduce their feelings of helplessness and hopelessness. Self-demeaning adolescents are convinced they are weak and incompetent. They feel inadequate to live life effectively. They believe they are unworthy of meaningful relationships. Remember, not all self-demeaning young people operate in the extremes of this personality orientation. While some experience severe incapacity, others demean themselves only when they are under stress.

Most self-demeaning teenagers feel helpless, and this helpless perception of themselves leads them to feel hopeless. Typically they don't believe they have the power or the ability to improve their situations. They see others as in control. Since having personal control over themselves and their world is central to healthy adolescent development, self-demeaning teenagers are often depressed. If anything positive is to occur in these teenagers' lives, they believe it must come through someone else's effort.

You can help your young people experience more control and power in their lives. Structure situations in which your teenagers can have success. Encourage your children to attempt tasks that help them develop positive self-esteem. When your adolescents perceive themselves as competent young people who can grow, develop skills and accomplish important achievements, their feelings of helplessness will wane. As they experience success and observe their own progress, their hopelessness will diminish.

Helpless and hopeless feelings are two of the most crippling aspects of the self-demeaning personality. Caring and insightful parental involvement is a powerful ally in your teenagers' battles against these barriers to personal growth.

6. Help your teenagers reduce their self-blame and direct their energies toward solving tasks.
Though some self-demeaning teenagers blame others for their unhappiness, most hold themselves at fault. They internalize their anger. Even when they should be angry at someone else who has wronged them, they usually redirect that anger back to themselves. These adolescents routinely internalize their anger and blame, an action that leads to strong guilt. Each personal failure confirms their

inadequacy, which reinforces their guilt and hopelessness.

You can be instrumental in helping your young people differentiate between the mistakes, errors, sins and failings *they* committed and the negative consequences *over which they had little or no control*. They *should* feel responsible for failing an exam after they decided to attend a football game instead of studying. They *should* feel responsible for being late to work when they decided to go shopping with friends rather than take their own car. But there is *no reason* for them to blame themselves for their parents' divorce. With your help and support, your self-demeaning teenagers can release this huge burden of personal responsibility. Instead of feeling guilty for *everything*, they can learn to hold themselves accountable for only their *own* actions.

Encourage your young people to concentrate less on blame and fault and more on solving tasks. Even though it is important for adolescents to learn from their mistakes and correct their destructive behavior patterns, self-demeaning adolescents are too focused on their *own* wrongdoing. Help them become more task-oriented. When something goes wrong, encourage them to think about *how* to correct the situation rather than *who* made the mistake.

"It doesn't matter who spilled the paint; we have a job to do. Let's work together to get this mess cleaned up."

"Blaming yourself for the brakes failing is not going to do any good now, Phil. Let's work out a transportation schedule for the time your car is in the repair shop."

Placing emphasis on the task that needs to be accomplished suggests you accept your teenagers and are willing to help them accomplish what needs to be done.

Self-blaming and repressed anger are destructive forces common to self-demeaning teenagers. You can help your adolescents turn these negative forces into positive task-directed energy.

7. *Help these young people become less sensitive to criticism.* Because self-demeaning teenagers already blame themselves and feel guilty, they have few defenses against the criticism and judgment that come from others. They *believe* all criticisms or accusations aimed toward them. They internalize all this negative input because it reinforces what they already believe about themselves. These young people do not possess the inner strengths necessary to evaluate, resist and reject untrue and unwarranted accusations. To evaluate and resist those kinds of accusations requires self-esteem, self-confidence and psychological energy. Self-demeaning adolescents do not possess these self-valuing characteristics.

You have a lot of control and influence over the atmosphere in your home. You can establish a positive, supportive environment or a negative, destructive atmosphere. Control your own attitudes, words and actions. Give fewer criticisms and avoid making accusations. Try to actively support your family members. Though brothers and sisters will typically be negative and critical toward each other, help your children lessen the frequency and intensity of their disparaging remarks.

When your self-demeaning son is criticized or faces a difficult accusation, encourage him to discuss his feelings with you. Let him talk while you listen. Try to respond to the pain you hear. Let him express *his* view of what happened. Support his efforts to explain his own opinions and perspective. Help him accept his part of the responsibility without accepting any overwhelming feelings of guilt and self-condemnation.

As your self-demeaning teenagers become less sensitive to criticism, they gain the personal strengths that can help them mature. You can be a primary source of support for your young people's efforts toward growth.

8. *Encourage your self-demeaning teenagers to be more self-reliant.* Independence is a difficult trait for these adolescents to develop. Since they have no confidence in their abilities and strengths, they find no reason to rely on themselves. Self-demeaning teenagers believe they must trust in someone stronger, wiser, older or better to give them directions or take care of them. Sometimes they depend on fate or chance.

Christian self-demeaning adolescents often exhibit an unhealthy reliance on God. This dependency is unhealthy because they treat God like a magician who takes care of *every* need, even if the adolescent is capable of handling the situation. For example, they may ask God to help them pick the right color of ribbon for their hair or tell them which jacket to buy. This type of reliance on God fails to stimulate personal growth and spiritual maturity. It assures self-demeaning teenagers they are inadequate and incompetent.

You can help your teenagers grow in self-reliance. Work with them to identify their strengths and competencies. When they accomplish a task or overcome a difficult hurdle, reinforce their efforts. Let them know you're proud of them and help them congratulate themselves. When you see them working independently instead of asking for assistance, bring it to their attention. Help them recognize their growth toward increasing self-reliance so they can experience pride in their independence.

Self-demeaning adolescents are convinced they are personally inadequate. Helping them grow toward increasing self-reliance is a powerful gift you can offer your young people.

9. Help your self-demeaning teenagers feel they belong in your family. Belonging is one of the fundamental psychological needs of human beings. The family is the first and most important group where children sense they belong. The way they seek to belong and the degree to which they secure their belonging has a great impact on their self-concept. Not feeling secure can be devastating to individuals' self-esteem and feelings of security.

Adolescents and children will do virtually anything to

ensure they belong. Their first attempts will be through positive efforts. They will offer their positive and unique qualities, talents and skills in an attempt to be valued and included in the family unit. These positive attempts are largely unconscious but still purposeful.

If their positive efforts fail, adolescents will turn to less positive or destructive efforts to get attention and position within the family. For self-demeaning teenagers, negative attention is better than no attention at all. These young people may be disruptive, slow, negative and even destructive if that is the only way they can get recognition. These young people can find extremely negative ways to belong in their families.

Reinforce the positive behavior of your self-demeaning teenagers. Ignore their negative behavior. When ignoring is impossible, strive to remove your negative reinforcement of their destructive and irritating actions. Remember, in these cases punishment actually *increases* the chances of their negative behavior continuing.

Find positive actions to reinforce.

"You sure had a good idea about how to prune the fruit tree."

"I really enjoyed your company on our shopping trip."

"Your sense of humor is delightful. You make our home so much more fun for all of us."

By encouraging their positive ways of belonging, you diminish the intensity and frequency of their negative behaviors.

You can help your teenagers find positive ways of establishing security within the family unit. By encouraging their positive approaches, you help your young people diminish their self-demeaning attitudes.

10. Support your child's friendships with teenagers who tend to build healthy relationships. Peer relationships are extremely important to an adolescent. Acceptance into specific peer groups and approval from selected friends are among a teenager's most highly prized experiences. The peer groups and teenagers selected by your young person will powerfully impact how he or she develops through adolescence. You will notice some friends have a positive effect on your child while others produce a negative influence. When you care about your child, you want to guide your young person into friendships that stimulate him or her in positive directions. It is wise to realize you cannot push certain relationships with much vigor or your teenager will react in the opposite direction. Selection of friends is a common issue in parent-teen conflicts. Your gentle encouragement toward healthy friendships and cautious discouragement of less favorable relationships is difficult but important.

Aggressive, competitive and unhealthy power-oriented adolescents often intensify the negative tendencies of your self-demeaning young person. Close association with these personality types depreciates your teenager's self-esteem and reinforces withdrawal and dependency. A self-demeaning young person forms his or her healthiest relationships with responsible teenagers and power-oriented adolescents who are extremely caring. These young people are less likely to reinforce your self-demeaning individual's negative traits. These friendships actually stimulate growth and self-respect within your self-demeaning adolescent. Since people with whom one relates have an impact on attitudes, actions and feelings about oneself, you will need to guide your self-demeaning adolescent into healthy friendships and associations.

11. Seek to ensure an accurate and healthy theology of Jesus Christ for your self-demeaning teenagers. Idealism is an important characteristic of adolescence. Teenagers tend to make heroes out of certain adults and seek to emulate them. They believe they will gain personal significance by acting like these special people.

Christian young people naturally idealize Jesus Christ (as they should) and seek to be like him. Jesus is an appropriate and positive identity to emulate. But many adolescents know Jesus *only* by what they read of him in the Bible and from what they hear ministers, teachers, other adults and peers say about him. Some young people have formed a partial or incomplete image of Jesus Christ. And sometimes this image contains significantly incorrect and unhealthy personality characteristics with which adolescents identify. Self-demeaning teenagers are particularly vulnerable to incorporating these misunderstandings into their own personality because of their dependency on others and their hesitancy to trust their own judgment and thinking.

These young people will strongly defend their self-depreciating attitudes when they see Jesus as self-demeaning. Some misunderstand the meaning of his meekness and love. They confuse Jesus' meekness with weakness. They mistakenly think of Jesus as a "nice" person rather than a strong, assertive, loving individual.

You need to *know* what image your children have of Jesus Christ. During home Bible studies and spontaneous times of discussion, listen to what they say about who Jesus is. Then correct their misperceptions. Work with your teenagers to develop a positive and accurate image of Jesus Christ for them to emulate.

12. Help your self-demeaning young people accept God's love. With all our awareness of psychological principles and attendance to intellectual sophistication, it is vital we do not lose sight of our central source of healing. There is absolutely nothing more healing or releasing than direct confrontation with God's love. Spiritual and psychological wholeness cannot be attained without the love of God.

Self-demeaning teenagers desperately need the freedom and energy resulting from opening themselves to receive God's care. Pray for your children and seek ways to expose them to God's love. Regularly attend church together as a family. Encourage your children's involve-

ment in Sunday school, youth groups and church retreats.
Help your children develop comfortable relationships with
your minister, the youth director, and other Christian
adults by including these people in your family activities.
Establish times for Bible study and prayer within your
home. One of your most vital tasks as a parent is to help
your self-demeaning children experience and respond to
God's love for them.

**13. *Patiently continue expressing love to your
self-demeaning teenagers.*** Self-demeaning young
people typically sabotage your efforts to love and encourage them. To accept love means to risk rejection; to
respond to encouragement means to risk failure. These
teenagers fear rejection and failure and may go to
extremes to avoid both.

These teenagers will usually try to get you to give up
on them. They initiate behavior intended to frustrate your
efforts. When you give up and withdraw your love and
support, these teenagers are left without *anyone* to help
them.

Self-demeaning adolescents *need* you to be stronger
and more tenacious than they. They need your love to be
stronger than their self-directed anger. Be patient when
you seek to help. Allow God the time he needs to use
your and others' efforts to help your teenagers.

**14. *Consider professional help for your self-
demeaning teenagers.*** When young people's
self-demeaning patterns become extreme or highly resistant
to your attempts to help, consider professional counseling.
Trained therapists understand the psychological and socio-
logical issues your children are confronting. Professional
counselors who are also Christian can help your teenagers
with their spiritual struggles as well. Rely on therapists to
be additional support for your teenagers while they
struggle through the developmental tasks of adolescence.
Self-demeaning teenagers often cannot escape their crip-

pling attitudes without the help of a professionally trained third-party. Ask your priest, minister, youth pastor, pediatrician or your child's teacher for names of therapists they would recommend.

Only a small number of adolescents identify themselves as self-demeaning personalities. (See Appendix.) If you have been a youth sponsor, minister to youth, teacher, counselor or parent for several years however, you probably have experienced contact with several of these young people. When you can accurately identify them, you will be better equipped to meet their needs. They may function in a healthy, well-adapted pattern like "modest" Jill or Walter the "servant." Or you may struggle with unhealthy self-demeaning adolescents like the "recluse," the "martyr" and the "masochist." A thorough understanding of the dynamics of self-demeaning teenagers has been outlined in this chapter. This information will increase your effectiveness in working with these young people.

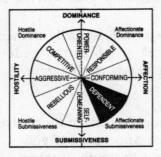

■ C H A P T E R   9

The Dependent Personality

Dependent personality types model behavior typical for the old dictum, "Children should be seen and not heard." Some adults still think *all* children should follow this rule. They believe the preadult years are for silence, staying out of the way and not causing any problems. These adults think children should receive attention at their parents' and other adults' convenience since their needs remain secondary to the needs of adults.

All adolescents experience the dependence-independence conflict as they move through their teenage years. When young people encounter excessive problems or failure in this developmental task, they become increasingly dependent. Located in the middle of the submissive-affectionate quadrant, dependent teenagers have particular difficulty gaining personal strength and independence. Through their behavior these young people say: "I am a weak person with little personal worth. But I admire others and need their support to feel secure in this world."

Dependent teenagers primarily fear they will be inadequate or fail if placed in positions of power, responsibility or leadership. Therefore, they prefer to rely upon someone else who will assume responsibility or adopt the leadership role. They avoid personal accountability by being dependent upon others. They truly believe in their own helplessness and reinforce this belief each time they avoid leadership or responsibility.

■ Development of the Dependent Personality

Gaining a strong sense of independence is one of the essential developmental tasks for adolescents as they grow successfully toward adulthood. Young people must begin to believe in themselves as individuals who need less and less of another's advice or guidance. Because dependent personality types tend to develop more slowly, they fail to grow toward this independence. They are overly agreeable, easy to influence and more than willing to follow another's lead. Usually they are easy children to parent or work with as part of a group, but some of them may also experience difficulty with their social and personal adjustments. And if these needy teenagers do not receive help, they are destined to have serious problems in the future. Understanding the source of their problems is often the first step toward knowing how we can help. Here are some of the most common experiences that contribute to adolescents developing a dependent personality style:

First, failure to nurture and support children early in their life stifles their ability to develop strength and independence during later years. Many tragic case histories of dependent personalities reveal insecure teenagers and adults who never received adequate love, affection, touch, conversation or other forms of caring during their childhood. Instead of strengthening or toughening these children, this lack of human warmth weakened development of their self-esteem and confidence and destroyed their trust in themselves and the external world. Lack of adequate care and attention during early months and years deprives people of the internal building blocks necessary for establishing enduring personality strengths. This failure to nurture also fosters dependency as children grow older.

Second, adults sometimes discourage adolescents' attempts to develop and express their personality strengths. Parents may react negatively to their children's early assertive expressions of their opinions, ideas and feelings. Some parents may misperceive these early expressions of personal strength as sinful pride, while others may feel personally threatened or uneasy when confronted with their children's self-assertions.

Many parents require their children's behavior to be excessively well-ordered and structured. Intense emphasis on rules, routine, a controlled noise level and how things should be done properly can stifle ingenuity, creativity and spontaneity. Rigid behavioral controls can thwart children's willingness to risk, accept responsibility and take initiative. These problems may intensify if these children experience the same rigid structure within their school classrooms, Sunday school classes, child care facilities or other supervised settings.

Third, sometimes young people's timidity, insecurity and excessive modesty are mistakenly reinforced as positive examples of spiritual meekness. Remember, spiritual meekness never implies weakness. Unfortunately, some testimonies of God's faithfulness falsely glorify humanity's passiveness which is quite different from an energized faithful patience while trusting in God's leading.

Patiently waiting on God is not passive. It is not motionless. Neither is it without action and direction. Read what James writes to us about patience: "Be patient, then, brothers, until the Lord's coming. See how the farmer waits for the land to yield its valuable crop and how patient he is for the fall and spring rains. You too, be patient and stand firm, because the Lord's coming is near. Brothers, as an example of patience in the face of suffering, take the prophets who spoke in the name of the Lord. As you know, we consider blessed those who have persevered. You have heard of Job's perseverance and have seen what the Lord finally brought about. The Lord is full of compassion and mercy" (James 5:7-8, 10-11).

Certainly, farmers are not passive while they wait for their fields to yield their crops. They work busily at numerous tasks while "patiently" waiting for their harvest. The prophets surely were not idle as they delivered their messages of what was to come. They persisted in spite of continual suffering and persecution.

We dare not squelch our children's spirits. We must not sabotage their drive toward individuality. If we discourage assertive individuality as an unhealthy spiritual value, we may encourage our children's development into dependent personalities.

Fourth, some adolescents have been negatively impacted by their own misperceptions of themselves or others' reactions to them. Psychologists have studied the intricate relationships between brothers and sisters as one of the most powerful sources of influence upon children's developing personalities. Children naturally compare themselves with their siblings. They learn to value or devalue themselves largely according to how they think they compare with the other children in their family.

"I don't think I'm as smart as my older brother."

"I don't understand it. I'm nowhere near as popular as my younger sister."

"I'm a lot stronger and faster than my brother."

These comparisons serve as powerful building blocks in young people's identity formations.

Comparisons young people make with friends and other peers also have a strong impact. A major danger is that many children make grievous mistakes in their personal perceptions. For example, many teenage beauty-contest winners honestly evaluate their physical appearance as average or below average. One junior high boy told his teacher he thought of himself as a dumb student.

Compared to his older brother who had a straight-A average, he incorrectly thought his B+ average was worthless. Many second-string quarterbacks struggle with self-depreciating attitudes because of their inaccurately low perceptions of their athletic prowess. They feel worthless because they are not "the best" in their schools.

As you listen to teenagers talk about their childhoods, their families and their early life experiences, listen carefully for indicators of their reality perception. Does what they say *fit* with your knowledge about them and their families? Are there inconsistencies between their evaluations of themselves and what they have actually accomplished? Significant misperceptions and erroneous self-evaluations during childhood can have dramatic, far-reaching effects on personality formation during adolescence and into adulthood.

Fifth, dependency can become self-reinforcing behavior. Remember, since using dependency as a defense mechanism reduces young people's anxiety, there's an increased chance that their dependent behavior will repeat itself. Defense mechanisms are used because they work well. Forming dependent relationships with individuals perceived as strong and responsible creates a sense of security for some young people. During adolescence when there is so much personal trauma and anxiety related to social situations, dependency may become an effective maneuver to reduce anxiety levels and feel safe.

When working with dependent teenagers, find out if there are any intensely dependent relationships in their personal histories. Check to see if this type of relationship has become their pattern. A long history of dependency usually indicates a more intense development of this personality type.

Sixth, we must remember that dependent people can successfully fulfill several different interpersonal functions. Many of these teenagers have had good experiences with being dependent throughout their childhood. They would argue that the world needs followers as well as leaders, and there cannot be leaders without a plentiful supply of followers. These young people have found a sense of value through following and attaching their loyalty to others. They feel most comfortable when they support the efforts of others rather than promote their own cause.

Energetic followers and supporters gain much reinforcement from following others. Appreciated and reinforced for the support and help given their leader, these adolescents experience external praise and internal good feelings that promote their dependent behavior. Evidence of these social patterns suggests early development of dependent personalities.

Effective work with teenagers requires some knowledge of how they have become who they are today. Investigate and examine their social histories. Find out about their family relationships. Probe gently into the way they perceive themselves. As you discover some of the origins of their social orientations, you will be better equipped to help them be more constructive in their current interpersonal relationships.

■ Healthy Forms of the Dependent Personality

Each of the eight personality types we are studying represents tendencies or trends that reflect extremes of normal, healthy behavior even in their adaptive forms. A central issue for all adolescents' development is the movement from being dependent on others toward greater equality within their relationships. When this movement stalls, slows or is nonexistent, a dependent personality probably exists. There are several healthy, positive expressions of this personality orientation as long as individuals do not become excessive or overly rigid within their dependency.

The Follower. Fifteen-year-old Ed appears to be a typically involved sophomore in high school. When he and his youth group recently attended their denomination's large regional youth conference, Ed participated in as many activities and meetings as he possibly could. He was pleasant, his attitude was cheerful and the other kids who met him at the conference seemed to like him. Outwardly, Ed related quite well within the large group. He was also supportive of others within the small groups. During one of the small group sessions, several of his new acquaintances used words like "happy," "encouraging," "good-natured" and "helpful" to describe him. But his youth leader noticed that Ed revealed very little about himself or his ideas when any personal sharing occurred.

Ed grew up in a strict family environment. His parents administered fair discipline and taught him traditional values. As the sixth child in a family of eight, Ed had little opportunity to exercise his leadership muscles. Instead he learned how to depend on others who were older and stronger. Relying on others and following their lead had resulted in good experiences, positive relationships and pleasurable feelings of belonging and acceptance. His mother and all the children attended church regularly, and his dad joined them occasionally.

Since both parents had to work, everyone shared household responsibilities. The children were raised to cooperate and help each other. If someone shirked his or her duties, group pressure became intense. However, the family atmosphere was usually pleasant and happy. There was ample love and commitment from each parent and mutual caring among the children. Aside from the typical sibling rivalry, brothers and sisters usually supported each other, and they became good friends as they matured into adolescence.

Ed learned how to adapt to other people from his childhood and early teenage years within his family. As he advanced in school, he continued to relate with others in much the same way he had learned at home. He was socially successful at school and in his neighborhood, and he was also popular in his church youth group. Ed was known for his encouragement, support and loyalty.

Though he hesitated to offer his own opinions, he eagerly affirmed someone else's.

Ed had found dependence a comfortable, successful way to interact with others. He gained his feelings of acceptance and belonging through following the lead of those around him. He also learned to believe in others' strengths more than his own. He found meaning in being a supportive and loyal follower.

The Admirer. Esther entered counseling at age 15, when she was a sophomore in high school. Although she wasn't in a crisis or severe trouble, she gained from the experience as her counselor helped her search for ways to prevent more serious problems in the future. Although many of her friends described her as easy to get along with, Esther's counselor saw her as passive and dependent.

Born as the youngest of two girls, Esther was only 3 years old when her parents divorced. Both girls lived with their mother, but their father visited them regularly once or twice a month. As a single parent, Esther's mother was determined her daughters would grow up with a high value for responsibility. She firmly enforced all rules and required prompt completion of routine chores. Strict and demanding, she succeeded in teaching her children the importance of responsible behavior, but her approach partially sabotaged her purpose. Her own strength and intensity overpowered Esther and her sister. Thus, Esther learned to take responsibility for her behavior, but her personal strength was crushed. Unable to produce the inner strength necessary for initiating her own actions and desires, she learned to identify with and depend upon someone else she perceived as powerful.

Esther's stepfather, who entered her life when she was 7, unwittingly intensified her dependency by his own role modeling. A kind and generous man, he passively accepted the decisions of Esther's mother about family finances, social life and vacations. He happily allowed her to manage his wages, and each weekend he responded readily to her "Honey-do" list. Unconsciously, Esther's stepfather proved to her that life is best when you can depend upon someone else who is strong, capable and trustworthy.

Since she was 11 or 12 years old, Esther has periodically attached herself to one or two special people whom she deeply respects and admires. Even though she doesn't understand why she is attracted to certain people, she has selected several teachers, youth leaders, Sunday school teachers and some of her mother's adult friends as special. She has also elevated several of her peers to this exalted position. Boys who show a lot of masculine bravado particularly catch Esther's attention. She has attracted four older boyfriends, each of whom has been either physically, athletically or socially more capable than she. She is especially drawn to responsible, power-oriented and competitive individuals because of their strength and self-confidence.

When Esther admires someone, she is a "one-girl fan club." She tells everyone how great her hero is. Through her identification with the other person's power and influence, she also feels powerful and influential. By sharing her admiration for another, she generates enthusiasm and exuberance from others. She then identifies with the admiration they experience and accepts it for herself. Esther handles these complex personal dynamics in such a successful manner that everyone feels better. She feels stronger by caboosing on another's glory. Her admired one feels better because of the increased notoriety and respect her relationship brings. And other people feel better because they have had the opportunity to affirm another person.

Esther is generally liked and accepted by other teenagers. They enjoy having her around, but her peers usually do not have *strong* feelings about her. She is described as "sweet," "kind," "nice" and "a good person." She is easy to have around, fits in well with most groups and adapts readily to different types of people. Unfortunately, these same positive qualities create some of her potential problems.

Even though Esther is passive and dependent, she is successful because she is not extreme enough to be destructive to herself. The goal of her counseling is to help her find, develop and rely upon her own inner strengths.

The Imitator. At age 19 Sean started seeing a professional counselor. Upon graduation from high school, he had taken a full-time job as a plumber's helper, a position he held for one year. Then he entered the local community college. Halfway through the first semester, he encountered an impasse. Unable to concentrate, he dropped two of his courses, thinking this action would relieve some of the tension. A few weeks later he could no longer force himself even to attend his remaining classes. He was depressed, anxious and temporarily incapable of coping with even the slightest stress. He felt this way for almost two weeks before his first counseling session. But within six weeks of twice-weekly sessions, Sean was feeling much stronger. With his newly acquired self-confidence, he enrolled and successfully completed his classes during the next semester.

What had caused this temporary break in Sean's effective functioning during his late adolescence? With no indication that he was headed for trouble, why did this happen to him? After a few counseling sessions with Sean, his therapist was able to answer these questions for him and for his parents and help them understand the effect of his personality development.

Sean was the second of three boys in his stable middle-class family. His older brother had always been an excellent student, and his younger brother was an outstanding athlete. From his elementary years on, Sean could not claim to be the "best" in any activities that typically affirm teenagers' self-esteem. He felt outclassed by both his brothers. It was bad enough when he couldn't match his older brother's straight-A average, but he felt totally humiliated when his younger brother surpassed him in athletic accomplishments. By the middle of eighth grade, Sean realized he couldn't compete with either brother and win.

Another major factor influenced Sean's personality development. When he was 8 years old, his mother experienced a deep depression. Because she was suicidal, her doctors hospitalized her for six weeks. Her outpatient psychotherapy continued for another two years until she had overcome her serious depression. During her illness Sean worried excessively about her. When she refused to get out of bed, when she was angry and complaining and when she didn't have enough energy to complete her household tasks, Sean blamed himself. He suffered guilt feelings, thinking he ought to be able to do something about her situation. These thoughts and feelings led him to even deeper self-doubts.

Sean handled his discouragement and guilt feelings through the formation of a dependent personality. However, his personality orientation was somewhat different from the teenagers we met earlier in this section. Instead of just becoming a follower or an admirer of others, Sean began imitating those people he respected and valued. Like Ed's and Esther's social orientation, his adaptation was healthy because it wasn't sufficiently extreme to destroy his social relationships. However, his own acute depression was a spinoff, resulting from his use of imitation. As he gained feelings of significance through imitating others' gestures, verbal characteristics and behaviors, he hindered the development of his own identity. The natural pressures of moving from late adolescence to early adulthood created more stress than his limited identity could handle. His adaptive functioning broke down, and he regressed in an attempt to regain his psychological balance.

In junior high and early high school, Sean had tried to imitate outstanding athletes and some of his other class leaders. He chose to wear the same clothes they did, use the same language and participate in the same activities as much as possible. He became a keen observer and sometimes unconsciously replicated their actions, attitudes and interests. Even though this adaptation brought him success and acceptance from others, he still felt empty and unfulfilled. At some level of consciousness, he realized he was not developing an identity that was uniquely his own.

During his junior and senior years in high school, he chose to identify with a group of heavy drug users. He dressed like them, picked up their style of speech, changed his personal habits to mirror theirs and then began using their drugs. Although at first he felt good about his acceptance into a new group of friends, he felt uneasy about giving up his loftier ambitions and ideals.

During the latter part of his senior year Sean became involved in church and his youth group. He made a strong commitment to Christ. Sean's youth minister took special interest in him, spending much time counseling and discipling him. Sean developed great respect for this young adult. Because he meant so much to him, Sean naturally began to imitate his youth minister as an expression of his desire to be the person God wanted him to be. Though certainly a more positive role model than his drug-using buddies, his youth minister still wasn't who God created Sean to be. Sean needed to seek his *own* identity. Instead of imitating those around him, Sean needed to discover his own way of uniquely reflecting God in whose image he was created.

Ed, Esther and Sean each exemplify primarily healthy, adaptive forms of the dependent personality type. All three relate well with others, they aren't destructive in their relationships and they are pleasant and enjoyable to be around. The "follower," "admirer" and "imitator" are often productive, healthy expressions of the dependent social orientation.

■ Unhealthy Forms of the Dependent Personality

When dependency becomes excessive, teenagers' social adaptations cease to work well for them. Their perceptions of their inner weaknesses prevent them from establishing relationships based upon their own strengths. Social contacts are characterized by adolescents' dependencies and thereby lose their ability to be healthy, well-balanced and nourishing. In this section we will examine three case studies of unhealthy, maladaptive forms of the dependent adolescent personality type.

The Helpless. For most of her life Rhonda has been the epitome of helplessness. Her social behavior expresses one overwhelming message, "I must have your advice, direction and strength, or I absolutely cannot survive." Rhonda was a 17-year-old senior in high school when she initiated therapy. She was suffering severe anxiety attacks and had pervasive fears about being around people. She felt terribly alone and saw herself as isolated in an uncaring, dangerous world.

The immediate cause for her symptoms was readily evident. Her anxiety attacks began a few days after her boyfriend broke up with her. They had been very close, and she was extremely dependent upon him. For the past two years, she had relied on him for almost everything she did. She used him to provide for all her social needs, going out *only* when she could be with him. She could get passing grades *only* when she studied with him. She finally learned how to drive *only* when he took the time to teach her. During evenings and weekends when he was unable to be with her, she chose to sit at home, bored, listless and unproductive.

When Rhonda started dating this young man, she slowly let go of her relationships with her girlfriends. She stopped going out with them, failed to return their phone calls and avoided them at school and church in an attempt to spend more time with her boyfriend. Therefore, when she lost him, she no longer had other people to whom she could immediately turn for support.

We can understand how Rhonda developed her helpless dependency if we look into her family dynamics and the childhood social experiences that affected her early life. Her father styled himself after the classic benevolent dictator. He found his pride in providing financially for his family and protecting them from harm. In return for these services, he required his family's trust, loyalty, obedience and dependency. Since their church heavily emphasized the authority of the husband and the submission of the wife, Rhonda's mother gladly fulfilled the requirements. She vividly modeled the role of helpless dependency for her three daughters. Thus, Rhonda learned to associate helplessness with desirable femininity and appropriate Christian behavior.

Rhonda developed great skill at positioning herself in a helpless role with other people. As the youngest of three girls, she made good use of her older sisters' abilities and willingness to do things for her, many of which she could have done for herself. As a result she began to falsely believe in her own helplessness. When she started school, she transferred her needy social behavior to this environment as well. Her teachers described her as "charming but passive." She had successfully learned how to ask favors from others without them resenting her. And when her friends would tire of her helpless demands, she would find others who were happy to feel needed.

By the time she reached her teenage years, Rhonda was especially adept at attracting power-oriented and responsible young people. The central basis for all of her social relationships continued to be her helpless dependency. She felt included and accepted only when someone helped her. She experienced her own strengths only when she could pull helping responses from others through her own display of weakness and helplessness.

The Gullible. From all appearances, 18-year-old Salvadore was making a positive adjustment to life throughout his mid-adolescent years. Popular among his peers, he was also well-liked by his teachers and other adults. He had always been friendly, warm and easy to get along with. But during his senior year of high school, he began to struggle with his inability to determine what was real. And his gullibility began to interfere with his interactions with others.

In a family of seven children, Salvadore was born second to the youngest. He was the younger of only two boys and received a great amount of love and attention from his mother and four older sisters. Because he was cute and charming as a small child, Salvadore learned early how to entice older children and adults to respond to him. He learned how to get attention without doing anything constructive or helpful for either himself or others. He remained passive in his social relationships because everyone else was so willing to do all of his work and carry responsibility for their relationship with him. Playing the role of the adorable child was all Salvadore had to do. He performed so well others were delighted to have him around.

Like most gullible people, Salvadore learned too well how to work the system. He used his own dependent style of relating so often that he increasingly narrowed his range of possibilities for social responses. He slowly became utterly dependent upon others to assume the lead in any of his interpersonal interactions. Encouraged by his protective home environment, he became overly trusting. No matter what others said, he believed them. And he would, without question, do almost anything someone said he should.

Since others took care of most of his needs and wants, Salvadore developed few skills and no special abilities. There was virtually nothing he could do well or significantly better than others. He had no hobbies and his few efforts to do something constructive during his childhood were largely unsuccessful. This lack of success resulted in his feeling discouraged and giving up. He learned not to trust himself. He discovered others were more skilled, more interesting and often more correct than he. This dependence on others and their abilities began early in his life.

Salvadore's adorable nature allowed him to progress through elementary school without any sense of personal pain or interpersonal problems. As he moved through junior high, however, he began to feel empty and insecure. Still active and popular in his relationships with both his peers and adults, he internalized his pain and hid it beneath his charming exterior. Finally, during his senior year his internal void collapsed, and his growing expectations and needs for independent functioning within relationships broke through his thin defenses. His lack of confidence and his minimal abilities, skills and talents were inadequate to sustain him through late adolescence. Salvadore's personality development had been stalled psychologically and socially at the preadolescent stage.

The most visible symptom of Salvadore's unhealthy personality development was his extremely gullible reaction to what others said or did. His friends had a great time when they wanted to get a reaction out of him.

"Hey, Sal, are you ready for the English midterm today? You didn't know about it? Boy, are you in for it now!"

"Sal, you know that awesome cheerleader, Brenda? Well, she thinks you're something else. She really likes you. She wants you to ask her to homecoming next week."

"Gee, Sal, we better get home. I just heard on the radio a big tornado is expected to strike any minute. We better leave and warn our families even if the principal won't let us out of school."

With no inner strength or confidence in his own thinking, Salvadore merely accepted being set up by his friends. Instead of evaluating the situation, Sal simply believed whatever someone told him. Rather than think for himself about what was or was not real, he relied on what others said. Lacking the inner strength to disagree or question, he passively accepted what he was told. Even though these incidents were innocent and meant for fun, they served to intensify Salvadore's conviction that he was inferior and inadequate.

As each year passes, Salvadore's dependency becomes more inappropriate and increasingly maladaptive. His gullible style of social interaction increasingly evidences his inner weaknesses and personal ineptness.

The Clinging Vine. Carmen was born to an unmarried teenage mother who elected to keep her child. The young mother lived at home with her own mother who had been divorced several years earlier. When Carmen was 2 years old, her grandmother developed breast cancer, underwent extensive surgery followed by eight months of chemotherapy and was unable to return to work. This unexpected illness and lack of any extended family support forced Carmen's mother to work to support her small family. When the young mother finally recognized her inability to handle the combination of working, caring for her ill mother and mothering her toddler daughter, she placed Carmen in a receiving home hoping to find acceptable adoptive parents for her.

Reacting to the instability and trauma surrounding her young life, Carmen developed severe temper tantrums. Potential adoptive parents were repelled by her behavior, so she spent the next seven years living in a series of foster homes. Several of these homes offered her love and structure, and none of her foster parents were abusive. But most families provided little more than food, clothing and shelter.

Shortly after her ninth birthday, Carmen was placed with an unusually loving and nurturing couple who also had a 13-year-old natural daughter. Almost immediately, Carmen felt like she had "come home." Her temper tantrums subsided, and she began to feel more and more secure with this new family. After just 10 months her foster parents applied to adopt Carmen as their own. And by the time she was 11 years old, she had a new mother, father and sister who were legally hers.

As Carmen's temper tantrums disappeared, a new behavior characterized her social interactions. She began to attach herself to one friend at a time. While dependent upon that one person, Carmen cared nothing for anyone else. She wanted to do everything with that one individual, and she became depressed and obviously upset when that person would do things with others. Her continual need for contact and attention strained her social relationships. Most of her friends could not tolerate this much intensity for more than a few months, so they withdrew, usually with some form of meanness in an attempt to discourage Carmen's clinging. But without fail, she would enter another mutual pact of loyalty and friendship with someone else just a few days after one of these traumatic episodes had ended.

In addition to clinging to her peers, Carmen also developed a similar pattern of clinging to adults. For the first two years following her adoption Carmen clung tightly to her new foster parents. When she finally felt secure within that relationship, she began parceling out her loyalty among the adult friends of her parents, her teachers, Sunday school teachers and neighbors. These hand-picked adults would temporarily provide her with further security and stability until they, too, would disappoint her by their imperfection in meeting all her needs.

When she was 15 years old, Carmen's parents took her to see a professional therapist who specialized in treating adolescents. During the first few sessions the therapist discovered that her "clinging vine" pattern of social interaction began in her extremely insecure early childhood. Her repeated loss of loved ones during her early years reinforced her belief that there are no stable relationships upon which she can depend. As most children do, Carmen internalized the problem—she blamed herself. She thought there must be something terribly wrong with her that made her unlovable and made other people leave her.

Carmen's response to this feeling of inadequacy was to tighten her grip on anyone who showed interest or befriended her. She exaggerated small signals of liking into commitments of loyalty and exclusiveness. Her clinging was an attempt to control and possess all the other person's time and resources for the purpose of befriending her.

We have observed three types of maladaptive or

unhealthy forms of dependent interpersonal behavior. Helpless Rhonda and gullible Salvadore are extremely passive in their dependency. Carmen, the "clinging vine," is much more active yet is still as dependent as the other two. These three adolescents find no strength or personal value within themselves. They rely totally upon external sources for their sense of identity. Their personal identity development is in serious trouble. All three must develop more of an internal sense of control and personal power before they can successfully advance both psychologically and relationally into early adulthood.

■ Effects of Dependent Behavior on Other People

Each of the eight personality types presented in this book elicits both positive and negative reactions from others. Usually, intensity of behavior determines whether these reactions will be favorable or unhappy. Others' reactions to the intensity of a dependent teenager's behavior are usually quite clear and fit logically with the needs the dependent behavior expresses.

A "follower" like Ed often elicits strength and leadership from others. This dependency maneuver especially affects power-oriented and responsible people. An "admirer" like Esther will often stimulate feelings of self-respect and self-affirmation within the individuals he or she respects. And in return, these people enjoy being around an individual who admires and looks up to them. An "imitator" can have the same impact on others that an "admirer" does since imitation is recognized as one of the finest forms of a compliment. If taken to an extreme, however, an imitating teenager may draw feelings of irritation and rejection from others.

Even an unhealthy form of dependency will draw positive responses, especially from responsible and power-oriented individuals. Many people *want* to provide some form of help, a friendly response or nurturing support to an individual who is dependent within the relationship. Some need to offer direction or advice to an adolescent who appears helpless. Others may extend sympathetic understanding plus an offer for support or reassurance to a young person who exhibits dependent behavior. These positive responses usually turn into negative reactions, however, when the dependent behavior takes an unhealthy form or becomes maladaptive in its intensity.

Like the unhealthy self-demeaning teenager, a dependent adolescent will sometimes refuse help from others. When offers of assistance repeatedly fail to bring a positive response or change, the helping individuals often react with frustration, anger and withdrawal. In the example of Salvadore, we saw how a gullible individual could bring a derisive, "making fun of" reaction from friends. In this way "gullible" Salvadore is similar to the clown type of masochist within the self-destructive personality type in Chapter 8. Rather than confront or question the social relationships offered by others, Sal merely accepts the dependent role his friends have chosen for him.

As a teenager's dependent behavior becomes more extreme, other people usually choose one of two types of responses. Most will finally push the dependent teenager away or withdraw in order to regain their personal freedom. Others, especially those who are less competitive, power-oriented or responsible, may initially try to foster even more dependency. When this happens, an unhealthy symbiotic relationship develops which is destructive to both people. Each individual reinforces the unhealthiness of the other. Usually in these cases, the healthier of the two individuals finally rebels against the controls of the other and pulls away from the relationship.

One of the clues to identifying a particular personality orientation is the reaction most commonly drawn from other people. When the primary responses outlined in this section are characteristic of reactions given to the adolescent you know, he or she may be a dependent teenager.

■ Guidelines for Working With Dependent Adolescents

The primary problem dependent teenagers deal with is their lack of strength or trust in their inner power. Most of their interpersonal difficulties and problems in adjusting to the world around them relate to this issue of strength vs. weakness. Youth ministers, teachers and counselors can dramatically affect these young people's lives. We can help them remove the blocks that hinder their personal development and assist them in their growth toward greater personal strength and self-control.

1. Learn what historical events and pressures have influenced these teenagers to develop dependent personalities. Our first step toward helping dependent teenagers is to learn how they have developed this social orientation. Dependency often suggests certain kinds of earlier life-learning experiences. Some parents demand and expect dependence from their children. They are over-protective, smothering and refuse to let go of their young people. Other dependent teenagers were forced into too much self-reliance too early in their lives. Their dependency needs were inadequately met earlier in their childhood, and they seek to satisfy those needs through their dependency.

Seek to know the answers to the following questions in order to better understand why a particular adolescent has developed this personality type.

What significant events in their past influenced their perceptions of the world?

Who were the important people who impacted their lives, and what were they like?

What have these young people learned about themselves during their childhood and adolescence?

By gaining this kind of knowledge we are more capable of understanding what dependence means to the teenagers we are trying to help.

2. Try to understand what messages dependent teenagers' behaviors communicate about them.
Teenagers express many of their emotions, attitudes and thoughts through their actions. Unlike adults who tend to *talk* about how they feel, adolescents are more likely to *act out* those feelings, at least initially. Dependent behavior sometimes expresses feelings of inadequacy; it may also reflect patterns that were modeled by parents. For other teenagers, dependency expresses their desire for security and their wish to be taken care of or protected. Since the same behavior can express different needs, it is very important for us to learn how to discover what dependent young people are really communicating through their actions. Therefore, we need to develop our own ability to "read" the behavior of these teenagers with an increasing comprehension level.

3. Encourage these young people to assume some leadership responsibilities. Recognizing dependent teenagers' central difficulties as their lack of trust and confidence in their own strengths gives us guidance on how to help them. People gain self-confidence only by testing their fears. Therefore, young people who are convinced they are personally inadequate must test themselves to find they can accomplish goals they thought were unreachable.

Let a dependent member of your group be co-organizer of a social event, a Bible study or a worship experience. Encourage your young person to serve on a decision-making committee for organizing class activities. Assign your dependent adolescent responsibility for bringing a list of three things to talk about at the next counseling session.

These young people usually resist our efforts to help them exercise their personal strengths. We have to be stronger and more tenacious than their resistance. Our task is to encourage, cajole and even pressure them to test their limits. However, we also must be sensitive to how much anxiety they can handle. If we push too hard, they may fail miserably, feel more guilty and then have even more proof of their inadequacy.

4. Assist and support dependent teenagers in their quest to find a sense of personal significance and value. An essential element in adolescent identity formation is a growing sense of having personal value within one's self. This sense of personal significance must be separate from any athletic prowess, academic achievements, political advancements and other skills, talents or hobbies. Though all of these external behaviors affect a person's self-evaluation, belief in one's own personal value needs deeper roots than just personal accomplishments or abilities.

The wonderful fact that we are individually created in God's image is a great place to start in helping dependent adolescents develop stronger evaluations of themselves. If we have been created and judged as acceptable by a God who created "man (and woman) in his own image," how can we question our value? There is no stronger basis for building healthy self-esteem. How can we discount human beings, no matter how they appear or operate, when at their core they are created in the image of perfection? We must share and teach that truth to our young people.

In working with teenagers, we must also help them experience their value as we express our appreciation for them. Essentially, we are teaching these young people how to relate to themselves. If we are impatient, intolerant and irritable with them, our behavior suggests they really are not worthy of our time, energy and best efforts. However, when we are tolerant, kind and respectful, we indicate these adolescents are just as valuable and important as we are. The old adage "Actions speak louder than words" is certainly true in this respect.

5. Encourage young people to become as fully as possible the people God created them to be. Most teenagers willingly conform to peer pressure in exchange for acceptance into a desirable group. Dependent youth, especially, are willing to sacrifice their own identity for the security of belonging. They have failed to discover they can be accepted, loved and valued for who they really are. They believe they are accepted only *because of* their conformity and their dependence upon others.

We need to spend extra time with these young people. Listen to them. Give them time to express their thoughts— their likes and dislikes, their preferences and opinions, their attitudes and feelings. These teenagers desperately need opportunities to share who they really are. They need to discover they are valuable without trying to be someone else. As they express themselves more fully and still experience your unqualified acceptance, they become increasingly open to developing their own identity. Movement from excessive dependency into personal strength requires a frightening amount of growth and a great sense of personal risk. A caring adult who will draw close and be supportive can make the difference between success and failure for these teenagers.

6. Dependent teenagers need to learn to value their differences from their peers rather than be embarrassed by them. Many adolescents, especially dependent young people, feel awkward and uncertain about how they differ from their friends. To these young people, their individual differences threaten their okayness. These adolescents see differences normally considered positive— such as early physical maturation, academic excellence, outstanding musical talent and exceptional physical attraction—as negatives. They usually interpret these unique personal characteristics as potential social hazards which can separate them from their friends.

Simply telling teenagers it is okay to be different will not resolve all their anxieties. However, helping them understand the necessity of individual differences to facilitate functioning as a group, a class and a church may help.

Work with them to discover value in their differences which seem weaker and less useful than others. Use television shows and movies to initiate discussions about the importance of people who follow and support leaders. Help them identify the positive contributions they make to your youth group or class. Teach them to respect their own differences and the differences of other people.

Make sure your young people are familiar with Paul's teaching about individual differences.

> *Now the body is not made up of one part but of many. If the foot should say, "Because I am not a hand, I do not belong to the body," it would not for that reason cease to be part of the body. And if the ear should say, "Because I am not an eye, I do not belong to the body," it would not for that reason cease to be part of the body. If the whole body were an eye, where would the sense of hearing be? If the whole body were an ear, where would the sense of smell be? But in fact God has arranged the parts in the body, every one of them, just as he wanted them to be. If they were all one part, where would the body be? As it is, there are many parts, but one body.*
>
> *The eye cannot say to the hand, "I don't need you!" And the head cannot say to the feet, "I don't need you!" On the contrary, those parts of the body that seem to be weaker are indispensable, and the parts that we think are less honorable we treat with special honor. And the parts that are unpresentable are treated with special modesty, while our presentable parts need no special treatment. But God has combined the members of the body and has given greater honor to the parts that lacked it, so that there should be no division in the body, but that its parts should have equal concern for each*

other. If one part suffers, every part suffers with
it; if one part is honored, every part rejoices
with it (1 Corinthians 12:14-26).

7. *Teach these teenagers how to express their*
disagreements with others in a constructive man-
ner. Dependent young people usually struggle to gain
sufficient courage to openly disagree with others. Since
disagreeing means to set one's self apart from another person, dependent young people fear any separation because
it removes the external source which helps establish their
sense of personal value. They also fear that if they strongly
disagree with another person, that individual will reject
them. Though some people cannot tolerate anothers'
disagreement, most relationships can survive these differences. We must help these young people understand that
their insistence on others' agreement is simply another
form of control over other people.

Help the dependent teenagers in your group practice
expressing their disagreements. Coach them, and above all,
encourage them to practice with you. Set up role plays
where you assume the role of the person with whom they
disagree, and then switch roles. In this way you can model
constructive methods for handling disagreements and provide opportunities for these adolescents to experience
being disagreed with. Allow time to talk about how they
felt playing both roles. Be sure to listen, hear and respond
to their expressions of fear, anxiety, insecurity and weakness. Reinforce any revelations of inner strength, security
and assuredness these teenagers may experience during
these practice sessions.

Be sure to encourage these dependent young people to
express themselves when they disagree with what you say
and do. They are sure to have differences of opinion; they
are just so accustomed to repressing or denying them that
they may not volunteer. If there is no response to your invitation, check out their feelings.

"Do you agree with this plan?"

"I wonder if you have a different opinion about that?"

"Your body language seems to indicate you are uncomfortable with that idea. What do *you* think we should do?"

Let them experience open discussion and disagreement with you without experiencing any loss of your contact or caring. Be sure to praise their positive methods of handling their disagreements. And guide them to correct any misunderstandings or negative reactions to expressing their differences so they can learn and grow from their mistakes.

8. Encourage dependent teenagers to take minor risks to develop their personal inner strength. Risk-taking is difficult for all of us. Fear and anxiety usually accompany whatever risks we contemplate. Dependent teenagers have a particularly difficult time with interpersonal risks. Because they see themselves as incompetent and inadequate, they are afraid others might also discover this truth about them. To assume positions of leadership, power or individuality is to risk exposure. While risk-taking is necessary for continued growth, we must guide these young people regarding the kinds of risks they should take.

Suggest small risks at first. Reduce chances for an early failure that might discourage any future growth. Point out their successes and reinforce the courage it took for them to try. For example, encourage your dependent youth to meet and talk with the school's student government adviser before campaigning for a school office. The chances of his or her successfully initiating a relationship with the adviser are far superior to winning a school election.

Be sure to reinforce *any* gains. Many young people are excessively critical of their accomplishments and feel discouraged because they recognize their task is incomplete. Help these young people feel good about what they *have* accomplished and who they are for doing it.

As these young people take risks and accomplish their goals, support their enhanced images of themselves. Help them see how they have broadened their collections of skills, abilities and talents. Then help them move on to progressively more difficult challenges.

Sometimes when young people take risks, they do fail to accomplish their goal. Dependent teenagers have a terrible struggle with failure. They jump to the conclusion that they really are incompetent. Help them realize that most people's successes come only after a series of failures. Are your young people aware that famous inventors often fail many times before they succeed? Politicians may lose several elections before they are elected to office. Help them see it is usually far better to try and fail rather than to shrink from trying at all. Explain and support the belief that failure and success are seldom all-or-none concepts. Usually, there is an element of both success and failure in all we do.

9. Encourage these young people to understand the power of their words. "This is difficult" should replace "I can't" within their personal vocabulary. Listen carefully to what dependent teenagers tell you. When they say they can't do something, they are communicating a myth they believe about themselves. Essentially they are telling us where they feel inadequate, and they need us *not* to be convinced. They need us to believe in their abilities so they can begin to embrace a more confident view of themselves.

Words have great power, not only for the person who receives them but also for the individual who speaks. "I can't" reinforces a feeling of helplessness within the speaker each time he or she utters that message. Alert dependent teenagers to the dangers of these disparaging messages about themselves. Help them recognize that what they say reflects what they believe about themselves.

Then help them change their messages. Even if they really believe "I can't," work with them to say something like, "This sure is hard for me" or "This is really a tough project." "I can't" says something about themselves, but the latter two messages simply make statements about their tasks. The helplessness of the "I can't" message suggests that effort and risk-taking would be foolish. But the descriptions of the tasks as "hard" or "tough" merely indicate the tasks are difficult, and difficult is not at all hopeless. Difficult tasks are accomplished every day!

When these teenagers do change their statements from "I can't" to "This is a tough one," support their efforts to tackle difficult challenges. When they succeed, give them strong affirmation. And if they fail, help them examine and identify parts of the project where they did well. Reinforce their efforts whether they succeed or not. This support will help them believe more in their strength and ability.

10. Encourage dependent teenagers to think and express their own thoughts. Dependent young people are afraid of placing too much confidence in their *own* thinking or reasoning. They don't trust their mental abilities. They feel more comfortable relying on someone else's thoughts and beliefs. Dependent teenagers often respond to the question "What do you think?" by replying "Well, Sue says . . . ." They prefer quoting a friend, their parent, the newspaper or some other authority so they don't have to account for their own thoughts.

When interacting with these teenagers, let them know that you want to hear what *they* think. Carefully assure them that if you had wanted to know what a friend thought, you would have asked the friend. When encouraging these dependent teenagers to share their thoughts, be careful not to judge or evaluate what they share with you. Give them positive comments that encourage them to think of themselves as people who have interesting things to say. Here are some examples.

"That's interesting. Tell me more."

"You sure have an interesting point of view. Can you explain that idea further?"

"You're a stimulating person to talk with. I always enjoy these kinds of discussions with you."

"Gullible" dependent teenagers have a particularly difficult time expressing their thoughts as valuable. Having been the victim of many jokes that made them appear foolish, silly or unthinking, they have learned through painful experiences not to trust their own thinking abilities. These young people especially need our help and support to develop more trust in their ability to reason and think logically.

In private discussions ask them what they think should be done about situations that arise at church, at school and within the community. Be careful not to evaluate or judge their responses. As they gain confidence in expressing their opinion in a private situation, include them in open discussions during Bible study or a discussion group. Go slowly. Work with these young people to make sure they don't get set up again for being seen as gullible or unable to think well.

11. Dependent teenagers need to learn how to "let go" to give their friends a chance to initiate a relationship. Teenagers like Carmen, the "clinging vine," provide a vivid picture of the fear dependent teenagers have about losing contact with a significant person. Their imagined inadequacies force them to tighten their grip on that special person and their unique relationship. Afraid of losing that social contact and extra attention, dependent teenagers cannot tolerate separation of any kind. Therefore, instead of allowing the other person to initiate getting together or starting a conversation, dependent young people always act first; and the other individual is left with no space to move within the relationship. This form of overdependence drives people away. They must eventually escape the relationship to avoid psychological suffocation. Clinging teenagers actually bring about the loss of the relationship they worked so hard to obtain.

Youth ministers and lay youth sponsors often observe "clinging vines" in action within their groups. In fact, these caring adults are often the targets of these adolescents. If you are the victim of this type of social maneuver, respond with love that has firm limits. Neither you nor your ministry can afford enslavement to only one person. *You* must be in charge of the amount of time and energy you spend with these young people. Decide in advance *when* you will be involved, *where* you will spend your time and *how often* you can be available. These adolescents will test your limits, so prepare yourself to be firm. Remember, saying "no" can be the most caring thing you can offer dependent personality types. Your consistency and firm decisions show you can be trusted. These qualities also give clinging adolescents limits which help them feel more secure in the relationship. Be prepared for some guilt-inducing maneuvers, but don't fall prey to them.

"You're my only hope. If you don't help me, I don't know what I'll do."

"You are the only one who cares about me."

"I just knew that you would never turn me down, especially since you're such a good Christian."

Again, let them know your limits. Do them and yourself a favor by withstanding their manipulation.

When you observe these interactions between dependent adolescents and someone other than yourself, try to help clinging young people adopt a more objective perspective of their behavior. Help them see they are robbing themselves of the pleasure of being approached by their friend. Help them realize their own fears may bring about the very thing they want to avoid—the loss of this friendship. Encourage them to let go of the relationship they value so highly so that the other person may return to them by his or her free will.

12. When teenagers' dependencies reach unhealthy levels of intensity, consider referral to a professional counselor. Dependency can sometimes reach unhealthy levels of intensity. When this happens, a professional therapist who specializes in working with adolescents may be helpful. They are accustomed to dealing with the various maladaptive styles of social interaction these young people sometimes use. Plus, the added structure of therapy sessions often helps place and enforce limits upon which these teenagers can depend.

Dependent teenagers may heavily resist your attempts to refer them to a professional counselor. They may misinterpret referral as another form of rejection. Tell them that you are referring them because you care. Offer to go to the counselor's office with them. Let them know that you are interested in how the sessions are progressing. Ask questions but don't pry. Continue in other aspects of your relationship. Your reassurance and continued support can help these needy young people to be confident that your relationship with them as youth worker, teacher or adult friend will continue.

■ Guidelines for Parenting Dependent Adolescents

As a parent of dependent teenagers, you are in a delicate position. Your children are struggling to gain independence from you, and you want to help them with this developmental task. But your assisting efforts seem to enmesh them into further dependency. You may feel frustrated, but you can help your dependent adolescents in numerous ways.

1. Carefully observe what your teenagers say through their actions. Teenagers function developmentally between children and adults. Even though they can *talk* about their inner experiences, they are more likely to *act out* their feelings, attitudes and opinions. You can usually discover more about your teenagers by observing their behavior than by listening to their words. As you watch *what* they do and *how* they do it, recall past experiences that could have contributed to your children's dependent personality development. Your awareness of their past helps you understand what you observe in the present.

Your careful *listening* to your teenagers' behaviors can provide deeper understanding of your teenagers' feelings and thoughts. Donny's lack of interest in school and his sudden drop in grades might be saying: "I've missed Dad so much since the divorce. I just don't want to try anymore." Marcia's exuberance and eagerness to help in the kitchen might be verbalized as: "I'm so happy that Bill asked me out for Friday night. I want everyone to be as happy as I am."

Behavior motivated by dependency needs often exhibits young people's desires for approval, imitation of others' actions or reliance upon another person's directions. By carefully observing your teenagers' behaviors and relating them to their pasts, you will gain your best understanding of why your teenagers act the way they do.

2. Treat your teenagers with respect. Your teenagers learn how to look at themselves largely from the way the family treats them. Dependent young people usually do not regard themselves highly. Nor do they typically recognize their personal strengths. These adolescents believe they are weak and incompetent. They choose to depend on someone else rather than rely on their own abilities. Often they idealize one or two people and constantly seek their company. Dependent teenagers experience success and adequacy by associating and identifying with other people who are ambitious, popular or successful.

One effective way to help your dependent young people is to be consistent about treating them with respect. Let them know you think they are valuable. Help them realize that *what* they do or *how well* they perform isn't nearly as important to you as *who* they are. Spontaneously express your love and high regard when they have done nothing to earn it. "Felippe, I just want you to know how proud I am to be your dad."

Show your teenagers respect by recognizing and considering *their* needs. Think of the variety of needs common to adolescents and respond appropriately. A closed bedroom door may reflect your teenager's need for privacy. It may be saying, "I need to be alone right now." Respect your own rule of courtesy that tells you to knock before entering another person's space.

Remember, the way people feel about themselves usually reflects the way others treat them. Dependent adolescents need to increase their level of self-respect. You can help them accomplish this goal by offering the same respect you expect from them.

3. Encourage your dependent teenagers to develop inner strengths and self-reliance. The central issue with dependent adolescents is their lack of confidence in their own strengths and skills. They do not believe they have the ability to function adequately in life. Challenges and opportunities normal for most teenagers seemingly overwhelm these young people. Fear, shame, guilt, panic and feelings of inadequacy often cripple these adolescents while their peers operate comfortably in similar situations.

To protect themselves from the weight of life's demands, these young people depend on others' strengths. They maneuver themselves into positions where others feel they must watch over them. This positioning reinforces both their own and others' images of them as inadequate and protects them from further stress. Dependent teenagers strive to convince others they cannot handle life without excessive help, support and protection. As a parent, you may be a primary target for this display of dependency.

Refuse to accept your dependent teenagers' perceived inadequacies. Without arguing the issue, support the development of your teenagers' inner strengths. Give your young people responsibilities that stretch their concepts of what they can accomplish. Don't move too quickly. Enhance their chances of success by enlisting their help with things you know they can accomplish. Planning an evening meal, reorganizing the garage, taking care of errands, helping younger siblings find lost items and scheduling a family outing are examples of tasks that exercise these young people's self-reliance.

Dependent adolescents want their parents to rescue them when things become frightening or difficult. Unless the situation is extreme, refuse to save them. Don't reinforce their belief in their own helplessness.

Fifteen-year-old Marty was house-sitting for some vacationing neighbors. Since he was afraid he hadn't done things correctly, he wanted his parents to do a final check to make sure everything was okay before the neighbors returned. His parents gently refused, telling him they were confident he had managed things well.

Dependent young people like Marty need your support and assistance to build their confidence in their personal strengths. Your trust and confidence in their abilities can have a powerful, positive impact on their self-confidence.

4. Allow your young people to make mistakes while they are still within the supportive environment of their home. When you see people you love experience failure and negative consequences for their mistakes and poor choices, you hurt too. You feel especially bad when your dependent teenagers, who already struggle with self-doubts and low self-esteem, experience failure. But do you help them by unnecessarily protecting them from reality? By shielding them, you essentially teach them a false impression of the world in which we live. They mistakenly learn they can make unwise decisions and proceed carelessly without negative consequences. That type of unrealistic concept could seriously thwart them for the rest of their lives. Part of your task as a parent is to equip your children to live effective lives in the *real* world. Just as your relationship with God equips you to live effectively for him, God expects you to help your children do the same.

Overprotection teaches dependent adolescents they are inadequate. When you reinforce your teenagers' false perceptions of their abilities to learn and grow, you breed more dependency into personality structures that are already overly dependent. Remember Marty, the young man we met in the previous guideline? While Marty was housesitting, he forgot to water several plants, and they died. He also neglected the goldfish, and they became ill. Since his parents didn't cover for him, he had to face his employers and his own irresponsibility. Even though his experience was extremely painful, it was better for him to learn the importance of carefully following directions now rather than later when his failure might affect a career.

Florence's parents encouraged her to organize the family's Sunday picnic. She did an admirable job; she remembered everything—everything *except* something to drink. When Florence's parents gave her responsibility for the picnic, they didn't step in and remind her of the details. The family went on the picnic and had a great time, even though everyone was thirsty. With her family's support, Florence learned she could handle a large responsibility by making a list and checking it carefully to be sure she collected all the necessary items.

You don't want your children to experience pain. But a little pain now may prevent more serious consequences later when the security of parents and home is not available.

5. Discipline in ways that enhance personal accountability and self-respect. Think of your discipline as more than behavior control. The *way* you discipline your children impacts their self-concepts; it affects how they see the world and reinforces or alters their attitudes toward authority figures and other people. The Bible clearly supports parental authority, but you need to vary your *methods* of God-given authority to meet the personality needs of each of your children. Since dependent teenagers already believe they are inadequate and possess little self-worth, be extremely careful that your method of discipline does not reinforce these negative attitudes. Do not demean or belittle them. These adolescents experience harsh, authoritarian methods of discipline as further proof that they are hopelessly inadequate. This severe discipline makes these young people feel even more helpless. They fear they can never become worthwhile or valuable.

Discipline your dependent teenagers with logical, natural consequences which help these young people feel more responsible for their actions. When you discipline with consequences, you effectively gain control of behavior without destroying fragile self-concepts. While punishment places responsibility on the adults, logical and natural consequences place responsibility directly on the adolescents.

"Tony, you got home an hour after your curfew last night. Your actions told me you're having trouble handling your freedom responsibly. You won't be going out next weekend, so you'll have some time to think about your situation. We'll talk Monday evening, and you can tell me what you think you can handle. Then we'll decide what to do."

"Sandy, your grades took an obvious nose dive this quarter. The teachers' comments indicate that your main problem is incomplete homework assignments. We will reserve the hour between 7 and 8 each school night for your homework and studies, and we'll see how that system works. At the end of next quarter we'll evaluate this program for your studies."

Each of these approaches used logical consequences that made sense in relation to the teenager's behavior. The changes instituted by the parent resulted from *hearing* what his or her young person's behavior was saying and then responding directly to that message.

Remember to discipline with concern rather than anger. Use your discipline as an opportunity to teach and train as well as a way to control. Dependent teenagers need your assistance. One way you can help your young people develop confidence is by disciplining with care and instruction on how to improve. In this way your teenagers can learn valuable lessons about personal responsibility.

6. Communicate acceptance to your dependent teenagers and let them know that you love them just the way they are. Young people who continually underrate themselves benefit greatly from consistent messages that others value them. They need continual assurance that you are delighted to have them in your family. Belonging is a central human need, and these teenagers find little within themselves to assure them that they belong. They passively involve themselves in family activities and pleasantly go along with what others want or suggest. But they never initiate anything on their own nor do they invest much of themselves in what is happening. Therefore, they gain little in return. With so little involvement or investment of their time or feelings, they receive little assurance that members of their family appreciate their value.

Take the initiative to involve your dependent young people in your family's interactions. Invite them to help you with your projects and chores. Suggest doing something together just to have fun. Ask to join them in their room, and chat about the day you both had. Your willingness to initiate activities and your consistent approaches for contact will help your young people believe they really *are* important to you.

You can also help your dependent teenagers by pointing out any of their personal characteristics that you especially enjoy. These young people need to know that you appreciate them, and they benefit even more from knowing specifically *what* you like about them.

"Lamont, your neat sense of humor and quick wit keep our home an interesting and fun place to be. We sure enjoy having you around."

"This place just wouldn't be the same without your quiet way of helping and loving. I think you bring out the best in all of us, Paula."

Make sure you specify *real* characteristics. Don't be phony. Help them identify their best personal traits, and then encourage them to develop them further.

Dependent teenagers need to know that you enjoy and value them for who they are. Your actions and words to reassure these young people of their valued place within the family can do much to help meet this need.

7. *Help your dependent young people develop their individual differences.* Dependent teenagers don't value their individuality. They devalue themselves to the point they must rely on another's strength for their *own* personal significance. They see their individuality more as a threat to their "okayness" than an asset they can nurture and develop. Often these adolescents are unaware of their unique qualities. When you comment on specific personal characteristics you admire, they may be surprised. They honestly believe there is nothing intrinsically worthwhile or noteworthy about them.

After helping them identify what differentiates them from others, encourage them to feel positive about those differences. Your consistent expressions of appreciation and enjoyment will help them begin to value their individuality.

Support your dependent teenagers' attempts to express their unique qualities. Reinforce their forms of self-expression and inventiveness, especially in areas of lesser importance like dress, hair styles and music. Tolerate your teenagers' less offensive forms of self-expression as a part of their process of developing a healthy adolescent identity. As teenagers grow into mid- and late adolescence, the more extreme expressions of their individuality begin to subside. Console yourself with the fact that most young people gradually return to the values, interests, beliefs and activities that are closely related to those of their parents.

Encourage your dependent teenagers to identify and develop their own areas of special interest and talent. Help them experiment. Let them try several musical instruments. Suggest they take classes in photography, mechanics, graphic arts or performing arts. Encourage their involvement in student government, science projects and various sports. Place your focus on their enjoyment rather than their expertise. Ask them what *they* like, and allow them to choose the things that stimulate *their* interests.

Dependent teenagers need to discover what makes them different from others. They need to realize that their unique qualities help make them special to you. Guide them to see how their individuality adds to the family unit. Help them see how their good characteristics contribute value to the family.

8. Refuse to believe your dependent adolescents are helpless. Many dependent young people have convinced themselves they are helpless. They honestly believe they do not possess the inner strengths necessary to be significant people. They recognize personal strength only through their identification and dependence on others.

Dependent teenagers desperately need your refusal to accept their helplessness. They need for you to believe in their inner strengths; and this is hard work. Each time you push and prod your dependent teenagers to take risks, you have to overcome their resistance. These adolescents will try to convince you to give up on them by failing. Be sensitive to your children's real limits, but patiently encourage them to try new tasks.

You *can* help your teenagers find and develop their inner strengths.

● Refuse to believe them when you hear, "I can't." Encourage them to understand the difference between "I can't" and "This is hard for me."

● When you hear them protest their helplessness, try responding with something like: "I know this is scary for you, and I know that you truly believe you can't do it. But I want you to know that I think you *can* succeed. It will be difficult, but I believe in your ability to accomplish this task."

● Be gentle and firm at the same time. While your gentleness communicates your compassion and warmth, your firmness will communicate your belief in their strengths. Your affirmation will also support the intensity with which you want them to try. Neither gentleness nor firmness can be as effective alone as when you combine these forms of support.

Help your teenagers realize that being afraid to try something is never a good reason not to attempt it. Your children can develop their inner courage by trying difficult tasks while they have your immediate support and encouragement.

9. Practice letting go of your dependent teenagers so they can develop greater trust in their own strengths and abilities. Adolescence is a developmental stage normally marked by a gradual movement toward independence. Dependent young people resist this normal development because they lack self-confidence. They try to maintain their dependency to avoid the anxiety that independence brings them.

As a parent of dependent young people, you may have difficulty letting go because these adolescents present a dependent front and do not appear ready to assume more responsibility or freedom. *Gradual letting go* is the underlying principle in helping dependent teenagers. While encouraging your children to handle more autonomy, you must maintain the amount and intensity of the love and affection you offer. These teenagers may feel rejected if their greater freedom includes less contact with you. Freely express your pride and happiness with their growth and increasing maturity. Your positive responses to their normal development will assure them that they need not equate their independence with rejection.

There are numerous ways to gradually increase your teenagers' freedoms and responsibilities.

● With each birthday extend the limits of your dependent adolescents' curfews. Reward their continuing responsible behavior with expanded opportunities and freedoms.

● As your adolescents gain driving skills and experience, gradually expand their freedom to drive more frequently and increase their opportunities to use the car in a wider variety of situations.

● With your children's progression through each grade level, decrease your amount of supervision for their academic performance. Remember, the grades they earn belong to them, not you. An important aspect of your adolescents' maturation process is increasing responsibility for their grades at school.

● Be less demanding and controlling about how your teenagers keep their rooms. As a vital part of their growing up, teenagers must become increasingly responsible for their immediate living environment. Though you may require some minimum standards because their rooms are still part of the family home, you must allow your young people to establish their personal standards. After all, these young people are growing toward adulthood.

Dependent teenagers can handle progressive movements toward increased freedom and responsibility far better than sudden increases or no freedom at all. Letting go should be a gradual process that both matches and encourages your adolescents' maturation.

10. Encourage! Encourage! Encourage! Encouraging your dependent teenagers has been stressed throughout this parenting section. Because these young people possess minimal self-confidence, they need your support and encouragement to meet the developmental challenges of adolescence.

Encourage them with your words. "We love having you as part of our family." "It's really gratifying for me to see you developing into such a wonderful young lady."

Encourage their growth by giving them increased responsibility within the family. Assign them meaningful chores, and include them in important decision-making as ways to reinforce their growth.

Maintain or even increase the amount of love, affection and attention you normally offer your dependent teenagers as they take steps toward independence. Remember to encourage their increased self-esteem by showing them your respect. Your encouraging responses to your teenagers must be honest and come from your heart. You express your good will, love and desire for your young people's success by your actions.

11. Consider the possibility of professional counseling for your dependent teenagers. There are both healthy and unhealthy forms of the dependent personality. Your dependent teenagers probably exhibit some of both. Your support, love and encouragement can do much to help them become healthier and more adaptive within their personality type. And you can guide them toward more independence through your positive parenting.

You may find, however, that your teenagers appear stuck within their personality development. Their dependency might become so rigid that these young people will refuse to take the risks required for growth toward their independence and maturity. When this rigidity exists, professional counseling can be helpful. Therapists that are specially trained in adolescent psychology can understand the special needs and fears of dependent teenagers. They not only help these young people, but they can also work with the rest of the family.

View the option of professional counseling not as a sign of your failure as a parent, but as an option you can choose to help your children. Pastors, priests, youth ministers, teachers and family physicians can often provide the names of competent psychologists and therapists who can offer the help needed.

Dependency during adolescence can have several

adaptive forms. The "follower," "admirer" and "imitator" can serve positive functions in our youth groups, classes and families. But we must continue to help these young people develop greater internal strengths and higher levels of self-esteem. The less healthy forms of dependent teen-agers, including the "helpless," "gullible" and "clinging vine" are in even greater need of our help. For these young people, dependency can become a permanent method to avoid the anxiety of social confrontation and leadership. With encouragement from caring adults and our refusal to believe in their inadequacy, dependent young people can develop self-reliance and learn to use it effectively.

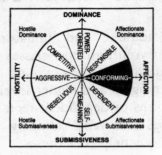

CHAPTER 10

The Conforming Personality

Conforming teenagers are usually delightful to have in youth groups, classrooms and families. They seldom create disturbances and are rarely the source of behavior problems. They actively seek to get along well with others and thrive in friendly, positive social environments. They are cooperative and try to support those around them. They care about other people and want to help whenever they can. These young people are generous, selfless and willing to sacrifice for another's benefit. They strive for peaceful resolutions to conflict and feel most secure when their social relationships exhibit positive feelings and a spirit of good will. These young people assume the most affectionate position of all personality types.

Conforming adolescents enjoy adherence to tradition. They like knowing the rules and social conventions so they can adapt comfortably by meeting expected standards. They feel most comfortable when they fulfill others' expectations of them.

The underlying purpose of conformity is to reduce the level of anxiety aroused by close contact with other people and stresses in life. This social orientation seeks to reduce anxious feelings by assuring adolescents they are accepted and liked. Through their behavior, conforming teenagers present the message: "I feel good about myself and most comfortable when I know I am meeting your expectations of me. When I please you, I assure myself that I can secure your acceptance and know that you like me."

The potential difficulty conforming adolescents encounter is sacrificing too much of themselves in an attempt to gain others' acceptance. If they reach the extremes of willingness to be whatever another person wants them to be, they lose sight of their own identity. This is extremely dangerous during adolescence when developing one's personal identity is the main task of psychological development. Some teenagers so fear confrontation, disagreement and rejection they willingly sacrifice their own likes, preferences, opinions, thoughts and feelings for acceptance. When this social action continues for too long, teenagers may experience identity panic and role diffusion. Feelings of anxiety and fear may overwhelm them when they realize they have no central identity, but are playing out a collection of roles with different people in different situations.

Conforming young people tend to be very optimistic. They need a positive outlook on life to feel okay. This dynamic forces these teenagers to be enthusiastic and fun. However, their need for optimism may sometimes blind them to the real problems and negatives with which they should be struggling. They would rather avoid and deny unpleasant realities rather than confront and resolve them.

"Time is a great healer."

"I'll be okay. I just won't let it upset me."

"If I just let things go, they always turn out all right."

These are just a few of their rationalizations for avoiding conflict or negative realities.

Another potential problem for conforming adolescents is rigidity in their personality structure. When they cling too tightly to conformity and see everything as positive, they lose their ability to be different. They forfeit the opportunity to stand up for what *they* think is right. They also sacrifice their chance to be original or creative. Their personalities become bland, their thoughts are impoverished, and they develop into boring individuals who have little originality, no uniqueness and few inherently interesting qualities.

■ Development of the *Conforming Personality*

Adolescence is a stage of development known for its conformity. Teenagers conform rigidly to peer group dress and hair styles. They adopt strict standards for their music, interests and activities. Conformity is one of the most powerful forces shaping their behavior.

Yet, for healthy balanced development to continue, teenagers must also have the ability to be different. They must be assertive enough to risk conflict and rejection as they develop their own individuality. When they characteristically bend to most pressures to conform, they are probably best described by the contents of this chapter. To more fully understand conforming personalities, we need to understand what early life experiences have directed their development. We will examine forces which have reinforced these conforming tendencies as well-established patterns of response.

First, some parents value conformity, avoidance of conflict and optimism as a preferred life pattern. They live out these values in their own relationships and teach them to their children. Parental modeling is an especially powerful teaching tool because of the numerous opportunities parents have to reinforce their behavior. Parents may avoid conflict with unruly neighbors, decline returning defective store items they have purchased or remain unrealistically optimistic when losing a job even though no new employment appears imminent. These parents may also tell their children to ignore the neighbor boy's selfishness, to always "turn the other cheek" if attacked on the playground and never to get discouraged.

Second, households run by a tight schedule and a regulated routine can influence children to order their lives accordingly. Young people who grow up in homes like these learn to value order, routine and structure. They learn to be efficient and not get sidetracked by impulses. They maintain good behavioral control and can delay personal gratification for the good of the group or future benefit. As these children express their learned behaviors, their parents reinforce these values of order and routine.

"You certainly are developing good self-control."

"I really like the way you're able to avoid getting into fights with the children across the street."

"You showed a lot of maturity by saying 'no' even though you really wanted to go with your friends."

Third, children are often heavily pressured to conform to the power of older brothers and sisters. Sometimes that pressure is subtle and loving.

"Bill, let's help Mom with the dishes. She's really been working hard. It's the least we can do."

"I think that's really selfish not to let your cousin play with your doll. Next time you should be more generous."

At other times the pressure to conform to an older sibling's wishes can be overt and difficult to defend against.

"If you tell Mom and Dad, I'll beat you up."

"I'm going to make sure every kid at school knows what a creep you are if you do that."

Some younger children learn their lesson too well. They learn life is much safer if they only do what pleases people who are older or more powerful than they. The pain of confrontation, disagreement, anger and rejection has proven too much for them. They have decided early in life to succumb through conformity to those around them.

Fourth, some younger children simply learn that a happy way to be part of the family is to adapt to what is already happening within the family environment. If the family is sports-minded, the children may join soccer, tennis or Little League baseball. If their family chooses the outdoor life, they may learn to enjoy hiking, camping, fishing or even three-wheeling. If born into a musical family, they may select their own instrument and begin lessons early during their elementary years. Excessively adaptive children often mature into conforming teenagers. They feel comfortable only when they alter their behavior, adjust their expectations or delay their wants in order to please others.

Fifth, severe family conflict or parental separation and divorce sometimes lie at the root of adolescent conforming behavior. Belonging can be threatened by rejection or a breakup within the family. Children desperately need to belong. When the stability of the family unit is challenged, their sense of belonging is severely shaken.

Certainly, severe parental fighting, physical violence, separation and divorce are major threats to children's security at home. But there are other threats as well. When a parent travels frequently or is out of town for long periods of time, young children experience inner disruption and feel anxious. The same feelings occur when an older sibling leaves for college or the military. Even more trauma occurs when an older brother or sister is forced to leave home because parents can no longer tolerate or control the son's or daughter's behavior. Many times severe or long-term fighting between parents and older siblings causes younger children to adopt a conforming, "no waves" policy of dealing with parents.

Sixth, inadequate nurturing is sometimes part of conforming teenagers' developmental history. Perhaps their parents were raised in relatively non-nurturing homes and could not teach their children how to feel or express physical and emotional affection. Maybe these significant adults have been too hurt or too frustrated to freely demonstrate softer, more vulnerable feelings. Whatever the cause, many children who grow up without adequate affection experience difficulty developing healthy identities during adolescence.

Some teenagers see conformity as a way of getting close to others. "If I can be like them, maybe they will like and accept me." For these young people conformity represents an attempt to gain intimacy and identity at the same time. Of course, results from this effort cannot be very positive or long-lasting. True intimacy can exist only when *both* people have fairly well-developed identities.

Seventh, excessive and possessive nurturing, which tends to retard children's emotional growth, can facilitate the development of a conforming personality pattern. This kind of parental attention is usually quite controlling and often passive-aggressive in its orientation. Overprotection is a common form of parental attention that communicates the parents' distrust in their children's abilities and skills.

"Mommy can't let you ride your bike. You might get hurt."

"I don't want you to play with those children. They're too mean."

Children learn inaccurately that they are inadequate and must stay under the protective care of their parents. As they grow older, they learn to fear separation from their parents and seek to remedy that situation by becoming whatever type of people the parents want them to be. The same dynamic is often transferred to other adults and peers whose opinions may dictate conforming behavior for these teenagers.

Eighth, some parents and other adults criticize children who express their individuality. They are threatened by young people who state their feelings with intensity. They misinterpret their determination for stubbornness. These adults forget children are not experienced in their social skills, that their assertiveness is sometimes simply over-stated because of their lack of experience. Reacting to

these children in a strong, punitive manner is inappropriate and may discourage further expressions of their
feelings and opinions. During therapy sessions some conforming teenagers can recall specific frightening episodes
of how adults harshly punished them for expressing their
individuality. Some vividly remember the exact incident
that prompted their decision to conform to others' expectations rather than risk further assertions of their own
identities.

Ninth, peer groups have a powerful force on their
members to conform to their specific standards. Peer pressure heavily influences clothing fashions and hair styles;
selection of friends, music and cars; choices of classes and
churches; gestures, facial expressions, behavior, language
and levels of academic achievement. Though virtually all
teenagers are impacted by peer pressure, some are far less
capable of resisting than others, even when such resistance
is desirable. Some adolescents find it intolerable to resist
their peers' expectations. Their anxieties about rejection,
being alone, and alienation prevent them from differing in
any significant way from members of their peer group.

Tenth, the teachings of some churches heavily influence and reinforce adolescents' conforming behavior.
Young people are taught to avoid conforming to the
world. "Do not conform any longer to the pattern of this
world, but be transformed by the renewing of your mind.
Then you will be able to test and approve what God's will
is—his good, pleasing and perfect will" (Romans 12:2).

The admonition not to conform to the world's standards is well-taken. However, problems arise when
teenagers are taught to conform to *everything* the minister
preaches, *everything* the youth leader says and *everything*
the Sunday school teacher teaches. The scripture says we
are to be "transformed by the renewing of (our) mind,"
not conformed. Conforming is much too shallow compared to being transformed and renewed. To conform is
something people do by an act of will. Being transformed
and renewed is a process generated by the Holy Spirit; it is

already happening. The person's choice in transformation is whether or not he or she will acknowledge the Spirit's influence within his or her life.

Youth ministers and volunteer youth leaders should be sensitive to the tendency for new Christians and new group members to overidentify with the group's standards and beliefs. Teenagers do this to ensure being approved of and accepted. New members in a group will often appear extremely "spiritual." Their religious language, regular Bible study, daily devotions, intense prayers, Bible memorization, and sharing of their faith may be motivated by their need for acceptance as much as by their love for Christ. The same religious activities may display deep spiritual growth or express one's need for acceptance; or in some cases these activities may indicate both.

Eleventh, teenagers use the conforming social orientation because it works. As it significantly reduces anxiety for young people, they use it again and again.

Now that we have a clearer picture of some of the root causes for the development of conforming as a defensive orientation, we are better prepared to work with these young people. Recognizing the forces that operated in the past to direct their psychological and interpersonal growth helps us understand the meaning of their conforming behavior in the present.

■ Healthy Forms of the *Conforming* Personality

The conforming personality tends to be a very sociable individual. These young people know how to make their defensive orientations work for them. They typically get along well with others. It's easy to spot healthy examples of this social orientation. You may have one in your family. And you probably have noticed several in your youth group or classroom.

The Counselor. Seventeen-year-old William is a good example of a healthy, productive form of the conforming adolescent personality. As a senior in high school, he volunteered for a peer counseling class at his church. Because of his apparent maturity, he was one of only five high school young people allowed to participate; the rest of the class were adults. As the 13-week training period progressed, he discovered a lot about himself and shared these discoveries with the rest of the class.

William was the oldest of four children. His dad was a career Navy man who had served sea duty during much of William's childhood and adolescence. As the oldest child with a continually absent father, William voluntarily took on many responsibilities to help his mother. Because he was especially kind and patient with his younger brother and sisters, his mother often requested his help with the other children while she shopped, cooked, cleaned house or ran errands. Usually he happily complied. He became adept at helping them solve their problems and creative in discovering ways to resolve their conflicts. Recognizing his efforts, the younger children usually responded well to his attempts to calm them after getting hurt or when feeling sick.

When William was 13, his youngest sister, just 9 years old, suddenly became ill with meningitis and died within two weeks. His father couldn't get home until a week after her death. During her illness and the week following her death, William was a major source of support for the rest of the family. Fortunately, there were several friends from their church who drew close during those difficult weeks. William accepted their support and compassion and was also able to give of himself to his mother, brother and sister.

Because he spent so much time helping his mother and assisting his younger siblings, William socialized very little with friends his own age. He felt uncomfortable at school because he was uncertain about how to act. Unstructured times, particularly lunch, were difficult for him. He wasn't quite so ill at ease within his church youth group, but he still felt somewhat awkward.

William's solution to his social uneasiness was to be as kind and helpful as he could. He believed if he were thoughtful, helpful and cheerful, others would always like and appreciate him. At home, at church and at school, William sought to please everyone. He was so comfortable and easy to be around that many of his friends sought him out when they needed to vent their frustrations. His attentive listening, genuine concern, patience and helpful suggestions gained him a reputation for being a good friend to talk with about problems.

William wasn't aware of the motivation that caused him to develop these constructive, helpful personality traits. He didn't realize his social orientation was helping him just as much as it was serving others. "Counseling" became his way of making social contact with his peers. This role gave him enough structure to feel secure with others. Being gentle and encouraging enabled him to make the only social contact that was comfortable for him. Because he was friendly and supportive, he could almost completely avoid harshness, conflict and confrontation with his peers and also with adults. His optimism was also a useful, appropriate response. Being optimistic when helping others enabled him to deny his own personal pain and avoid problems within his own life.

William styled himself as a peacemaker. He consciously sought to model his life after Matthew 5:9, "Blessed are the peacemakers, for they will be called sons of God."

The Greeter. When arriving to address an urban church youth group, the special guest speaker met 16-year-old Samantha at the door. She greeted him with a bright friendly smile, sparkling eyes and a bubbling: "Hi! How are you? We're so glad you can be with us tonight. I'm Samantha. I'm really looking forward to hearing what you have to say. Let me introduce you to our youth pastor." From that time on until 15 minutes into the program, Samantha stood at the door, greeting people as they arrived. She welcomed everyone and spent more time with first-time visitors and new members, making sure they were introduced to others within the group. She was marvelous! What a blessing to have someone like her to help people feel comfortable and welcome the minute they walk through the door!

After the meeting the speaker and youth pastor went out for dessert. During their conversation they talked about Samantha. Her youth pastor related the fact that Samantha always acted like she did that evening. At virtually every youth meeting, Bible study and social event, she happily assumed the position of greeter and welcomed people. She had never been appointed to that position nor had anyone ever asked her to do it. But her youth pastor remembered she had started welcoming people within a few short weeks after her graduation into the high school group.

When not fulfilling her self-appointed role as greeter, Samantha was rather quiet. She was always there and obviously interested in what was happening, but she was not actively involved. She was a great listener but volunteered few comments of her own in group discussions or even casual conversations among her friends. She felt most comfortable with others when she was in the greeter role. That is when she felt the personal freedom to interact and be spontaneous with others. Some of her personal history and family background helps us understand how Samantha developed her interpersonal orientation of conformity.

She was born the fourth of five children to her parents. Her mother and father were extremely different from one another. Dad was a free spirit, uninhibited and wanted to live for today. Mom was exceptionally conscientious, conservative and believed in living rationally and cautiously to guarantee the future as much as possible. Their marriage seemed destined to end, and it did.

When Samantha was 5 years old, her parents divorced. She and her four brothers and sisters lived with her mother. They seldom saw their dad after the divorce. He never played a major role in supporting the family, nor did he participate in caring for the children. Her mother dated other men only a few times but never remarried. She didn't trust men and felt more in control by being single.

Samantha never dealt with the psychological pain caused by her parents' divorce. She never talked with anyone about her feelings of loss and sadness. Her mom became very protective of the children, carefully monitoring their activities and their choices of friends. She also supervised their bedtimes, homework schedules and household chores, while making sure they ate well and wore proper clothing. Observing her mother, Samantha learned that life and relationships were quite fragile, that much care had to be taken to protect and preserve both.

Samantha also learned not to get too involved with friends. She found she could be liked and accepted when she gave people what made them feel good. When she smiled, others smiled back. When she talked in a friendly manner, most people reacted with friendly responses. She also learned that when these shallow relationships broke up, there was less pain than when deep friendships ended.

Becoming a greeter suited Samantha's needs. It allowed her to make contact with large numbers of her peers as well as adults, and she could use her limited social skills to their maximum benefit. By smiling and being friendly, she elicited the same responses from others. An additional benefit to her role as greeter was her lack of time to enter into deeper relationships, even though she did find opportunities to facilitate her friends' relationships with each other. She remained cheery and positive and was happy to have the sense of belonging and relationship she had.

We have met two teenagers who represent healthy, adaptive forms of the conforming personality. Both William and Samantha fulfill valuable social functions within their youth groups and circle of friends. Their style of interaction is useful and pleasant to those around them. It also helps them fulfill their own social needs. There are limitations to their social orientation, but there are limitations to *every* style of social interaction. Our hope for these teenagers is that as they continue to mature, their range of social skills will broaden and they will more fully integrate their own identities into their social relationships.

■ Unhealthy Forms of the Conforming Personality

Each of the personality orientations discussed in this book have both healthy and unhealthy forms. Teenagers are seldom completely described by only one type of personality. Most people have elements of two or more of the orientations in their personalities. They also usually possess both adaptive and maladaptive characteristics of their particular orientations.

We have seen two examples of healthy conforming teenagers. Conformity becomes unhealthy when young people feel they are incapable of confronting others or when development of their individual differences is severely hampered. Conforming then becomes a prison which confines teenagers to a narrow range of social behaviors, thought to be safe and acceptable. When this limiting occurs, young people's quality of life and level of fulfillment are seriously limited. Now we will meet two unhealthy forms of this defensive structure.

The Yes-Man. At age 18, Solomon went to see his guidance counselor at the community college he attended. At the beginning of his second year, he had no idea what career path he wanted to follow. As he entered the counselor's office, he was extremely nervous, not knowing what was expected of him or how to proceed. But as soon as the counselor initiated the conversation and began asking pertinent questions, Solomon relaxed and began to feel more secure. He answered the inquiries as accurately as he could and tried to assist his counselor's efforts to guide him. His personal history and family background helped the counselor understand why finding his career orientation was so difficult for him.

Solomon was the younger of two boys in his family.

Both parents were disciplinarians but operated differently. His father was firm and at times harsh in his demands. He posted household rules on the kitchen door and insisted both boys obey them. He handled all infractions quickly through spankings, restrictions or loss of privileges, in addition to intense and lengthy verbal tirades.

Solomon's mother also expected strict obedience to rules; however, her discipline and disapproval were more subtle. She demanded that her boys respect *all* authority, especially their parents. She based her life on the premise, "It is always best to follow rules, to fulfill what is expected and get along with others, no matter what the personal cost." When Solomon and his brother disobeyed, she disciplined primarily by withdrawing her affection. She became silent, looked disapprovingly at them, stiffened her neck, slowly shook her head from side to side and walked out of the room. The only avenue back into her favor was through apologies, admissions of guilt, promises it would never happen again and numerous requests for her forgiveness. She made it clear that any forgiveness she offered was neither deserved nor warranted by either of the boys.

Both parents' methods of punishment carried messages of rejection and separation. Both approaches to discipline suggested that misbehavior made the boys unacceptable and unlovable. The only way to be okay again was to subjugate themselves completely to the conditions and perceptions of their parents. They had to reject any sense of individuality, differences and dignity to again be acceptable for a friendly relationship with either parent.

In addition to this atmosphere of harsh discipline, it was even more difficult for Solomon to develop adaptive behavior because of the instability of his home life. His family moved approximately every two years because of his father's searches for employment. As a semiskilled laborer, his father had difficulty keeping a job for very long. He usually began to experience conflict with his supervisors within the first year and then was either fired or quit his job sometime during the next year. Solomon's childhood was a long series of changes in schools, neighborhoods and friends. He learned how to meet new people but never developed any long-term relationships.

In junior high school he experienced a series of heavy, painful rejections. One of his most traumatic experiences occurred near the end of seventh-grade shortly after his family had moved to yet another new city. Within a few weeks after starting school, he became infatuated with a girl in his humanities class. He knew he would have to make his move soon because school would be over in less than a month. So he took the risk and asked her to go to the movies with him. She smiled, and then her smile broke into laughter. To intensify the situation, she then told some eighth-grade boys who were friends of hers. And for the rest of the school year, they ridiculed and made fun of him. He imagined it was because of his accent and his different style of clothes. But this rejection and intimidation intensified his feeling painfully odd and out of place.

Solomon's guidance counselor realized this young man's problems went much deeper than his reported difficulty in deciding on a career. He exhibited an extreme fear of rejection. He was terribly hesitant to develop relationships, fearing he would lose them. He was extremely self-conscious and very sensitive to any differences he perceived between himself and others. He dared not state his opinions or attitudes very strongly and would never consider openly disagreeing with anyone. He felt most comfortable when he was in a structured social situation where there were rules to observe and clear expectations to follow. He readily did what teachers and others told him to do; and in group discussions he openly agreed with the points made and opinions given by others, rather than share his own.

Solomon could not tolerate his own negative feelings; they were just too threatening. Feelings of dislike for someone, disagreement with what was being said, anger about what was being done and unhappiness with part of his life produced terrible anxiety for him. He would quickly repress these impulses and consciously deny them. They threatened his tenuous sense of security in his relationships with people. Solomon could not tolerate any indication that he might be different from others. External indicators like dressing differently or internal signals like feeling angry at someone frightened him terribly. He forced himself into perpetual optimism and positive thinking to guard against the threat of any negative thoughts or feelings.

The Chameleon. This is probably the least healthy form of the conforming personality orientation. The "chameleon" is similar to both the "imitator," a form of the dependent orientation, and the "yes-man" we just met. The primary difference is the level of consciousness individuals have while defending themselves. Both the yes-man and the imitator are aware of what they are doing. The yes-man consciously decides to protect himself or herself from rejection. The imitator chooses to imitate those he or she respects in order to vicariously experience some of the same respect and admiration he or she has for others. Chameleons, however, operate their defenses almost completely without conscious awareness. Psychologists would consider these conforming teenagers to be more primitive or less psychologically sophisticated. The less conscious people are of their defenses, the more likely it is that intense pain or trauma occurred earlier in their lives.

Gina was 16 years old before she saw a professional therapist. She came first with her mother and half sister and then saw the therapist for several months alone. Later, she joined with her mother, half sister and stepfather in family counseling sessions. The events which led to her therapy encompassed most of her life; they are typical of the level of trauma that usually causes self-damaging and rigid personality orientations.

When Gina was just three years old, her parents divorced. Her father moved out of state, and she had few memories of him. During the next few years her mother had two live-in boyfriends. The first man offered Gina some parenting, but was primarily involved with her mother. After Gina's half sister was born two years later, the couple's relationship deteriorated, and he left. When the second boyfriend came to live with her family, he was also very involved with Gina's mother. However, after a short time his interest turned to Gina, too. Before her mother had broken off her relationship with this second boyfriend, he had sexually molested Gina three times. Frightened and confused, Gina did not know what to do about the genital fondling she had experienced. She never told anyone, including her mother, because the man had threatened to beat her if she told.

When Gina was 7 years old, her mother married again. Everything progressed quite well for about the first year, then life caved in on Gina. One evening while her mother was bowling on her league night, her stepfather came into her room and lay down beside her on her bed. He forced her to manually stimulate him while he did the same to her. He said nothing until he got up to leave her room, "You better not say anything that would hurt your mother, or you won't live through it!" Gina was frightened, hurt, angry and thoroughly confused. Memories of her earlier molestations overwhelmed her. It was happening again! And she didn't know how to stop it!

Her stepfather continued this sexual harassment, molesting her as many as three times a week. After several months he increased his demands to oral stimulation, and within a year he was having genital intercourse with her on a regular basis. She was terrified he would hurt her, and she was even more fearful that her mother might find out.

Gina was also angry that her mother had never discovered their "secret." "Wasn't it obvious? How could she live here and not know?" Gina lived with this confusion, plus a sense of dread, anger and guilt. She dreaded being alone with her stepfather. She avoided him whenever she could, but he would have sex with her in the house, in the car or wherever he could get her alone. She was angry at him, and she was also angry at her mother. She was caught in a position where she could not keep from betraying someone she loved. By keeping the secret, she had already betrayed her mother; and if she told, she would betray her stepfather.

One Saturday morning when she was 14, her stepfather told her this would be the last time he would have sex with her because he was afraid she might get pregnant. She felt a great sense of relief, but she also experienced rejection and betrayal. Within a few days he approached Gina's half sister. Several years before, she had figured out what was happening between Gina and their stepfather and had vowed never to let it happen to her. After the second time he made advances toward her, she told their mother who called the Child Protective Service. The police investigated, removed the stepfather from the home and initiated counseling for the entire family.

During the time Gina was in therapy, she became involved with a nearby church which had an active high school youth ministry. She felt safe there and attended regularly. As she participated more, the severity of her social impairment resulting from her trauma became increasingly apparent. When she was with a group of girl-friends, she became giggly, happy and fun, *just like they were*. When she was around a group of boys, she was boisterously loud and mischievous, *just like them*. And when she was with a group of adults she was thoughtful and pensive, *modeling the behavior she saw around her*. Unconsciously she assumed the characteristics of the people with whom she associated. When asked about her behavior, she had no idea she was acting this way.

The counselor clearly understood Gina's situation. The vast majority of Gina's elementary school and early adolescent years had been overshadowed by her ongoing trauma. The impact of her sexual abuse had affected virtually every area of her life. She felt embarrassed and ashamed around other girls, fearing they could sense what she had been doing. She also felt intensely uncomfortable and guarded around men and boys. Because of her past experiences, she mistook any interest from them to be sexual and realized that was the only way she knew how to relate with men and boys.

Gina had repressed, controlled and denied her emotions and impulses for so many years she often could not even recognize what was going on inside of her. In order to survive through those six years in her incestuous home life, she had psychologically anesthetized herself to her own thoughts and emotions. Now, she was unable to regain her lost self-awareness. Increasing her level of consciousness became one of the major goals in her therapy.

Gina had essentially lost herself. Since she had so little control over what was happening to her, she lost her own sense of individuality and had yet to begin developing her own identity. Her only way of relating was to automatically become like the people she was with at the time.

We have seen two examples of the conforming orientation at its worst. On the surface even unhealthy conformity can look okay. As parents, teachers, counselors and youth ministers, we need to look beneath surface behavior. We need to develop the capacity to understand young people's behavior so we can know what these teenagers are really saying about themselves. Then we are in a better position to respond to their needs.

■ Effects of Conforming Behavior on Other People

The purpose of conforming behavior is to avoid any confrontation and diminish interpersonal differences to facilitate comfortable social relationships. Therefore, we would expect the major effect of this personality orientation to be positive. And as long as a teenager doesn't become extreme or rigid in his or her use of conformity, this young person will have positive experiences with others.

Most teenagers and adults like to associate with conforming adolescents. This personality type makes others feel comfortable and relaxed. The conforming adolescent makes sure conversations are light and pleasant; he or she says only nice things or compliments others to make them feel good. This type of adolescent often expresses tender, warm and caring feelings to illustrate his or her support, care and respect for others. William the "counselor" offers us a good example of how this type of teenager can offer genuine and helpful care for others. A conforming adolescent knows that when you show appreciation, value and acceptance for others, they will respond cheerfully and positively. This personality type exemplifies the lesson that smiling at someone usually draws a smile in return.

Another common effect from being with a conforming teenager is feeling happy. Everything looks better and we feel more hopeful when we are around an individual who has positive perceptions and cheerful responses to life itself. However, if this optimism is too unrealistic, it can be irritating. Remember, for this type of young person, optimism is a defense against personal pain or discomfort. Sometimes he or she carries that positive outlook to an extreme and loses the ability to respond appropriately and meaningfully to worries and concerns. In working with one of these young people, we may experience irritation or aggravation and not feel heard as a response to his or her extreme optimism.

Another negative reaction we may have to this conformity is frustration. Since this personality orientation adapts so readily to the current rules, expectations and needs of others, it is difficult to know *who this young person really is*. The need for comfort and ease within relationships creates a major block to any deeper self-disclosure and development of intimacy with others. Risking our inner feelings is serious for each of us, but especially for a conforming teenager. Fear that others won't like or respect something he or she values is just too overwhelming.

After frustration we may experience boredom if we spend much time with a conforming adolescent. The inability to get past his or her rigid defenses leaves only limited opportunities for personal interaction. This young person's lack of creativity and spontaneity leaves us with a bland feeling. A conforming teenager doesn't offer much fun or excitement; he or she is *just nice*.

Power-oriented people sometimes take advantage of this teenager's conformity in much the same way they use the dependency of other teenagers. In an effort to get along and avoid conflict with others, a conforming adolescent will allow himself or herself to be used by these strong personality types.

■ Guidelines for Working With Conforming Adolescents

Our approach toward ministering, counseling and leading conforming adolescents will be somewhat different from the way we work with other teenagers. Their needs, fears and defenses are unique to their personality orientation. Since conformers are typically pleasant and non-threatening, their needs and personal struggles often go unnoticed. Their feelings of insecurity and fears about interpersonal conflict are often well-hidden beneath their cooperative, helpful, agreeable behavior. Though there are basics to helping almost anyone, we should consider some specific factors when working with these teenagers.

1. Seek to understand the family background and personal history of your conforming teenagers and how these experiences have affected their personality development. In order to clearly understand why teenagers behave the way they do, we must have a fairly thorough knowledge of their background. Get to know the parents of young conformers. How do they relate socially? Can they disagree with each other? By observing and talking with parents, brothers and sisters, you can gain valuable insights into the family atmosphere in which the conformer lives. Sometimes conforming young people have experienced intense pain from earlier social rejection. Their family may also struggle with unhealthy patterns for resolving conflict and personal differences. The more we understand about *why* young people do what they do, the better equipped we are to meet their inner needs.

2. Try to accurately understand what teenagers say about themselves through their behavior. Adolescents often express their thoughts, feelings, emotions and attitudes more through their actions than through words. In addition, teenagers often act before they speak. Observe what they do, when they do it and under what circumstances. Look for patterns of meaning.

Does their behavior seem to express anger, fear or confusion?

Do certain people seem to stimulate particular behaviors?

How regular or unpredictable are their behavior patterns?

As we more accurately understand the meanings and messages of teenagers' behavior, the more helpful we can be to them.

3. Reinforce the positive and constructive contributions conforming teenagers offer to relationships. Much of what these young people do in their social relationships has a positive impact on others; therefore, our approach to them must also be positive and reassuring. They feel very uncomfortable with probing questions, confrontation or evaluation. Our initial relationship needs to offer acceptance and reassurance to help these young people relax their defenses when they are with us. With this positive support, they can begin to believe in themselves. Nothing helps people believe in their ability to change more than feeling affirmed about their personal worth and value. Since so much of conforming adolescents' behaviors are directed toward maintaining positive, comfortable relationships, we need to compliment and reinforce those positive attributes.

4. Support conforming teenagers' efforts to develop their own identities and individualities. Conforming teenagers develop their own identities slowly. Their defensive orientation causes them to focus on external issues rather than their own internal world. How other people think, feel and act greatly concerns them. They take their cues from what others say and do rather than from what they experience or need within themselves. To the conforming adolescent external peace and security are more important than internal fulfillment.

Help them see and value differences between themselves and others. Emphasize the value of individuality. During Bible studies, stress the importance of standing up for what they believe, even when it is unpopular. Cite Noah, Joseph, Paul and other biblical examples of this kind of strength.

Then help these young people relate the concept of individuality to their everyday lives. How can they assert their individual differences in their families? school? church? their neighborhoods? Don't overspiritualize. Get them to talk about how scary it feels and discuss how they might accomplish it anyway. Support the concept that it's okay to be different. Help them see that individual differences are necessary. Work with them to feel more accepting and better about their own individuality.

5. Help conforming teenagers increase their awareness and expression of their own thoughts, feelings and opinions. While talking with these young people, continuously check out what *they* think about a situation. Get them to express *their* feelings about what has happened. Encourage them to verbalize *their* opinions about what is going on. Help them differentiate between what someone else thinks and *what they think*.

"That's really great that you have your own thoughts about this."

"You really have a creative way of looking at things."

"It's fun to talk with someone who doesn't always agree with me."

Help these teenagers feel more comfortable within themselves even when there is tension between themselves and others around them. Gradually encourage them to enjoy the feeling of knowing who they are more than the security of being like someone else. Probe, accept, reinforce and encourage these young people as they develop their own sense of identity.

6. *Gently question and confront these teenagers along with reassuring them of your acceptance.* Conforming young people avoid intimacy with others partially because they fear confrontation, questioning and evaluation. They are apprehensive that people will discover things about them they won't like. They are afraid of the alienation, separation and rejection that may occur because of who they are. Conforming defenses protect these young people from self-awareness as well as the rejection they fear.

These teenagers need to experience confrontation by people who will not reject them so that they can begin to trust themselves in relationship to others. Offer them some confrontive experiences in your own relationship with them. After you establish a firm basis of caring and acceptance, gently begin to express some of your own views which may differ from theirs. Then in a non-challenging way, ask them why they believe as they do. Without criticizing their ideas, suggest some different ways of looking at an issue. Be careful not to act in a derisive, sarcastic or demeaning way. In an objective manner, simply state an alternate position. Then, encourage them to discuss the various ideas presented without concluding which is "best." Try not to make this a win-lose issue. Focus on how interesting it is that two intelligent people can see things so differently, yet recognize the validity of some of the pros and cons for both points of view.

7. Encourage creativity within your conforming teenagers. Some hazards of this personality development include a lack of creativity and ingenuity. Creativity requires the courage to be different. Even more, it necessitates an acute awareness of one's thoughts and feelings. Conforming young people find their own feelings, attitudes and impulses threatening because they don't know if it's okay to have these internal experiences. These teenagers lack the ability to affirm their own okayness. They have to receive confirmation from external sources to feel good about themselves. And that requires letting others see what is inside. This necessity for openness creates great anxiety when young people are dependent upon another person's reaction for their own self-concept.

Always be sensitive to conforming teenagers' levels of readiness for creative expression. At first, they may not be aware of any creative thoughts. Patiently wait and encourage them to try to come up with their own ideas on how or what can be done. Later, they may have some great ideas and not feel strong enough to express them openly. Again, patiently wait for that open door and then coax them through it at the right moment. Creativity takes time, especially for conforming young people.

Creativity can occur within groups or when one is alone. Invite your conforming teenagers to participate in committee work. Let them help make posters and worship banners. Enlist their skill in writing skits. Let them get involved with program planning. Encourage their participation in assembling the group's yearly calendar of social events. There are numerous opportunities for creative expression. The classroom and youth group provide exceptional settings for both individual and group creativity.

8. Set up opportunities for conforming adolescents to experience their own and others' spontaneous expressions. Adolescent young people struggle with being spontaneous for the same reasons they have difficulty being creative. Spontaneity suggests a freedom from their defenses. It requires self-acceptance and secure feelings and necessitates a comfortable level of trust in one's self and others. Teenagers with strong conforming defenses do not trust themselves or other people. They view the world as potentially rejecting and hurtful, and they perceive themselves as not having much personal value to warrant their own secure place in this world.

These young people need our help in developing their spontaneity. Help them react spontaneously and impulsively in their interactions with you. First, make sure you have a solid foundation of trust and caring within your relationship. Then, in small ways and a friendly, caring atmosphere, surprise them. Be careful not to say or do things conforming young people might perceive as self-demeaning or devaluing. Give them spontaneous hugs that catch them off guard. Pop a serious question when they least expect it. Introduce them to someone without first warning them. These and other surprises express your admiration and value for their ability to accept the unexpected.

When your teenagers respond to these friendly surprises, respond immediately in an affirming manner. Show delight in their freshness. Let them know how much you enjoy them. Help them see they are even more fun, refreshing and enjoyable to be with when they relax. Your happy reactions will affirm their spontaneity and allow them to piggyback on your acceptance to develop greater self-acceptance.

9. Help them admit to and accept their occasional negative thoughts and feelings. All of us have times when we think negatively toward other people, events and even ourselves. We also experience anger, jealousy, envy, bitterness, resentment and hatred. At other times we may also feel depressed, sad, gloomy, hopeless and unhappy. These kinds of thoughts and feelings are common human experiences. Yet, conforming adolescents are afraid to admit, even to themselves, that they *have* these inner experiences. They are afraid that the presence of these emotions and attitudes makes them bad and unacceptable to others. Since they are overwhelmingly concerned about being seen as nice, kind and caring people, they feel they must hide these *unacceptable* aspects of their inner life.

When working with these young people, be somewhat transparent with your own negative thoughts and emotions. Let your upset or angry feelings surface occasionally. Tell these young people when you are feeling depressed or blue. Let them know you feel jealous or envious of certain people. Suggest to them that these and similar experiences are normal. Let them see you can still accept yourself even though you know that you have these *bad* thoughts and feelings at times.

After sharing your negative feelings, gently ask these teenagers what makes *them* feel angry, depressed or frustrated. Treat these experiences for what they are—normal human behavior. Help conforming young people not to fear and concern themselves with these aspects of their humanity. Help your Christian teenagers realize it is what they *do* with their feelings and attitudes, not merely experiencing them, that God judges as righteous or evil. When conforming teenagers gather the courage to express negative attitudes and feelings, be sure to communicate to them your continued acceptance and respect. They will need to know that seeing those negative aspects hasn't changed your opinion of them.

10. Encourage healthy adolescent rebellion within your conforming teenagers. Remember, rebellion is a healthy aspect of adolescent development. It plays a vital role in positive identity development when it is kept within constructive limits. Teenagers must distance themselves far enough away from their parents to see themselves as separate entities. They must develop the ability to differentiate between their parents' values, morals and principles and their own.

Because conforming adolescents fear being different from others, they often resist and repress any rebellious impulses. Since being different represents a threat of being rejected, rebellion seems to assure certain alienation and isolation from others to these insecure teenagers.

Encourage conforming teenagers to admit and express their rebellious feelings and impulses. Disagreeing, refusing to do what is requested of them, expressing negative feelings, and offering other alternatives are healthy forms of adolescent rebellion. Help these young people recognize these experiences as normal and healthy for them during this time of their life. When these young people finally do begin to release some of their repressed rebellious impulses, accept them and their rebellion with no hesitation. Help them explore ways to express these rebellious feelings and attitudes in positive, constructive ways.

We must also help parents understand the importance rebellion plays in their adolescents' development. As teachers, youth ministers and counselors, work with parents to help them accept this new behavior in their children.

11. Help conforming teenagers feel comfortable about receiving kindness and help from others. Conforming teenagers feel most socially secure when they *give* to others. The young people described in this chapter feel best when they obey rules and fulfill others' expectations. Being warm, expressing kindness, giving with generosity and extending themselves in numerous ways for another's benefit are examples of how conforming teenagers grasp interpersonal security and feel okay about themselves.

Certainly, we need to reinforce these young people for the good they do. Encourage them in their strong values and good efforts, but teach them the value and blessing of receiving, too. We can arrange situations for these adolescents to receive from others without reciprocating. We can help them become more comfortable in social situations when they are not the ones who do the giving. Arrange surprise birthday parties for them. Give them little gifts for no special reason. Surprise them with kindness through spontaneous gestures like a hug or a pat on the back. Help these teenagers learn the wonderful truth that they are loved and accepted, even when they aren't working to earn that reward.

12. Refer conforming teenagers to counseling when you think professional help is needed. Review the case histories in this chapter as well as the descriptions of these teenagers. Familiarize yourself with this defensive pattern so you can identify and respond more immediately to the needs of the less healthy, maladaptive conforming young people who may be in your class or youth group. When you recognize conforming adolescents, work with them, using some of these guidelines. Try several approaches, remembering the major dynamics of this personality pattern. Don't get discouraged if the first steps you take don't work. Just try something else. Your love and genuine interest are the most effective tools you have.

Because conforming teenagers' behavior patterns are so socially acceptable and valued, these young people are among the least likely to be referred for professional counseling. However, when their psychological defenses cause these teenagers' conforming orientations to damage their social relationships, professional counseling may help.

■ Guidelines for Parenting Conforming Adolescents

The teenagers described in this chapter make parenting seem pretty easy. Since they rarely rebel, if at all, their presence within the family doesn't strain relationships like other adolescent types do. When there is no turmoil surrounding your adolescent children, you may be tempted to "let well enough alone." Unfortunately, a lack of problems *can* indicate inappropriate and unhealthy adolescent growth or development. If you lack *any* tension or stress during your childrens' adolescent years, look for arrested personality development or passive behavior. An almost complete lack of turmoil or problems during adolescence may indicate the presence of conforming personalities.

After reading this chapter, you may conclude that your teenagers are primarily conforming personalities. The following guidelines should help both you and your adolescents work to meet their needs.

1. "Listen" carefully to the meanings your teenagers' behaviors are expressing. You know your adolescent children better than anyone. Their gestures, facial expressions, postures, behavior patterns and special words contain certain meanings. Their past histories and early-life experiences usually shape their behavior patterns in unique ways. Teenagers' current actions often express much of how they feel about themselves and others and how they perceive the world in which they live.

You dare not *assume* you understand your teenagers' motivations or meanings expressed through their behavior. Recognize the fact they can often surprise you. Even though you may formulate your own thoughts about what they are doing, be sure to *check* with them to find out if your perceptions are accurate. Sometimes *they* may be unsure of why they act the way they do. But you can still learn something from their responses.

"When you stay in your room instead of eating dinner with us, it usually means you're upset about something. Is something happening that we can talk about?"

"You certainly seem bubbly and cheerful this afternoon. Did something special happen at school today?"

Finding specific meaning for conforming teenagers'

behavior is particularly difficult because in a sense their behavior doesn't really belong to them. They have *imitated* or *borrowed* it from someone else, and therein lies its primary meaning for them. Seek to understand why your adolescents need to conform so strongly to others.

2. Continually reassure your conforming teenagers of the important place they have in your family. Teenagers need to know they are valued members of their families. Conforming adolescents are excessively sensitive about their acceptance and belonging. They need constant assurance that they are valued and have an important place in your home. Encourage them, and let them know they would be greatly missed if they weren't there.

Belonging is an important issue for most adolescents. Conforming teenagers are especially concerned about *fitting in*. They seek to be like others in their attempts to be accepted. They are afraid that any significant difference will lead to their rejection. You can help your teenagers actively gain value as a member of the family while they grow in their abilities to express their individuality.

Try to surprise your conforming adolescents with statements that indicate their value when they have done nothing to earn your admiration. "I really like having you as a part of our family." "You know, things wouldn't be the same around here without you." "Do you have any idea how much you'd be missed if you weren't here?" Mix in bear hugs, a few warm nudges and some friendly pokes and pats to help them believe you really *do* mean what you're saying. Periodically you might write your assurances in a note or on a special card and put it in their lunch sack or tape it on their mirror.

Another way of helping your conforming teenagers feel secure is by making sure they fulfill some significant roles in the household. Let them do certain chores that make a difference to the smooth functioning of the family. Cooking, laundry, ironing, dusting, vacuuming, shopping, doing the dishes, mowing the lawn and being responsible for regular errands are examples of meaningful tasks that teenagers can assume. Reinforce and affirm their efforts when they fulfill their responsibilities. In addition, let them see the disadvantages others in the family experience when they don't carry out their duties. Take care not to manipulate your children's behavior through guilt.

Recognize the importance of belonging for your conforming teenagers, and help them feel secure and important as a part of your family. With this kind of support you can help these young people fulfill some of their deepest needs.

3. Reinforce your teenagers' expressions of their individuality and uniqueness. Conforming young people experience great apprehension about being different from others. Even positive differences threaten them. Sometimes they will purposefully do poorly on an exam, intentionally come in second in a race or quietly decline an opportunity to tell a party joke rather than call attention to their special skills or talents. These teenagers take conformity to their peer group to the extreme. Not to conform lowers their defenses and seriously threatens the development of their identity.

As a parent, you are in a strategic position to help your conforming teenagers. Use your relationship to help them develop a personal identity. Since conforming teenagers struggle with being different, let them know how much you enjoy their unique qualities.

Think about those special characteristics, habits and modes of expression that make your adolescents one of a kind.

● What things about your children do you especially like?

● What is it about them that makes you enjoy having them around?

● When they are gone for a period of time, what do you miss about them?

Think about your teenagers' style of communication and decide what seems special about each one.

● Do they have a unique sense of humor?

● What about their ability with words? Can they choose just "the right word at the right time"?

● What about the uncanny way they express their thoughts and feelings with accuracy and insight?

Consider the physical appearance of your children. Is there something about them that you think is especially neat?

● What do you notice about their hair? their eyes?

● Which facial expression or gesture seems unique to them?

● What about the way they walk or their body movements?

Let them know you think they have something special about them that sets them apart from others. Conforming teenagers value their individuality, yet they are also frightened by it. Your parental encouragement and reinforcement of their uniqueness can strongly influence their identity formation.

4. Encourage your conforming young people to express their own thoughts and feelings. Conforming adolescents are afraid of being different from their peers because they might be rejected. Because of their apprehension, these young people often withhold their attitudes, opinions and feelings from others. By not volunteering how they really think and feel, they protect themselves from the rejection and isolation they fear. Their feelings of insecurity and self-doubt often build as these teenagers suppress their insights, perceptiveness and individual attitudes.

Your conforming teenagers need you to help them to identify and express their thoughts and opinions. You may provide the extra *push* your conforming young people need to get them over their hurdle of fear. Accept and reinforce their thinking. Provide opportunities for your children to express themselves with minimal risk. Establish regular family meetings to discuss vacation plans, chore assignments, weekend activities and so on. These meetings offer an excellent non-threatening environment for your teenagers to say what they really think. For more specific ideas on how to run successful family meetings, look at *Counseling Teenagers*.[1] Another good source is *How to Live With Your Teenager: A Survivor's Handbook for Parents*.[2]

Be willing to search for your young people's thoughts. Assure them you *want* to know what is going on inside their head and heart. Be tenacious, but not pushy. Develop the art of probing, but not so forcefully you cause your children to back away. Be persistent, and your patience may be rewarded. When there is something that is especially important to talk about, find a way to be alone with your teenager. Go for a ride in the car, or take a walk together. Go out for a hamburger with your son, or take your daughter shopping. Do something enjoyable that allows time for talking about thoughts and feelings.

Let your young people know you find their thoughts interesting. Don't be threatened by what they think. All of us experience thoughts and feelings that we would never act on. Teenagers need to think through the full range of options open to them. They need time to mentally work out the possible consequences of their various actions. The more comfortable they feel talking these things over with you, the more you can help them. Accept and encourage their openness instead of judging and correcting their ideas. "That's an approach I've never thought of. Tell me more about how that might work." This kind of support is more accepting than: "That idea has already been tried before. It never works."

Conforming teenagers hesitate to express their own thoughts, attitudes and opinions. Their fears of rejection cause them to suppress any individualistic thinking. As their parent, you can help them develop confidence as they explore their own abilities to think.

5. Encourage your teenagers' creativity. Creativity suggests doing something differently, a frightening and threatening concept to conforming adolescents. This personality type fights all creative freedom because of their fears of rejection if others see them as different. By encouraging their originality, you actually support your children's healthy identity development. The supportive family within the home is perhaps the safest environment for these young people to venture into their creativity. These young people need a non-judgmental atmosphere where they know they are safe from being laughed at or being thought of as stupid. This supportive atmosphere is vital for conforming teenagers' continued growth toward mature identity development.

Involve your teenagers in brainstorming sessions where all ideas are considered and enjoyed. Brainstorming demands two things: no one can make fun of any idea and no one can ridicule anyone who suggests an idea. Families can enjoy these sessions. Individuals can offer a wide range of silly as well as serious ideas, fun as well as serious considerations. Once your family has experienced the fun and value of these creative sessions, give your adolescents actual tasks around the house that require their creative thoughts and actions. Let them rearrange the storage area in the garage, the tool shed or their own closet. Let them design the art work for your family's Christmas letter or have them create a custom Christmas card. Perhaps they could construct a unique address marker for the front of your house. Maybe there is a small section of your yard where they could landscape and maintain the plants on their own. The possibilities are endless, limited only by your own creativity.

Conforming personalities resist their creativity because they fear being rejected because of their uniqueness. You can provide a safe environment within your home where creative thoughts and actions are stimulated and reinforced.

6. Encourage your teenagers to be spontaneous. Spontaneity is important to teenagers' psychological health. It helps them express their full range of emotions and enhances their capacities for creativity. It helps them communicate their real thoughts, attitudes and feelings to those around them. Personal spontaneous expressions help teenagers develop their self-concepts.

Conforming adolescents fear spontaneity the same way they fear creativity. For them, spontaneous actions present such dangers as being different, standing out in the crowd and getting attention. These teenagers need to control their words and actions and seal off their spontaneous reactions before others recognize them.

Conforming young people need your help to develop spontaneity. Home is often the safest place for them to try their varied forms of self-expression. You can supply encouragement, suggestions and, most importantly, acceptance of your teenagers as they experiment with spontaneous self-expression. You can protect your young people from ridicule and derision as they seek freedom from their overcontrolling defenses. The following ideas may stimulate your own strategies for helping your teenagers.

● Use material from television programs, movies, songs and books to elicit spontaneous expressions from your conforming teenagers. For example, when you are watching television together, ask your young people about their reactions to particular scenes—both dramatic and comedy. Make your request in an offhand, non-imposing manner.

"I can't believe he did that! Did you see that coming? . . . What did you think of that?"

"This *has* to be the funniest show on television! I love her sense of humor. What part did you like best?"

● Encourage your conforming teenagers to outwardly express their inner reactions to events around them. When you hear the loud screech of screaming brakes, you might ask, "What's the first thing you think of when you hear that?"

● In situations that typically elicit strong emotions,

366 ■ *WHY TEENAGERS ACT THE WAY THEY DO*

check with your teenagers to see how they're feeling. Let them see and hear how the same situation affects you. Help them understand that spontaneous emotional responses are normal and healthy. When they do risk sharing their own spontaneous feelings and thoughts, offer them assurance that they are okay. They need to know *right away* that you don't think less of them because of their spontaneous reactions.

Conforming adolescents lack the normal capacity for spontaneous reactions. They need and can benefit from your encouragement and reinforcement of their efforts to develop more spontaneous freedom.

7. *Help your teenagers know it's okay to have and express negative feelings.* Conforming young people are apprehensive about anger, depression, resentment and other negative feelings because they are afraid something is wrong with them. They fear expressing their negative feelings because they don't want others to think badly of them or reject them. We must help our teenagers learn how to deal with their negative emotions, even though their struggle will not be pleasant to experience. Allow them to express themselves at home. Help them discover appropriate ways to release their feelings and impulses.

When your conforming teenagers are upset with individuals in the family, encourage them to express their anger. Then talk with them about their feelings until the intensity is gone. This process helps conforming adolescents build confidence in their abilities to handle feelings successfully. It also helps them realize that intense and painful emotions are usually temporary.

You can help your adolescents by modeling healthy expressions of your own negative emotions. Let them hear you raise your voice. Allow them to see your tears. Your transparency will show them how it's done. It will also help them understand that horrible things don't have to happen just because we sometimes feel bad.

Conforming teenagers need encouragement, reassurance and examples to follow to feel more comfortable expressing their own negative emotions. You can make a big difference by helping your young people develop healthy ways of handling their emotions.

8. Encourage and support your conforming teenagers' attempts to rebel. This suggestion will make no sense to parents of most other adolescent types. But conforming teenagers find it difficult to actively push against anyone. In their minds, rebellion seems a dangerous and foolish thing to do. To rebel would bring the very thing they fear most—separation and alienation from others. They are also afraid that if they start rebelling, they may not be able to control their aggressive impulses.

Conforming young people need your support and reassurance. They need to know you will not reject or severely punish them when they do exhibit rebellious behavior. They need reassurance that you will help them control their rebellious impulses.

Try to recognize their subtle expressions of rebellion. These teenagers will be cautious and wary when they start rebelling. They will test the waters of your response before diving into full adolescent rebelliousness. Show acceptance and genuine concern for their well-being during their initial ventures into rebellion.

Allow and encourage your young people to express differences of opinion. They may find it easier to *talk* about their differences before they can *act* on them. Accept what they say as valid for them. This doesn't mean you have to agree with their position. If you did agree, there would be no differences and no rebellion. So let the difference in opinions remain. Discuss the issue with them, and then say something like, "Well, I guess we disagree about this. But then we're two different people, and we're not going to agree about everything, are we? Maybe we can just agree to disagree on some things, and go right on loving and accepting each other." This kind of statement helps them learn that differences between people are important. Your response also reaffirms your continued acceptance and models your willingness to listen to other opinions.

When you are the parent of conforming adolescents, encourage not only *verbal* differences, but allow your children to *act* differently as well. This position is tough. This is where your insecurity begins to show. This is where you have to trust your teenagers' abilities to handle more responsibility for their own lives. This means you're letting go while they grow up. Don't wait until they are adults; it's too late then.

When their rebellious expressions produce too much trauma, disrupt the household or stimulate disrespect toward others, you must put limits on what behavior is and is not acceptable to you. Clarify your standard that while rebellion is necessary and allowable, disrespect and violence are not. Be careful not to overreact. Overreaction has two possible responses: you may push your teenagers back into extreme conformity, or you may push them into more extreme forms of rebellion. Your task is to be encouraging and supportive while providing security through safety limits.

9. Help your conforming adolescents learn how to graciously receive good things. Most conforming teenagers feel uncomfortable receiving from other people. They enjoy giving because that act confirms their goodness, kindness and generosity, but receiving leaves them in a vulnerable position. When these young people are receiving from others, they aren't doing anything to affirm their personal value and "okayness." When they receive with no opportunity to give in return, they feel insecure. As a parent, you can help your conforming teenagers become good receivers as well as generous givers.

Arrange opportunities for your teenagers to receive from others. Birthday parties and other special events which focus on your teenager offer the easiest possibilities.

Observe how your adolescents respond at parties given in their honor. Embarrassed? Low key and cool? Excited? Talk over their responses at a later time. Encourage them to express how they felt about the experience. Gently let them know what you observed.

You may express your love and caring for your children by giving to them in many ways. Things like money, clothes, sporting equipment, school supplies, stereos and cars are typical gifts for special occasions. But don't forget your gifts of time and energy like preparing meals, running a taxi service, helping with homework, listening to problems and counseling on what to do with painful friendships. These are some of the most valuable gifts you can give your adolescents. Your continued giving will help them gradually feel more comfortable as a receiver.

You can also coach or teach your conforming teenagers how to receive gifts from people. The art of gracious receiving is a social skill that people must learn. No one is born with it. Let them know you realize that receiving can be an uncomfortable experience. Talk about their feelings with them. Tell them how you and some of your friends handle those kinds of situations. If they're willing, role play receiving situations with them. Be sure to talk about their experiences. Encourage them to share how they felt and discuss the new skills they learned.

Receiving from others makes conforming adolescents extremely uncomfortable. You can help your teenagers learning to handle these difficult experiences.

10. Consider the possible benefits of professional counseling for your conforming adolescents. The conforming personality orientation can disrupt teenagers' identity formations. In extreme cases these young people fail to establish a concept of themselves as different from other people. Some overidentify with another person as a way of avoiding the anxiety-producing work of establishing their own identity.

If your conforming teenagers request counseling, find a suitable person to work with them. If you believe professional help is advisable and your adolescents are resistive, try to find out why their resistance is there. Is it fear, mistrust, anger or self-rejection? When you uncover the reasons for their hesitation, assure your teenagers that you understand their feelings. Help them realize that part of your responsibility as a parent is to provide them with the help they need, sometimes even against their will. Help them see that you would provide medical and spiritual help in the same way you are trying to provide psychological or counseling help.

Professional counseling can help a teenagers struggle with establishing their own identity. When the conforming defense becomes too rigid or extreme, professionals may advise psychological help.

Teenagers who have developed conforming personalities can be delightfully healthy young people who relate well socially and build positive self-concepts. But they can also be relatively unhealthy individuals who have severely disturbed relationship patterns. Teachers, youth ministers, counselors and especially parents are in positions from which they can offer valuable help. After reading this chapter, you have become more familiar with conforming adolescents. In addition, you have learned some specific ways you can help these young people become increasingly adaptive in their personality orientation.

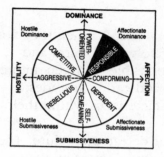

■ C H A P T E R 11

The Responsible Personality

*T*his personality type is as close to the social ideal as adolescents can get. These young people are typically successful, well-liked, respected and happy. They represent a blend of power-oriented and conforming personalities. In the middle of the affectionate-dominance quadrant, they possess capabilities for both leadership and friendship. They follow through with commitments, and they respect authority.

Youth ministers and teachers are happy to have a strong representation of responsible teenagers in their youth groups and classrooms. These young people are mature, they handle themselves comfortably in social situations and they impress others with their strength and self-confidence. These young people reflect good, logical reasoning and a sense of fair-mindedness. In addition, they maintain a capacity for compassion, sensitivity and a desire to help others.

Responsible teenagers appear to have few problems.

They feel most confident and comfortable when they are in control of their lives and operate within warm and pleasant social relationships. Responsible teenagers impress others with their inner strengths and caring attitudes, while reinforcing those same characteristics within their behavior.

Responsible young people fear defeat and failure. They strive to avoid rejection and isolation. Generally, they don't like confrontation, so they seek positive, happy relationships. They motivate themselves to be helpful, caring and supportive in their social contacts so others will respond and affirm them as good citizens. The behavior of responsible teenagers essentially says, "I feel comfortable when I am in control of my life, when I exercise strength and leadership and when I am warm and supportive in my social relationships." This personality type has many advantages. But when these teenagers uphold their responsibilities in a rigid manner or express them in extreme forms, negative results can occur.

■ *Development of the Responsible Personality*

Responsible teenagers often appear to be mature young people with no personal problems. Teachers and youth workers accept and welcome these adolescents because of the help they bring to the classroom or group. But we must remember that *all* social orientations attempt to diminish the anxiety of interacting with others and dealing with life's stresses. To understand why teenagers act the way they do, we need to know what has happened to them in their past. Knowledge of significant events and the people impacting them earlier in their lives gives us valuable insight into how we can best work with these young people. Several factors within these teenagers' personal histories contribute to the development of their responsible personalities.

First, most responsible teenagers are active and

energetic. This personality orientation requires a healthy body and at least an average level of metabolism. These young people usually involve themselves in many different activities. They are often leaders in clubs, athletics and the student governments within their schools. Frequently, they also participate in their churches and youth groups. Good academic performance, an active social life, involvement with family activities and perhaps a job keep these adolescents busy. A history of good health and a high energy level seem to be essential for this responsible personality type.

Second, we find that these children often emulate their parents. Children of responsible mothers and fathers learn their parents' style of relating with the world. Although adolescents rebel against their parents' values, some still exhibit the same underlying personality orientation. Instead of using their leadership and helping capabilities at school, these young people may attain their power and respect from their church, their social group or even another group of which their parents disapprove.

Modeling isn't the only way parents influence their children's movements toward certain personality orientations. They may actively "train" their children to be responsible types. Family schedules, regular times for eating and sleeping, homework supervision and required chores are all common in homes of responsible teenagers. Through these activities, parents subtly teach the basic value of responsibility.

Third, severe discipline and intense physical punishment sometimes impact young people's histories and personality development. Severe punishment will normally produce rebellious, self-demeaning or dependent teenagers. But when other psychological supports for adolescents are adequate, these young people can develop the traits their parents seek to instill within them.

Responsible teenagers seldom have physically abusive parents. Those situations are usually too damaging to produce the internal strength necessary to sustain this type of personality structure. But non-abusive, strong discipline can result in children's obedience to a value structure that supports responsibility.

Fourth, when parents fail to provide adequate care for their children, sometimes a responsible personality will develop. Most children express anger and depression through delinquency or destructive behavior, but sometimes young people find other sources of emotional support and respond by overcoming their negative feelings and experiences. When responsible personalities result from inadequate parental care, these teenagers have compensated or overcompensated for their early-life deficiencies. When this is true, unmet emotional needs plus repressed pain and anger accompany these teenagers' external presentations of strength, warmth and "having it all together." While responsible behavior in Teenager A may indicate development of a strong personality, identical behavior in Teenager B can signal overcompensation. This type of personal history is a powerful example of why we need to know something about the background of our teenagers.

Fifth, adequate nurturing is a common discovery in the backgrounds of responsible adolescents. Some degree of positive self-esteem is necessary to support the responsible social orientation. Strong parental interest and adequate nurturing are typical ingredients for developing this type of inner strength. Children learn about who they are and what attitudes to have toward themselves primarily from how their parents and other significant people treat them. This is why it is vital that parents respond lovingly and positively toward their children. Essentially, they are teaching their children how to think and feel about themselves. And by the time young people reach their adolescent years, these attitudes are well-established and difficult to alter.

Many responsible young people have grown up in families that reinforce responsible behavior. They have been taught to feel good about themselves when their attitudes and actions follow responsible patterns.

"You certainly do a fine job of keeping your room clean."

"I really appreciate your willingness to pitch in and help."

"I'm impressed with your grades! You're so conscientious."

These positive comments offer support for behavior common to responsible personality types.

Sixth, some of the young people described in this chapter begin adopting a responsible orientation early in life. For some, life presents situations that invite responsible behavior. Examples include young children who live in single-parent families. When single parents work outside the home, they have neither time nor energy left for normal household duties. They typically expect their children to help.

Older children often experience similar expectations from their parents. These teenagers may assume a variety of responsibilities like taking care of their younger brothers and sisters or assisting with numerous household chores. By completing their tasks, young people receive reinforcement for being responsible, contributing members of their families. In this way they also identify themselves as people who help others and take active leadership roles within groups.

Seventh, some responsible teenagers may have experienced pain and failure during their earlier childhood. They may have felt rejected by their friends and classmates. Others may have received poor grades or were chosen last when the class was divided into teams. Children who have felt put down, rejected or isolated by others often succumb to rebellious, self-demeaning or dependent personality adjustments. But *responsible* teenagers who experience these unfortunate childhood incidents have had enough inner strength and external support to compensate for their earlier pain. They have refused to give in to adversity. Their responsible orientation expresses their efforts to prevent a recurrence of those painful experiences. They believe that through self-reliance, personal strength, active involvement and warm friendships they can live happy and fulfilling lives. Their choice of a responsible life style represents an escape from pain and a commitment to positive, effective living.

Eighth, as preadolescent and early adolescent young people find that others rely or depend on them, their responsible social orientation is reinforced. They learn that others not only like and respect them, but seek to be with them.

Experiencing others' dependency enhances their good feelings about themselves. It reinforces their sense of personal value and helps them believe in themselves as people who have something valuable to offer. As long as others' dependency is not smothering, it can provide the basis for satisfying and meaningful relationships.

Responding to another's needs keeps responsible teenagers from thinking about their own weaknesses. When they are not confronted by their own pain, their internal feelings of failure or questions about their personal worth, they feel more comfortable. Focusing on the needs of another helps them avoid their own inner tension and reinforces their good feelings about their value to others. This reinforcement also increases the probability that the same types of responsible behavior will continue.

Ninth, a responsible social orientation sometimes develops during childhood or early adolescence when young people are exposed to others' pain or tragedies. Contact with people experiencing serious emotional or physical pain often draws intense feelings of compassion, sympathy and desires to help. A friend may suffer the death of a parent, brother or sister. A buddy's parents might divorce. A relative may develop and suffer through a terminal illness. Friends of the family might experience a severe financial reversal. There are also many less drastic but painful experiences that friends and relatives may confront. Breaking up with a girlfriend or a boyfriend, being cut from an athletic team, losing an important game, breaking an arm or a leg, having surgery, losing a school election or being rejected by an important peer group—all of these experiences are extremely painful for children and teenagers.

Responding to people in physical or emotional pain often brings feelings of satisfaction and fulfillment. To see the smile on another person's face or receive a hug of appreciation indicates the importance of our comfort and compassion. Helping other people causes young people to feel important and helps them recognize their value as they extend themselves to others. These types of experiences help to develop important parts of their self-concepts. "I am a compassionate and sympathetic person." "I am a generous and helping individual." Helping acts and concern prepare these young people to develop a responsible personality orientation as they move into their adolescent years.

Tenth, responsibility becomes a self-reinforcing pattern. Each of the eight personality patterns we are studying in this book are developed by different teenagers *because these behavior patterns work*. Each pattern reduces anxiety that comes from close contact with other people. Each orientation gives adolescents a way to view themselves. Each provides a pattern adolescents can rely on for interacting with others. The responsible orientation is usually heavily reinforced by adults and teenagers' peers. The responsible personality orientation works well in our culture because others value the behaviors and attitudes expressed by this personality type.

Identifying factors that contribute to the development of the responsible orientation helps us understand these young people. When we know where they have come from and what caused them to be the way they are, we are better prepared to help them meet their needs. Our knowledge and support can help these young people adapt more positively to this world.

■ *Healthy Forms of the Responsible* **Personality**

Some teenagers present healthy, positive functioning within their responsible adaptation. These young people have found ways to become valuable members of their group, class and family. They have adapted their personality type in ways that help them feel good about themselves. They have integrated the stronger values of responsibility into their identities. Even though not every aspect of their social and personal functioning is positive, the overwhelming picture is one of healthy adolescent development.

The Helper. Marvin is a 17-year-old junior in high school. He is an active member of his church youth group and is popular both at school and in church. During a recent consultation session with a group of youth workers, one of Marvin's adult youth sponsors talked about him as an example of the responsible type of teenager. She reported that he is actively involved in many kids' lives. Apparently, he is a good mechanic and freely gives his time and talents to repair his friends' cars. He's also excellent in math and regularly tutors others in his classes. Even when his teachers grade on a curve, he continues to help his classmates excel on their exams. He offers rides to and from school, youth meetings, Bible study, football and basketball games and other activities. And he provides interest-free loans to his friends.

In some ways Marvin reminds us of Walter the "servant," whom we met in Chapter 8 as a self-demeaning personality. Both find meaning in helping others. The primary difference is in the attitude each boy has toward himself. Walter believes the only thing he has to offer is his servitude. He has little belief in himself; and no matter how much he does for others, his self-esteem remains low and unsatisfactory. Marvin also helps his friends. Yet, there is a difference in the quality and attitude of Marvin's helping. Marvin *enjoys* everything he does. He is eager to help in almost any way he can. There is no hint of a self-demeaning attitude when he does something for others; in fact, he enjoys helping so much that he makes others around him feel better, too.

Marvin has been involved in his church youth group only since the summer before his sophomore year. Some of his friends, who were already members, invited him to join them on a 1,000 mile bike hike. During this experience he made a personal commitment to Christ and developed a close relationship with the youth minister. After the trip, Marvin began attending Sunday school and youth meetings. He quickly became a popular and valued member of the group.

Marvin grew up in a traditional family environment. His father worked on the assembly line in an automobile manufacturing plant. He worked shifts, so his schedule changed every six months. His mother stayed home, but contributed to the family's finances by taking in laundry, doing ironing and providing mending and seamstress services.

Marvin was the second of four children. Each child had regular chores and was expected to contribute to the family in whatever extra ways were needed. The values of working together, pooling their resources for the common good and helping each other were taught by example, direction and family structure. Marvin learned his lessons well. He embraced these values as important rules to live by. He also formed much of his interpersonal orientation and personality development around these integral principles evident in his family.

To Marvin, a good and worthwhile person meant being helpful and considerate toward others. It meant being responsible and following the rules. It meant expressing generosity and genuine concern. He felt good about himself when he acted according to these ideals. Pangs of guilt stabbed at him the few times he decided to place his own interests above those of his family and friends. Marvin's helping attitude and efforts won reinforcement from those around him; his social pattern became fixed. His style of interacting with others and adjusting to the world became central to the way he saw himself. He developed an adaptive, healthy form of the responsible personality type.

The Reliable. Wayne is a high school senior who lives with his mother and younger brother in a moderate-sized city. His mother is a clinical social worker, who works in private practice at a psychotherapy center. Wayne's father is an attorney who had problems with compulsive gambling and women. When Wayne's parents were together, their combined income was over $100,000 per year. Wayne's father squandered thousands of dollars each year on gambling, but they avoided financial ruin because Wayne's mother was a good money manager. Finally, after struggling through three of her husband's affairs, Wayne's mother filed for divorce. Following a 16-month settlement dispute, the court determined that she and the two boys could stay in the family home until the younger son graduated from high school. Wayne was 7 years old when his parents' divorce was final.

After listening to many parental arguments and discussions about the dangers of gambling, Wayne is well-aware of the risks of uncontrolled impulses. Even though he didn't understand the terms, from early childhood he was learning firsthand how compulsive behavior patterns and poor impulse control can destroy family life and personal happiness. From his mother he also learned the value of responsibility, consistency and reliability—strong traits that helped her family survive those difficult times. He observed her as she worked extremely hard, even increasing her caseload, to meet her family's increased financial demands.

As a young child, Wayne began to grasp the seriousness of their financial plight and learned to value his mother's wise and consistent managing of their family finances. He wanted to emulate her responsible attitude. He began looking for opportunities to help. During childhood and his early adolescence, he felt guilty when he shirked responsibilities, did a sloppy job or was lazy. He knew those actions let his mother down. He remembered how his father had repeatedly fallen short of her expectations, and he didn't want to be like his dad. He didn't want his mother to be angry with him the way she had been angry with his father. Unconsciously, Wayne was afraid that she would also leave him if he disappointed her too frequently. He resolved to do all he could to please his mother; he *had* to be a good person.

Wayne consistently completed his chores at home. He was equally reliable in being on time and turning in his completed school work. His teachers, as well as his mother, learned to depend on him. His word was totally trustworthy; he did what he said he would do. He wasn't as energetic or efficient as Marvin the "helper," whom we met earlier in this chapter, but he was a dependable, trustworthy and totally reliable 17-year-old.

The Overachiever. Sharon is one of the most outstanding members of her graduating class. She has been extremely active during all four years of high school. Although she has an IQ just slightly above average, she produces a straight-A average on almost every report card. She is active in her school's student government and every year has been elected to such positions as student council representative, class vice president, class president and student body president. Sharon's classmates recognize her as a great organizer and director of campus events and group projects.

She also participates in competitive team sports. She plays forward on the girls' basketball team, and she enjoys tennis. Her skillful serve and ability to rush the net have earned her the position of first singles player on the girls' tennis team. Volleyball and swimming round out her athletic activities.

Sharon's energetic lifestyle extends to her church youth group. Even though her primary focus is on school, she is also involved in leadership at church. She has taken piano lessons since she was in second grade and plays for her high school class on Sunday mornings. She is on the social committee and is one of two student representatives from the youth group to the church board. Sharon has also taken training to disciple new members on a one-to-one basis.

Where does Sharon get all of her energy? Why does she choose to be so actively involved? A look at her family gives us some clues. She is the elder of two children. Her 13-year-old brother is almost as busy as she. Their father is a corporate executive who has worked 10 to 16 hours a day six days a week until the past two years. As an executive vice president, he has finally delegated many of his responsibilities. He now works only10- to 12-hour-days, but has his weekends free. Sharon's mom does not work outside the home, but both parents are heavily involved socially, at church and in both of their children's schools. Her mother is also active in their precinct's political activities.

Sharon has inherited a high level of metabolism which contributes to her extreme activity. She has learned from her parents to look for and take advantage of new or exciting opportunities. Her parents have stressed the value of setting goals and achieving them. Her whole family seeks external symbols of success as indicators of their personal "okayness." Everyone in Sharon's family values having the *right* friends, being seen with the *right* people, wearing the *in* styles, driving the *right* cars and participating in just the *right* activities. Though Sharon enjoys her activities, she seems *driven* by a fear of missing out on something. Her need for personal affirmation makes it painful for her to let go or say no to any additional worthwhile activity.

The responsible personality orientation is a popular interpersonal style within our culture. Young people like Marvin, Wayne and Sharon can enjoy their adolescence and mature toward adulthood through constructive use of this social orientation. The "helper" finds value with other people by being useful to them. The "reliable" teenager develops strong self-control and consistent, responsible behavior. The "overachiever" strives in constructive ways to attain evidence of his or her personal worth and value. Each of these adolescents can experience personal success while reducing his or her level of fear and anxiety.

■ Unhealthy Forms of the Responsible Personality

Teenagers who have developed an unhealthy form of the responsible social orientation often go unnoticed by their youth ministers, teachers and even parents. On the surface their behavior may look not only normal but typical and responsible. The core of their problem is their *excessive need* to be normal and acceptable. Their behavior expresses an uncontrollable need to be liked and respected.

These young people restrict their actions to *only* those activities they perceive as acceptable to others. They do everything to please other people and lose contact with their own expectations and desires. They are no longer capable of establishing their own value system. Here are some examples which might help you identify and help these maladapted, responsible adolescents who function within your group, your classroom or your family.

The Little Adult. Fifteen-year-old Oliver and his parents met his counselor at their church while the man was presenting a series of meetings on parent-teen relationships. At the close of each of the six sessions, Oliver sought out the therapist and asked him several thoughtful questions about adolescence, families and communication. His parents joined their son's discussions with the counselor at the end of the last two teaching sessions. Within a few weeks after the series ended, Oliver's father called to initiate counseling for his son.

Oliver was well-liked by his teachers, youth minister and other adults who worked with him. He was also popular with his peers. He was a serious and contemplative individual, and at first appearance he seemed extremely mature. Even with limited contact, however, his counselor had discovered that Oliver's attempt to appear grown up was actually a "pseudo maturity." He could present a facade or a behavior that looked mature, but this was only a performance. There was no identity development within Oliver to give his behavior any real substance. All of his actions gave an *impression* of maturity without exhibiting maturity itself. Oliver had unconsciously designed his facade to present the very trait he lacked.

Oliver lacked the youthful spontaneity and exuberance normal for teenagers. He seldom joined others as they joked, teased and played around. He could handle group activities *only* if they were organized and structured, and then he demanded that rules be impeccably followed. He felt indignant when his sense of justice was violated, but he seldom released his anger where it could be seen by others. Oliver exercised tight control over *all* his emotions. He feared his anger might get out of control. He was also afraid others might reject him if they saw how he *really* was on the inside.

People seldom saw *any* emotional expression from Oliver. He always responded in logical, rational ways. He prided himself on his ability to think clearly. He felt superior because of his apparent exemption from strong, potentially disruptive attacks of extreme emotion so common among early and mid-adolescents.

Oliver's therapist quickly saw that Oliver was quite immature in his social development. Oliver represented a combination of the "helper" and "reliable" forms of the responsible personality type, but to an *extreme* degree. He felt free to interact with his peers *only* in safe, proper and almost formal ways. Otherwise, he was withdrawn and passive around other teenagers. He was especially immature in his relationships with girls. He could relate with them only within a caretaking or parenting role. According to Oliver's youth minister, girls respected him and liked him, although they thought he was a little "odd."

Several individual therapy sessions with Oliver plus

two family counseling sessions provided some family history and interpersonal dynamics which helped his therapist understand why Oliver developed the personality structure he did. Oliver's father had chosen a professional military career in the Army, and both of his parents had strong conservative religious commitments. Their home life and family expectations reflected the tight structure common to both disciplines. Oliver's parents fully expected him to meet their expectations and conform to their values, attitudes and perceptions.

Oliver's home was very loving. With no brothers or sisters, Oliver did not have to share his parents' ample affection and positive attention. They reinforced his conformity and good behavior with more attention and affection, but responded to his few episodes of misbehavior with temporary withdrawal of support, strong verbal reprimands and an occasional spanking.

The combined forces of Oliver's home environment strongly impacted his personality development. The tight structuring of the military and religious orientations, the heavy reinforcement of conformity, the threat of withdrawn affection and attention and the underlying assurance of his parents' love were key elements in Oliver's personality formation.

His family's frequent relocations necessitated by his father's military career also affected Oliver's social development. He was adept at forming new relationships, but had virtually no experience in developing long-term friendships. Therefore, his friendships and relationships were based on what he perceived others wanted, needed, or expected rather than expressing the person Oliver had developed into.

The Neurotic. Vanessa was a 17-year-old senior in high school when she entered professional counseling. Her youth minister had spent many hours counseling her, as had two women who served as volunteer youth leaders in her church. Finally, with the encouragement of the youth minister, Vanessa's parents took her to the Christian therapist he had recommended.

Several things about Vanessa struck her counselor as she entered her first counseling session. Vanessa's perfectionism was immediately apparent. Her skirt and blazer were freshly pressed and coordinated, her hair and nails were perfectly groomed and her makeup was flawless. Her tense body reflected the worry and apprehension she carried with her every day. Stress had etched lines of concern in her forehead and tightened every muscle in her body. She was extremely thin and taut. She was also excessively eager to please. She looked to her counselor for indications of what he wanted her to do. She desperately needed to know the rules for behavior. With no cues to guide her, she wasn't sure what was appropriate in this new environment. These initial impressions were merely surface indications of Vanessa's deep and enduring personality traits.

Vanessa was the youngest in a family with four children. Her parents, brothers and sister had been unusually eager to meet her needs and wants. While still very young, she had learned how to maneuver each family member into serving her. This ability to manipulate others had produced a strong egocentric orientation which worked throughout her elementary years both at school and church, in addition to her home.

As Vanessa moved into middle school, however, things began to change. No longer were her friends willing to treat her like a queen. They began to reject her demands for attention and service. By November of her sixth-grade year, she found herself isolated and rejected by her previously close school friends. And she experienced the same rejection in her church youth group.

Throughout the next few years, Vanessa floundered socially. She was confused, frustrated, lonely and depressed much of the time. During her sophomore year she finally began to change. Her biology teacher, Mrs. Bryson, noticed her struggling and asked Vanessa to help her with some special projects. While they worked

together in the lab, they talked. Mrs. Bryson listened carefully and gained Vanessa's trust. After a time this gentle
teacher helped Vanessa see how her self-centeredness had
turned others away. Vanessa gradually recognized she was
largely responsible for her friends' negative reactions. She
realized she would have to change the way she treated
others if she wanted them to accept her.

Vanessa consciously decided she would pattern her life
and relationships after her parents. Her parents had been
leaders in her church as long as she could remember. Her
father was a respected businessman in the community, and
her mother had served as a volunteer in several charitable
clubs and committees. Both were known, liked and well-
respected within their community. They seemed to have
their lives well-organized and under control. Everything
about them appeared stable.

As Vanessa recovered from her pain of rejection and
her exclusion from meaningful relationships, she adopted a
new social orientation. She decided she wanted to always
be appropriate and do what was expected. She didn't want
to disappoint anyone. She decided she would *always* be
kind, giving and helpful to other people.

Vanessa became intolerant of any weaknesses she perceived within herself. Personal weakness and inadequacy
represented major threats to her hopes for peer acceptance. She became extreme in her external presentation,
believing her worth came from the way others saw her.
Her excessive concern about her performance caused her
to lose sight of her inner being. She lost contact with her
inner feelings and motivations. She became excessively restricted, lacked creativity and began demanding perfection
from herself in everything.

Though she usually received straight A's on her report
cards, Vanessa dreaded every test. She was sure she
wouldn't pass. Following most of her examinations and
assignments, she was certain she had failed. She was
always surprised with each additional A.

Friendships provided another setting in which Vanessa

felt anxious and fearful. She was extremely nervous about what others thought of her. She felt she had to comply perfectly with all rules and expectations to be socially acceptable to her friends. Within relationships she could tolerate herself only as a helper or a giver and would never allow herself to receive from others.

Vanessa's level of anxiety had become destructive to her physical and emotional well-being. She experienced insomnia, loss of appetite, weight loss, an inability to concentrate, lack of interest in her daily activities and other symptoms of depression. She seemed agitated and nervous, talked compulsively and was unable to stop pacing and fidgeting. Her symptoms clearly resulted from her unhealthy intensity in being a responsible young person. Vanessa had become *neurotic* in her adolescent personality development; she was obsessed by her need to be responsible.

We have met two adolescent examples of unhealthy, maladapted responsible personalities. In both cases a potentially constructive and adaptive orientation to life became unhealthy because of the *intensity* of the teenagers' defenses. Oliver and Vanessa both lost themselves in the process of trying to be okay as they matured through their adolescent years. Their stories remind us that even extremely responsible young people can sometimes be unhealthy and maladaptive in their personality structure.

■ Effects of Responsible Behavior on Other People

The responsible personality type represents one of the most ideal and desirable lifestyles of our society. Our society (as well as the Christian community) generally prizes the values supporting this social orientation. Strength, self-reliance, self-control, reason, logic, helping others, obeying rules, respecting traditions and sympathetic concern for others are fundamental to this interpersonal orientation.

Because the underlying values of the responsible personality type are socially desirable, people typically respond positively to this type of teenager. Many young people like to form a dependent relationship with a responsible adolescent; they see the strength and leadership qualities and find security in relying on them. This dependency also fulfills the need of the responsible teenager by reinforcing his or her fantasies of personal strength, social power and helpfulness.

Cooperation is another common reaction others have to a responsible teenager. The affectionate-dominance tendency stimulates others to cooperate and align themselves with a benevolent leader. When young people can give their allegiance to a responsible-oriented adolescent without sacrificing their personal dignity or self-respect, they find it much easier to cooperate. With the responsible personality type, others do not fear losing their personal value.

A responsible teenager also receives respect, acclaim and popularity from adults and peers. This young person epitomizes the behavior and styles of interaction valued by most of our society. Adults are pleasantly surprised when they interact with one of these teenagers. They are impressed with the apparent maturity and competence. A responsible young person is often valued more highly by peers than by his or her personal evaluation. Peers assume the responsible teenager is brighter, functions at a higher level, and operates in a more competent social manner than they. Other teenagers like a responsible adolescent, consider him or her popular and seek that valuable friendship. The compassionate strength of the responsible adolescent draws respect and admiration from all with whom he or she associates.

Some teenagers, particularly competitive, aggressive and rebellious ones, often react with frustration and anger to a responsible teenager because they don't feel equal. Some of these reactions come from the personality struggles and defenses inside the other teenagers; however, some are responses to the power operations used by the responsible teenager. When this young person is *excessive* in his or her responsible behavior, he or she may receive negative reactions. When his or her actions become so extreme that they seem out of touch with reality, others may become bored or disinterested and are likely to withdraw.

■ Guidelines for Working With *Responsible* Adolescents

Responsible young people typically present themselves as competent, strong, consistent, compassionate and helpful. Adults often think they have little to offer these adolescents. We seldom see the needs of responsible teenagers within our classrooms, church youth groups, athletic teams and service clubs. These young people are usually self-sufficient. And when they do experience needs, they allow few people to know in order to preserve their self-sufficient image.

We must remember that the responsible personality type, like the others, is a defensive orientation. Responsible personalities are designed to reduce the internal tension and anxiety caused by the close interpersonal contacts in our daily lives. This orientation, especially when extreme or in an unhealthy form, can mask real and even desperate cries for help. Consider the following approaches when you strive to help responsible teenagers.

1. Learn how their personal and family history has influenced their personality development. There are always good reasons for the way people behave. Their actions may not be positive and constructive, and the reasons for their sinful, destructive actions do not excuse their behaviors. Nevertheless, identifying and understanding *how* people develop their particular behavior patterns is important if we are to meet our young people's needs.

The quality of family life and the parenting experienced during early childhood are particularly significant influences on adolescents' personality development. Social interaction patterns during elementary school also play a major role in developing teenagers' social orientations. Personal histories have a major impact not only on teenagers' personality types, but also on whether adolescents' behavior patterns are adaptive or maladaptive.

Invest in one-on-one time with the teenagers with whom you work. Get to know them deeper than surface level. Ask about their past experiences.

What do they remember about their early childhood?

How do they feel about their elementary-school experiences with their teachers and the other children?

What do they recall as their most life-influencing experiences?

Who are the people they see as having the most impact on their lives?

Understanding more about their past will help you meet their needs more effectively during their adolescence.

2. Recognize that most teenagers tell us more about themselves through their behavior than through their words. We know to *listen* carefully to our teenagers' behavior if we are to understand what they think and feel. Observe not only individual actions, but also significant patterns of behavior.

What reactions are typical of responsible teenagers in new social situations?

What is their usual response when receiving either praise or criticism?

How do they normally handle responsibility and leadership opportunities?

Carefully observe your responsible teenagers' behavior patterns. They may suggest the presence of strong self-confidence. You might also see indicators of learned patterns of responsibility and compassion. These patterns may express these teenagers' deep fears of their own weaknesses. Gently probe their awareness of their own behavior patterns. Try to help them gain insight into the meaning of their actions.

3. Reinforce the inner strengths evident in responsible young people. These teenagers usually possess adequate amounts of personal strength. They can make responsible decisions and carry them out. They often exercise their leadership abilities and can influence others.

While you help your responsible young people grow in other areas, remember to reinforce them in their areas of strength. Helping young people believe in themselves and increase their level of self-confidence is important in assisting their personal growth and development. Help them feel good about their positive accomplishments. Reinforce their good efforts and successes. Let them know you notice and are proud of their positive qualities. Build a strong, supportive relationship that will facilitate their efforts toward personal change and alteration in their unhealthy behavior patterns.

4. Reinforce the help, care and compassion these teenagers express toward others. Many responsible adolescents exhibit genuine concern for others. They truly care for their friends who suffer emotional or physical pain. They often extend themselves to help those in need. They may provide transportation for their friends who don't have cars or drivers licenses.

Selflessness is an important value for these young people. They need opportunities to practice this value so they can develop the compassionate part of their responsible personality. Place them in positions where they can lead in helping projects. They might set up a food drive or collect clothing for the poor. Let them assist you in your class or group and then experience the joy of stimulating a similar compassion within their friends.

As these young people feel valued by you and others

for their giving orientation, they will gain a higher level of self-esteem. Their self-value and personal appreciation will increase, yielding an improved willingness and ability to make *other* personality and behavioral changes.

5. Guard against these teenagers' tendencies to be overcontrolled. Responsible adolescents are extremely conscious of rules and other people's expectations. They exercise a tremendous amount of self-control to assure themselves they will stay within the bounds of expected and approved behavior. When they emphasize self-control excessively, adolescents risk focusing too intensely on their external behavior. They become rigid in their attempts to always be correct and appropriate. Their self-concepts depend upon how well their behaviors fit with their perceptions of what is expected of them. They lose sight of their value as a creation in the image of God. They either fail to develop or lose their internal thread of personal identity.

Our task is to help responsible young people relax the grip their personal controls have on their personalities. Without suggesting that self-control is undesirable, we need to help these adolescents realize how *too much* self-control can damage them. Let them know they are okay even when they make mistakes. Accept and encourage them when they make errors in judgment. Readily express your forgiveness when they commit a rare infraction against someone else in the group or class. Responsible teenagers are their harshest critics; they suffer from an overdeveloped conscience. Your acceptance and love which is not conditioned upon their perfect self-control can be used by God to free them to accept the perfect love of their creator.

6. Help these teenagers become less demanding of themselves. Remind them that perfection is not necessary for acceptance. Responsible teenagers often struggle with excessive personal demands for perfection.

This comes from their need to be sure they are okay. Responsible adolescents often demand personal perfection to allay their fears of being unacceptable. "If I'm perfect, then I am probably good enough."

We need to help these young people realize that their personal value does not rest in how close they come to some measure of perfection. Help them accept the human being God created them to be. Assist them in finding personal value not so much in their performance but in the quality of their being.

While it is fine to compliment these young people on their actions, they will benefit much more from our affirmations of *who* they are.

"I certainly enjoy having you in our youth group."

"You're a pleasure to have as a part of our class."

"You're one of the reasons I look forward to leading Bible study each week."

Each of these statements lets teenagers know they are valued and liked, not because of something they have done, but *because of who they are.*

7. Encourage responsible teenagers to enjoy spontaneity and play. Along with their excessive self-control and extreme need for perfection, many of these adolescents lose their freedom to relax and enjoy play. They control themselves too tightly to relax. They become too serious and adopt a "pseudo maturity" that robs them of their freedom to enjoy good times with friends. A volunteer youth leader recently said of a middle-schooler in his group: "He looks so pensive all the time. Sometimes I want to poke him in the ribs or do something to surprise him in order to get a reaction." These young people need to know they can be all right even when they aren't concentrating on being perfect and in control.

An alive sense of celebration and praise is vital to healthy worship, especially with responsible young people. Numerous church youth groups paralyze the atmosphere of their worship with excessive emphasis on what some call "spirituality and holiness." Design your meetings and Bible studies to include times of frivolity and joyous spontaneity as well as times for introspection and quiet contemplation about the nature of God. The most effective youth ministers know when to use their good sense of humor and when to help others laugh at themselves.

School classrooms should be primarily settings for academic learning. Scholastic endeavor is serious business; but an occasional spirit of levity, spontaneous laughter and the freedom to react to humorous situations provide a healthier learning environment. All young people need to develop the ability to laugh at themselves as a healthy part of their personality development.

8. Support responsible teenagers' freedoms to disagree and express rebellion in moderate ways. Within the responsible defensive orientation, many teenagers avoid risking adolescent rebellion as part of their identity formation. They fear being different. They are especially apprehensive about their own rebellion. Like conforming teenagers, they are afraid that their pushing away from parents or other authority figures will result in anger and rejection.

Unlike conforming personalities, responsible adolescents exert some individuality in the strength they express in leadership and helping. But they typically assert this strength only in ways approved by the family, church, school or organization of which they are a part. Rebellious thoughts, and even more, rebellious acts promote anxiety. Acting against approved behavioral regulations feels dangerous to these young people. They panic at the risk of losing others' acceptance and approval as the result of their behavior.

Reassure these teenagers they can be different and still be okay. Let them know that adolescent rebellion is an important aspect of identity formation. Instead of telling them what you expect, provide opportunities for them to determine courses of action on their own. Encourage them to let you know when they disagree with you. Help them realize that periodic disagreement with each other is completely normal within human relationships. Your acceptance and expressions of valuing them when they assert their independence will reassure these young people that developing their own identity will not threaten their relationship with you or others.

9. Help responsible young people recognize and accept their personal weaknesses. Responsible adolescents spend a lot of time and effort designing their interactions with others. They work hard to protect themselves from the anxiety associated with personal weakness and incompetence. Like power-oriented teenagers, they fear being exposed as incompetent or inadequate. They believe any personal inadequacy threatens their value and worth. Faults and weaknesses are obvious threats to their need to appear perfect.

Reassure these young people that they need not be perfect to be completely acceptable. They can receive nothing more convincing than your own love and acceptance. Entrust them with additional responsibilities immediately following any failure or mistake. As they experience your attention, trust and continued relationship, they will be better equipped to become more self-accepting.

10. Encourage these teenagers to feel okay about sometimes depending on others. Self-reliance and independence are so important to responsible adolescents that depending on another person threatens them. They prefer having others depend on them, for that type of relationship affirms their sense of personal worth and security. But depending on others raises questions about their own value and worth. To them, dependency symbolizes weakness and inadequacy. It suggests they have no value to others and, therefore, no basis for receiving others' esteem or respect.

Structure group experiences in a way your responsible

adolescents can depend upon others for leadership. Let them participate on committees in which they are not in charge. During one-on-one discussions, help them identify times when they depend on their friends. Maybe they get rides from someone, or perhaps they have borrowed a book or coat from a friend. Gently find out how they feel during and after these experiences of dependency. Suggest to them that depending on another person is perfectly okay. Help them realize that others need to feel valued and strong, too; other young people need to know they, too, have something to offer. Help your responsible teenagers recognize that part of their position in the body of Christ involves *needing* as well as helping others.

11. Help these young people learn to value their emotions as well as their thinking. Responsible teenagers tend to trust only the rational side of their being. They usually question emotions both within themselves and others and believe feelings should not be trusted. Churches often erroneously teach parishioners to distrust their emotions; basically, individuals are told that their *feelings* will lead them astray, but *thinking* will lead them in the right direction. This suggestion that emotions are not created by God or that emotions are somehow more corruptible than thinking is not founded in sound theological, philosophical or psychological thinking. This concept of a human dichotomy within each individual dangerously limits the basis by which we can find the truth. It also creates and holds the bias that our emotions are inferior and less important than our thinking.

Our task is to help adolescents enjoy and value their whole self which was created in God's image. Help these young people find fullness and integration in their personality development. Encourage them to learn from and more fully use every aspect of their created being. During personal discussions find out how your teenagers both *think* and *feel* about themselves, other people and relevant issues. Clarify the difference between thought and emotion. Help these young people discover that clear identification and expression of feelings can do much to draw people together. Help them see their emotions as friends rather than their enemies.

12. Support responsible teenagers' willingness to be appropriately confrontive and aggressive. Responsible teenagers are often capable of assertive behavior. But when they must be openly confrontive or aggressive, these young people experience great difficulty. Their fear of rejection creates strong anxiety when facing direct confrontation. They would much rather appease, skirt the issue or find a solution that pleases everyone. They cannot tolerate aggression within themselves because they fear others will reject them if they become aware of its existence. These teenagers also reject aggressive impulses because they are afraid of losing their self-control. They see loss of control over their aggression as incompetence of the most dangerous kind.

Allow these members of your group or class to express some aggressive impulses. Help them in their struggle to find positive ways to confront and disagree with both friends and authority figures. Accept and encourage them as they risk expressing their negative thoughts and feelings to you. They need to know that their reactions will not offend or repel you. They also need to know you can and will allow them to be different. They need assurances that you can accept their anger or disagreement.

13. Encourage greater self-awareness and deeper self-understanding. We have already discussed how this interpersonal orientation can cause responsible teenagers to focus on their external behavior and appearances to the point they lose sight of their inner feelings and experiences. Some develop this personality type as a defense against examining their own emotions and impulses. They feel anxious about their anger, insecurity, sexual desires, jealousies and emotional pain. These young people develop a responsible behavior to help them avoid conscious contacts with their internal conflicts and reduce their level of anxiety. They function with others as if their feelings and impulses do not exist.

Our task with these young people is to gently encourage them to gain deeper insight into themselves. During Bible studies, group discussions, youth meetings and individual sessions provide opportunities for them to discuss how they react emotionally to other people and various life situations. Encourage them to talk confidentially with you about their secret impulses and fantasies. As they realize you are not judgmental, condemning or repulsed by their sensitive personal disclosures, they will grow in their own self-awareness and learn to accept *themselves* as they are.

14. Help these teenagers focus more on their inner values than on their external performances. Help redirect responsible teenagers' attention and valuing onto their inner being. As they struggle through adolescence, they need to gain a more mature and correct perception of what makes them important people. Through Bible study, appropriate teaching and discussion groups, communicate to them the importance of finding sources of value within ourselves rather than only within our external behavior. During personal discussions try to focus on these young people's private perceptions, thoughts and feelings. Let them know what *you* think is most important by *where you place your emphasis.*

15. Be willing to refer your unhealthy responsible teenagers to a professional therapist. When responsible teenagers' behaviors become rigid and unconscious, they probably need specialized help. When their behavior consistently drives others away, professional counseling is advisable. A danger signal is evident any time young people seem unable to step outside their responsible personality orientation. When they find it impossible to depend on others, to allow others to be equal with them, to rebel or disagree, to enjoy spontaneous play or to express emotional reactions, these young people may be appropriate candidates for professional counseling.

When you identify teenagers in your class or group as responsible personality types, review these suggestions. Decide which ones are appropriate for you and your young people. Try several different approaches, and then use what works.

■ Guidelines for Parenting Responsible Adolescents

Parents are usually proud of their responsible adolescents. These young people often relate easily with most adults and are usually popular with their peers as well. Responsible-oriented young people present few behavioral problems; however, you can benefit from suggestions on how to meet your adolescents' special needs. After reviewing the contents of this chapter, the following suggestions will offer additional help as you parent your responsible teenagers.

1. Try to understand how your teenagers think and feel by carefully observing their behavior. Little children almost always express their feelings and attitudes *through their actions*. Adults usually *talk* about their opinions and emotions. Adolescents do some of both but will most likely express their *inner* thoughts and feelings through behavior. They may express their happiness and affection as well as their anger or uncertainty. When expressions of their internal feelings overcome their intended actions, we say these young people have a behavioral problem.

If you haven't already, now is a great time to observe your teenagers' behaviors. Use dialogue and discussion to check how accurately you understand what your teenagers are doing and why. Through verbal interaction you can provide opportunities for your young people to put their feelings into words.

"Each of us finds ways of relating to others that help us feel good about ourselves. I've noticed you really seem to enjoy helping some of your friends with their math homework. How do you feel when they call you for help?"

"Son, I think it's great you're so busy at school and church. It's neat to be popular and active. But are you finding any time just to slow down and think? Sometimes continuous activity protects us from getting to know ourselves better. What do you think?"

Share your observations of your teenagers' actions and prompt them to question their feelings of responsibility. Help your young people determine whether what they are doing is for themselves or because others expect it.

2. Reinforce your responsible teenagers' strengths. Teenagers, especially responsible-oriented young people, want to please their parents. They respond well to appreciation and compliments. The more you notice, accept and appreciate them, the more highly motivated they will be to make other positive changes. You're familiar with the phrase, "Nothing succeeds like success." Let your young people know that you see and value their personal strengths.

"Sue, I can't tell you how proud I am of how well you've handled your position as a student-body officer this year. It's put a lot of pressure on you, but you've managed extremely well! You've certainly developed a lot of personal strength during this experience."

"Mark, it must have been tough not to give in to the temptation to use drugs last night at the party. Sounds like almost everyone was involved. You showed a lot of character by saying no, and I'm proud of you."

In addition to sharing your appreciation for their strengths and accomplishments, emphasize your confidence in their abilities by letting your teenagers take leadership roles within the family. Encourage them to plan vacations, set up schedules for household chores and plan dinner menus. Let your responsible young people know that you value their abilities and strengths.

3. Encourage your responsible adolescents in their tendencies toward compassion and caring for others. Responsible teenagers feel good about themselves when they show love and kindness toward others. They feel comfortable when they give to others, even though they need to learn how to receive. Let your teenagers know how much you appreciate and value their compassion, care and help for other people. Reward their kind gestures and congratulate their willingness to extend themselves to their friends.

Do something special for your teenagers when they are kind to an unpopular child at school or church. Write them notes of appreciation to let them know you're aware of their special qualities. Take them out to dinner, or prepare their favorite meal at home.

Encourage your responsible teenagers to take leadership in a family helping project. Maybe they could be in charge of collecting items for the family's special package to send to missionaries. Perhaps they might research what it takes to support a needy child through an organized missions project or a nearby orphanage; then they could help the family implement this project. Ask your teenagers to manage the collection of canned food or toys for needy families in your church, community or neighborhood. Your responsible teenagers will benefit greatly from your encouragement as they lead your family in these caring projects.

4. Help your young people relax their self-control. While many parents are actively praying for their adolescents to *learn* self-control, many responsible-oriented teenagers hold themselves under controls that are *too* rigid. The extremity of their self-control expresses an underlying distrust in themselves. They are afraid that relaxing control over their feelings and actions will get them into trouble. Often they experience strong anxiety about their aggressive and sexual impulses which leads them to repress, deny and "overcontrol" their behavior. As a parent, you are in a key position to encourage them to relax their critical self-observation and tight self-controls.

Brenda presents a good example of an adolescent who takes self-control to an extreme. Brenda strictly adheres to a modest but well-balanced diet of fish, chicken, vegetables and fruit. In addition, she has designed an extremely tight schedule for herself. Each morning she spends half an hour reading her Bible and praying. Immediately after school she does her homework until it is completed. She practices her oboe for 45 minutes every evening, except on Thursday when she has her lesson. Every Saturday morning she cleans and straightens her room, does her laundry and then completes her ironing before she does anything with her friends.

Brenda's parents appreciate the self-control their daughter has developed, but they also recognize her unwillingness to make any exceptions to her routine. They have talked with her about their concerns and have encouraged her to allow some flexibility within her schedule. She has gradually gained confidence in her ability to continue being responsible while loosening her self-control.

You can provide the same kind of guidance to your own responsible teenagers. Help them question their rigid behaviors. Offer your acceptance and encouragement for a more flexible schedule. Your support will help these compulsive young people accept themselves without their extreme forms of self-control.

5. Help your responsible teenagers relax their demands for perfection. Many responsible adolescents become excessively perfectionistic in their personal demands of themselves. They feel highly threatened by any signs of their own imperfections, weaknesses or inadequacies. Their perfectionism may signal extreme insecurity and fear beneath their facade of competence and adequacy. Your parenting task is to help them become more comfortable and secure with themselves by assuring them that you unconditionally love and accept them. As they experience your care and acceptance, even when they make serious mistakes, they begin to learn that their inherent value does not come from their perfection.

When Mark began to demand straight A's of himself and berated himself for an occasional B, his parents decided not to differentiate between the two grades. They congratulated him in the same way for both A's and B's. They let him know they were proud of his ability to do well in school, but reassured him that perfect grades were not why they loved him.

Sheila's parents began to notice her drive for perfection when she insisted on always being the "perfect daughter." She became extremely rule-conscious. She chose only the *right* friends, participated in only *acceptable* activities, took *only* college-prep classes and wore *only* those clothes appropriate for her figure type. She also made sure her behavior was mature at all times.

Sheila's parents resisted her additional attempts to mold them into a perfect pattern. Even though they sometimes embarrassed Sheila, they chose not to always dress in the most appropriate style. They openly laughed at their own mistakes and tried to help Sheila relax and not take herself so seriously. In actions as well as words, her parents communicated that her perfection was not essential for their pride in her as their lovable, wonderful daughter.

Both Mark's and Sheila's parents acted to reduce their children's perfectionism. They displayed acceptable standards with their own behaviors and continued to maintain control of their lives according to their own rules. Both sets of parents modeled acceptable behaviors without the perfection upon which their adolescents insisted.

**6. *Encourage your responsible young people to
respond spontaneously.*** As a result of excessive self-
control and personal demands for perfection, these
teenagers lack the ability to express their feelings and
thoughts spontaneously. They become pensive, deliberate
and intense young people who need moments of spontaneous release and play. These adolescents tend to internalize and then repress their negative emotions. They
sometimes carry tremendous burdens of concern and
worry.

Part of your parenting task is to help your responsible
teenagers feel self-confident and secure enough to enjoy
spontaneity. Consider these various ways to help your
young people accomplish these goals:

● Remind yourself of the powerful impact of effective
modeling, and exhibit spontaneity in your own life.

● Tell a joke the moment you think of it, even if the
timing isn't quite appropriate.

● Laugh out loud sometime when it is socially correct
to be subdued.

● Decide to fly a kite, go roller-skating or play ball
with your young person instead of mowing the lawn, even
when the grass is threatening to swallow the flower bed.

● Illustrate in your own life what you want your
young people to express in their lives.

● Risk being lighthearted and tease them in a *gentle*
and *loving* manner. "You know, George, I'll bet going to
the game today wouldn't cause you to flunk out of
school." "Wait a minute, Barbara. What's the *worst* thing
that could happen if you did lose control and laugh during
prayer time?"

Help your teenagers see that periodic spontaneity will
not bring catastrophic results.

**7. *Allow and, if necessary, even encourage your
responsible adolescents to rebel in acceptable ways.***
Parents of competitive, aggressive and rebellious teenagers
will have difficulty understanding why parents would ever

encourage their adolescents to rebel. These parents **expend** tremendous energy and experience intense heartache when they try to control their excessively rebellious teenagers. But sometimes responsible young people are too insecure to actively rebel against anyone or anything. Rebelling against a parent or another authority figure feels too risky. The fear of being rejected and condemned is just too great.

With these young people your parenting task is to help them develop the courage to risk enough appropriate rebellious behavior to establish their own sense of identity. Resist telling your teenagers what *you* think about a situation until they have fully expressed *their own* thoughts and feelings. Don't make it easy for them to conform to your perceptions. Prod them to explore and discover their own feelings and attitudes.

"Josh, I'm really interested in what you have to say about this newspaper headline. You usually have some interesting ideas about this sort of thing."

"Sure, I'll tell you what I think. But *first* I want to hear what *you* think about it."

When your responsible adolescents finally express some signs of rebellion, reassure them it's okay to be different from you. Tell them you're eager to see how they will develop into their own adult personalities. Bring to their attention some of their perceptions and attitudes that are different from your own. Discuss these differences so they understand that being different does not threaten their sense of belonging and the parental relationship that is so important to your teenagers.

8. Accept your teenagers' weaknesses. Responsible teenagers typically feel threatened by their own weaknesses and inadequacies. They fear that the personal flaws they perceive within themselves will cause others to reject them. Their need for personal perfection prevents them from accepting areas of incompetence within themselves. This inability to accept their inadequacies seriously impedes their psychological and social development during adolescence.

You can dramatically influence your young people to accept themselves more fully. Through a parental attitude of acceptance, teenagers learn that self-rejection is unnecessary and undesirable. These young people can piggyback upon your accepting attitude while they develop their own self-acceptance.

You can help your responsible teenagers accept their own weaknesses. Remember to encourage and accept your young people when they fail. They may be cut from an athletic squad, lose a class election, receive a failing grade, be fired from a job or experience a good friend's rejection. These adolescents usually blame themselves for all the negative things that happen to them. Your love and emotional support at these sensitive times can soften your teenagers' tendencies to punish themselves.

Your teenagers will sometimes disappoint you and fail to live up to your expectations. Share with them how you feel, what you expected and what they can do to improve and correct the situation. Focus on your teenagers' behaviors, not on their character. You need to do this in a way that provides opportunities for reconciliation and new beginnings. "I want you to change your behavior" is a much better approach than, "You're really acting stupid." Always let your adolescents know that it is *your* feeling about their behavior you are having trouble accepting. Rejection limited only to their behaviors will continue to provide opportunities for reconciliation, new beginnings and growth for both you and your adolescents.

9. Encourage your teenagers to risk depending on someone else and still feel good about it.
Responsible young people usually feel guilty about their dependency needs. They feel vulnerable and insecure when they have to depend upon someone else. They unconsciously are saying, "I am secure only when I am strong, helping and independent." Dependency feels dan-

gerous to these young people. Reassure your teenagers that adolescence is a period of development when it is *normal* to fluctuate between independence and dependency. These young people need to know they have personal value even when they are dependent as well as when they are independent.

You can perform a valuable function when you help your teenagers accept their dependency needs. Provide opportunities at home for periodic discussions of each family member's strengths. Focus on the benefits the whole family gains from each member. Celebrate each person's special gifts and thank each one for his or her contribution. Discuss how your family represents the body of Christ with each member fulfilling his or her function. Stress your need for each other and emphasize the value of interdependence.

10. Help your responsible teenagers accept their emotions as well as their thoughts. Responsible young people need to learn that their emotions are as much a part of normal, healthy living as are their thoughts. These adolescents distrust their emotions and believe they must keep them under tight control. They feel insecure and vulnerable when they experience and express strong feelings. Fears and concerns multiply because of the heightened intensity and wider extremes of emotions prevalent during adolescence. When dealing with these strong emotional impulses, teenagers are threatened by their inability to maintain particular images. Responsible teenagers see any loss of control over their emotions as unacceptable.

You can help and reassure your young people. Express your own emotions in a constructive manner in front of your teenagers. Allow yourself to cry, laugh, raise your voice in anger, extend sympathetic compassion and admit to anxiety and fear. Let your teenagers see that strong emotions aren't always destructive. The way you handle your feelings can encourage your young people through the impact of your example.

Be open and accept your teenagers when they express their emotions. Don't expect perfect or appropriate behaviors. Allow them to make mistakes without strong disciplinary reactions. Remember these young people are just learning how to accomplish a difficult task that many adults have never mastered. They probably will shout too loud, feel sorry for themselves too long and become infatuated with partners who don't meet *your* expectations. Remember to respond to them with patience and understanding. Trust them to learn and mature through their experiences. Remain open and available when they need to talk or share their intense feelings and when they ask for your help or your opinion.

11. Allow and even encourage your responsible young people to experience and express some aggressiveness. Responsible-oriented teenagers have difficulty risking *any* confrontation through aggressive expressions, even in moderation. They hesitate because they fear rejection. They are also afraid of being seen as uncaring, selfish people. They willingly deny all their aggressive impulses to protect themselves from losing self-respect or experiencing condemnation from others. These adolescents need help to integrate their aggressive traits with the rest of their personality.

You can play an important role in giving these teenagers the help they need. Discuss openly the wide variety of aggressive models that movies and television present to us. Talk about how different types and intensities of aggression work in various settings. Point out the necessity of the more extreme types of aggression in hostile environments like war and violent crime. Discuss the appropriateness of milder forms of aggression like honesty and direct expressions of thoughts and feelings. Help your young people see that these milder forms of aggression contain no desire to hurt other people, but contribute to most social interactions, especially to the family. During these discussions be sure to ask what your teenagers think about these forms of aggression. Don't just lecture!

Allow your young people to make errors in judgment. Let them make mistakes without losing their dignity. First, listen to what they have to say. Talk about what happened. Then, sparingly and briefly, share your observations with them. Avoid making judgments. Assure them there will always be a next time to try again.

Encourage them to practice their aggression at home. Don't worry about these young people making the household a battleground. Remember, they are usually reticent to express even mild aggression, so let them practice their confrontive skills on you. It's better for them to make mistakes within their secure home environment so they can function with confidence in their other relationships.

12. Help increase the levels of your teenagers' self-awareness. The first step toward growth is to gain awareness. Confession cannot take place without consciousness about what one is confessing. Your teenagers cannot change their attitudes, perceptions, thoughts, feelings or behavior without first becoming aware of who they are and how they wish to be. The family should provide the most secure environment for this awareness to take place. Once teenagers feel safe and accepted as they are, subsequent movements toward change can occur.

You can facilitate your young people's increasing self-awareness. Encourage your teenagers to talk about themselves. Avoid the parental tendency to do most of the talking yourself. This is particularly important when your young people are quiet and withdrawn. Let them know you are genuinely interested in what *they* have to say. Don't hound and probe; rather, *invite* them to share their thoughts and feelings with you.

Then wait patiently as they slowly move into a position where they feel comfortable opening up to you. Remember, sharing, especially anything negative, is difficult for responsible teenagers because they often feel they are risking their dignity. Seek to accept and refuse to judge what they reveal. The amount of openness you experience from them will depend upon how well you receive what they choose to share.

Be more open about yourself. This will encourage openness in your teenagers. As your adolescents begin to know you as a real person with faults and weaknesses, you become less threatening to them. One early adolescent client recently told his therapist: "Since my dad started letting me see some of his faults, it's easier for me to let him see some of mine. I always thought he was almost perfect. Now I'm glad he's not. If he has problems, then maybe he won't be so critical of me!"

13. Encourage your teenagers to establish their own standards of acceptable behavior rather than accept those of their peers. Responsible young people are especially conscious of the current guidelines for appropriate behavior. As they mature through their adolescent years, they will need to develop inner strengths to determine what is right and wrong for them.

Effective parenting includes helping your teenagers become increasingly responsible for their own choices. During regular conversations with your adolescents, indicate an interest in knowing what they think.

"I'm curious as to what you think about that."

"You know how your teacher voted. Now how would *you* have voted if you were 18?"

"I think you know how we view having sex before marriage. But what's even more important is what *you* think about it."

Sometimes it is important for you to support your teenagers' strength to stand against their peers. Affirm them when they decide to live by their own conscience rather than that of their peers. Encourage them to talk about their temptations to conform. Invite them to share and recognize their fears of rejection. Remind them of your support and assure them of God's strengthening presence as they struggle with these difficult decisions.

14. Consider the possibility of professional counseling for your responsible teenagers. When responsible young people become deeply entrenched within this personality orientation, they sometimes benefit from a series of sessions with a professional therapist. Insecurity and fear may hide beneath their extreme forms of responsibility. Their deeper needs often go unmet because they function so successfully. As a parent, your task is to recognize and accept your children's needs. Do not be deceived by your need to raise perfect children. Nor should you deny your young people professional help because of apprehensions about your own parenting skills.

Responsible-oriented teenagers often resist counseling. They perceive a need for help as proof that their fears about inadequacy and incompetency are true. Their fears are not sufficient reason to delay or reject counseling. A competent therapist who works well with teenagers should help most young clients release those fears.

We have examined the responsible adolescent personality in some depth. We have surveyed ways of working with and parenting these young people. As you identify responsible teenagers within your class, your group or your family, review this chapter to prepare yourself to meet their needs. Remember to accept and build on their strengths. But prepare yourself to be supportive and trustworthy to help these young people struggle with their growth and maturity, qualities essential to their complete personality development.

■

A FINAL WORD

*T*he study of adolescent personality development is both fascinating and invaluable for effective youth ministry and parenting. If we are to sufficiently meet the needs of young people, we must accurately understand how they think, feel, and perceive themselves and the world around them. We must hear what they tell us, accurately *read* what their actions express about them and respond to the needs we discover. Helping you accomplish these tasks has been the goal of *Why Teenagers Act the Way They Do*.

The benefits of this book will be determined by what happens within its readers.

If you experience self-understanding about your own adolescent years;

If you increase your awareness of your own adolescent personality that still dwells within you;

If you gain an increased understanding of your teenage children;

If you attain a deeper understanding of the young people with whom you work and minister;

If you implement some of the practical suggestions offered within these pages;

If you are stimulated to creatively respond in new and healthful ways to your young people;

Then this book will have been worth writing and reading.

The Personality Types of Adolescent Christians: A Research Study

The eight personality types in *Why Teenagers Act the Way They Do* were studied extensively in the fields of research psychology. The Interpersonal Check List was the research instrument upon which these studies were based. (See sample Interpersonal Check List, Chart 6.) The author and the editors of Group Books decided to explore this research with adolescent Christians. The primary objective of the study was to discover the frequency of the eight personality types among these teenagers. Another objective was to learn whether a difference exists between the adolescents' "real self" personality (the way they actually see themselves) and their "ideal self" personality (the way

Chart 6
Interpersonal Check List
Side 1

Please fill in the "□" in front of each   Your name:_____
item which describes: Your Real Self.   Date: _____

□ 1 Able to give orders
□ 2 Appreciative
□ 3 Apologetic
□ 4 Able to take care of self
□ 5 Accepts advice readily
□ 6 Able to doubt others
□ 7 Affectionate and understanding
□ 8 Acts important
□ 9 Able to criticize self
□ 10 Admires and imitates others
□ 11 Agrees with everyone
□ 12 Always ashamed of self
□ 13 Very anxious to be approved of
□ 14 Always giving advice
□ 15 Bitter
□ 16 Bighearted and unselfish
□ 17 Boastful
□ 18 Businesslike
□ 19 Bossy
□ 20 Can be frank and honest
□ 21 Clinging vine
□ 22 Can be strict if necessary
□ 23 Considerate
□ 24 Cold and unfeeling
□ 25 Can complain if necessary

□ 26 Cooperative
□ 27 Complaining
□ 28 Can be indifferent to others
□ 29 Critical of others
□ 30 Can be obedient
□ 31 Cruel and unkind
□ 32 Dependent
□ 33 Dictatorial
□ 34 Distrusts everybody
□ 35 Dominating
□ 36 Easily embarrassed
□ 37 Eager to get along with others
□ 38 Easily fooled
□ 39 Egotistical and conceited
□ 40 Easily led
□ 41 Encouraging others
□ 42 Enjoys taking care of others
□ 43 Expects everyone to admire him
□ 44 Faithful follower
□ 45 Frequently disappointed
□ 46 Firm but just
□ 47 Fond of everyone
□ 48 Forceful
□ 49 Friendly
□ 50 Forgives anything

□ 51 Frequently angry
□ 52 Friendly all the time
□ 53 Generous to a fault
□ 54 Gives freely of self
□ 55 Good leader
□ 56 Grateful
□ 57 Hard-boiled when necessary
□ 58 Helpful
□ 59 Hard-hearted
□ 60 Hard to convince
□ 61 Hot-tempered
□ 62 Hard to impress
□ 63 Impatient with others' mistakes
□ 64 Independent
□ 65 Irritable
□ 66 Jealous
□ 67 Kind and reassuring
□ 68 Likes responsibility
□ 69 Lacks self-confidence
□ 70 Likes to compete with others
□ 71 Lets others make decisions
□ 72 Likes everybody
□ 73 Likes to be taken care of
□ 74 Loves everyone
□ 75 Makes a good impression

□ 76 Manages others
□ 77 Meek
□ 78 Modest
□ 79 Hardly ever talks back
□ 80 Often admired
□ 81 Obeys too willingly
□ 82 Often gloomy
□ 83 Outspoken
□ 84 Overprotective of others
□ 85 Often unfriendly
□ 86 Oversympathetic
□ 87 Often helped by others
□ 88 Passive and unaggressive
□ 89 Proud and self-satisfied
□ 90 Always pleasant and agreeable
□ 91 Resentful
□ 92 Respected by others
□ 93 Rebels against everything
□ 94 Resents being bossed
□ 95 Self-reliant and assertive
□ 96 Sarcastic
□ 97 Self-punishing
□ 98 Self-confident
□ 99 Self-seeking
□ 100 Shrewd and calculating

□ 101 Self-respecting
□ 102 Shy
□ 103 Sincere and devoted to friends
□ 104 Selfish
□ 105 Skeptical
□ 106 Sociable and neighborly
□ 107 Slow to forgive a wrong
□ 108 Somewhat snobbish
□ 109 Spineless
□ 110 Stern but fair
□ 111 Spoils people with kindness
□ 112 Straightforward and direct
□ 113 Stubborn
□ 114 Suspicious
□ 115 Too easily influenced by friends
□ 116 Thinks only of self
□ 117 Tender and soft-hearted
□ 118 Timid
□ 119 Too lenient with others
□ 120 Touchy and easily hurt
□ 121 Too willing to give to others
□ 122 Tries to be too successful
□ 123 Trusting and eager to please
□ 124 Tries to comfort everyone
□ 125 Usually gives in

□ 126 Very respectful to authority
□ 127 Wants everyone's love
□ 128 Well thought of
□ 129 Wants to be led
□ 130 Will confide in anyone
□ 131 Warm
□ 132 Wants everyone to like him/her
□ 133 Will believe anyone
□ 134 Well-behaved

AP = _____		HI = _____	
NO = _____		BC = _____	
FG = _____		JK = _____	
LM = _____		DE = _____	
Nic = _____		Ain = _____	
Dom = _____		Lov = _____	

Please fill in your: Age: _____ Sex: _____
City: _____ State: _____
Church Denomination: _____

Chart 6
Interpersonal Check List
Side 2

Please fill in the "☐" in front of each   Your name:_____
item which describes: Your Ideal Self.   Date: _____

☐ 1 Able to give orders
☐ 2 Appreciative
☐ 3 Apologetic
☐ 4 Able to take care of self
☐ 5 Accepts advice readily
☐ 6 Able to doubt others
☐ 7 Affectionate and understanding
☐ 8 Acts important
☐ 9 Able to criticize self
☐ 10 Admires and imitates others
☐ 11 Agrees with everyone
☐ 12 Always ashamed of self
☐ 13 Very anxious to be approved of
☐ 14 Always giving advice
☐ 15 Bitter
☐ 16 Bighearted and unselfish
☐ 17 Boastful
☐ 18 Businesslike
☐ 19 Bossy
☐ 20 Can be frank and honest
☐ 21 Clinging vine
☐ 22 Can be strict if necessary
☐ 23 Considerate
☐ 24 Cold and unfeeling
☐ 25 Can complain if necessary

☐ 26 Cooperative
☐ 27 Complaining
☐ 28 Can be indifferent to others
☐ 29 Critical of others
☐ 30 Can be obedient
☐ 31 Cruel and unkind
☐ 32 Dependent
☐ 33 Dictatorial
☐ 34 Distrusts everybody
☐ 35 Dominating
☐ 36 Easily embarrassed
☐ 37 Eager to get along with others
☐ 38 Easily fooled
☐ 39 Egotistical and conceited
☐ 40 Easily led
☐ 41 Encouraging others
☐ 42 Enjoys taking care of others
☐ 43 Expects everyone to admire him
☐ 44 Faithful follower
☐ 45 Frequently disappointed
☐ 46 Firm but just
☐ 47 Fond of everyone
☐ 48 Forceful
☐ 49 Friendly
☐ 50 Forgives anything

☐ 51 Frequently angry
☐ 52 Friendly all the time
☐ 53 Generous to a fault
☐ 54 Gives freely of self
☐ 55 Good leader
☐ 56 Grateful
☐ 57 Hard-boiled when necessary
☐ 58 Helpful
☐ 59 Hard-hearted
☐ 60 Hard to convince
☐ 61 Hot-tempered
☐ 62 Hard to impress
☐ 63 Impatient with others' mistakes
☐ 64 Independent
☐ 65 Irritable
☐ 66 Jealous
☐ 67 Kind and reassuring
☐ 68 Likes responsibility
☐ 69 Lacks self-confidence
☐ 70 Likes to compete with others
☐ 71 Lets others make decisions
☐ 72 Likes everybody
☐ 73 Likes to be taken care of
☐ 74 Loves everyone
☐ 75 Makes a good impression

☐ 76 Manages others
☐ 77 Meek
☐ 78 Modest
☐ 79 Hardly ever talks back
☐ 80 Often admired
☐ 81 Obeys too willingly
☐ 82 Often gloomy
☐ 83 Outspoken
☐ 84 Overprotective of others
☐ 85 Often unfriendly
☐ 86 Oversympathetic
☐ 87 Often helped by others
☐ 88 Passive and unaggressive
☐ 89 Proud and self-satisfied
☐ 90 Always pleasant and agreeable
☐ 91 Resentful
☐ 92 Respected by others
☐ 93 Rebels against everything
☐ 94 Resents being bossed
☐ 95 Self-reliant and assertive
☐ 96 Sarcastic
☐ 97 Self-punishing
☐ 98 Self-confident
☐ 99 Self-seeking
☐ 100 Shrewd and calculating

☐ 101 Self-respecting
☐ 102 Shy
☐ 103 Sincere and devoted to friends
☐ 104 Selfish
☐ 105 Skeptical
☐ 106 Sociable and neighborly
☐ 107 Slow to forgive a wrong
☐ 108 Somewhat snobbish
☐ 109 Spineless
☐ 110 Stern but fair
☐ 111 Spoils people with kindness
☐ 112 Straightforward and direct
☐ 113 Stubborn
☐ 114 Suspicious
☐ 115 Too easily influenced by friends
☐ 116 Thinks only of self
☐ 117 Tender and soft-hearted
☐ 118 Timid
☐ 119 Too lenient with others
☐ 120 Touchy and easily hurt
☐ 121 Too willing to give to others
☐ 122 Tries to be too successful
☐ 123 Trusting and eager to please
☐ 124 Tries to comfort everyone
☐ 125 Usually gives in

☐ 126 Very respectful to authority
☐ 127 Wants everyone's love
☐ 128 Well thought of
☐ 129 Wants to be led
☐ 130 Will confide in anyone
☐ 131 Warm
☐ 132 Wants everyone to like him/her
☐ 133 Will believe anyone
☐ 134 Well-behaved

AP = _____		HI = _____	
NO = _____		BC = _____	
FG = _____		JK = _____	
LM = _____		DE = _____	
Nic = _____		Ain = _____	
Dom = _____		Lov = _____	

Please fill in your: Age: _____ Sex: _____
City: _____ State: _____
Church Denomination: _____

they wish to be).

■ Research Sample and Method

During the summer of 1986 at GROUP Magazine's National Christian Youth Congress, the adolescent registrants were requested to participate in the research project by taking the Interpersonal Check List two times. The first time they took the test they were asked to check items that described their "real self." The second time they took the test they were asked to check items that described their "ideal self." They were also requested to provide demographic information: age, sex, state where they lived and their congregation's denomination. Their names were not requested in order to protect privacy. For this study's purposes, only the responses from 12-year-old through 19-year-old participants were accepted.

A total of 973 registrants turned in their testing materials. Some respondents failed to provide all or some of the demographic data. Some completed only the ideal or the real self rating. However, more than an adequate number of sufficiently completed answer sheets were acquired for valid statistical analysis of the data.

■ Research Results

The research results are shown in Chart 7. The results are listed from greatest to least frequency of personality types in the real self and ideal self ratings. In the real self rating, the numerals and percentages are based on 860 Christian adolescents. In the ideal self rating, the numerals and percentages are based on 853 Christian adolescents.

Let us now look at the findings regarding individual personality types according to the Interpersonal Check List Profile (Chart 8). This chart is further explained in the introduction to Part Two.

Power-Oriented. Characterized by dominance, strength and self-reliance.

Real self. A total of 170 (19.8%) of these young people saw themselves operating primarily from the power-oriented type. This was the second most frequently selected orientation, trailing behind the responsible type.

Ideal self. The power-oriented orientation was the second most frequently rated personality type for the ideal self rating. A total of 257 (30.1%) teenagers indicated they would like to have a power-oriented personality. This interpersonal style, then, is highly valued by Christian teenagers.

Responsible. Characterized by a blend of dominance and affection.

Real self. The teenagers in our study rated themselves as responsible personalities more often than any of the other types. A total of 235 (27.3%) teenagers placed themselves in this category. It is possible that these teenagers' real self rating may have been influenced by their thoughts about their ideal self.

Ideal self. The responsible personality was the overwhelming choice for these teenagers' ideal self. A total of

Chart 7
Personality Types Research Results

Real Self Rating				Ideal Self Rating			
Octant	Rank	No.	Percentage	Octant	Rank	No.	Percentage
Responsible	1	235	27.3	Responsible	1	486	57.0
Power-Oriented	2	170	19.8	Power-Oriented	2	257	30.1
Conforming	3	124	14.4	Competitive	3	51	6.0
Competitive	4	122	14.2	Conforming	4	23	2.7
Dependent	5	86	10.0	Aggressive	5	16	1.9
Aggressive	6	51	5.9	Self-Demeaning	6	9	1.0
Self-Demeaning	7	38	4.4	Dependent	7	7	0.8
Rebellious	8	34	4.0	Rebellious	8	4	0.5
TOTALS		860	100.0	TOTALS		853	100.0

486 (57.0%) desire the responsible orientation. It is interesting to note that 87.1% (743) either wish for the responsible or power-oriented type.

Conforming. Characterized heavily by affection, compliance and conformity.

Real self. In the research sample, 124 (14.4%) teenagers rated their real self with the conforming type. As the third most common personality type, conformity is apparently a more frequent mode of social adaptation of Christian teenagers.

Ideal self. The conforming personality was the fourth most common ideal self rating. In the sample, only 23 (2.7%) of the adolescents selected the conforming personality as their ideal. Social adaptation through conformity, affection and conflict avoidance is clearly less valued by Christian teenagers than interpersonal expressions of strength, independence, help and competition. Almost twice as many (51) of the adolescents who participated in our study preferred competition over conformity as their ideal interpersonal orientation.

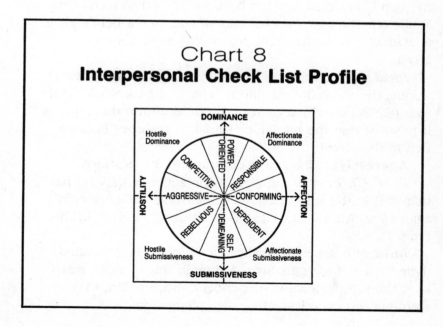

Chart 8
Interpersonal Check List Profile

Dependent. Characterized by a blend of submissiveness and affection.

Real self. Few adolescents in the study (86 or 10.0%) rated their real self as the dependent type.

Ideal self. An even smaller number of teenagers chose the dependent personality as their ideal self. With only seven (0.8%) young people choosing dependency as an ideal, it is clear most teenagers do not view this type as a good way to live one's life.

Self-Demeaning. Characterized by extreme submission.

Real self. The adolescents in this study infrequently described their personality as self-demeaning. Only 38 (4.4%) rated themselves in this self-humiliating orientation.

Ideal self. Only nine (1.0%) people in this sample chose this type as an ideal. It is clear that this submissive type is not valued by Christian young people.

Rebellious. Characterized by a blend of hostility and submissiveness.

Real self. In this research, the rebellious type was least frequently selected, chosen by only 34 (4.0%) teenagers. While rebellion is a normal part of adolescent behavior, it is evidently not a frequent personality type within this group.

Ideal self. As with the real self rating, teenagers least frequently chose the rebellious type as the ideal self. Only four (0.5%) of 853 adolescents scored within this type. Is it possible that the rebellious Christian teenager is more fiction than fact?

Aggressive. Characterized primarily by hostility.

Real self. A small number of the adolescents who participated in the study described their real self as primarily aggressive. A total of 51 (5.9%) placed themselves in this type.

Ideal self. An even smaller group of 16 (1.9%) rated their ideal self as aggressive. Although this number was low, the self-demeaning, dependent and rebellious types were chosen even less often than aggression.

Competitive. Characterized by a blend of dominance and hostility.

Real self. The competitive personality type was chosen fourth most frequently by Christian adolescents in the study. A total of 122 (14.2%) described their real self as primarily competitive. This orientation is apparently fairly common among Christian youth.

Ideal self. Of the sample, 51 (6.0%) rated their ideal self as competitive. Although this was the third most selected ideal, a very small percentage of the adolescents chose it. The large majority of ideal self ratings was the combined 87.1% of the power-oriented and responsible types. The competitive type was more often a real self rating than an ideal one.

■ Relationship Between Real Self and Ideal Self

There is an apparent correlation between the rankings of the real self and ideal self octant frequencies. The responsible and power-oriented orientations were ranked first and second for both the real and ideal results. The self-demeaning and rebellious orientations were ranked seventh and eighth for both the real and ideal results. The conforming and competitive were reversed as were the dependent and aggressive octants when comparing the octant rankings between the real self and ideal self.

Further analysis of the relationship between real self and ideal self was tested. The correlation between real self and ideal self octants was low, but significant ($r = 0.2226$, $p < 0.00$).

A regression analysis of the two variates was then performed between the octant ratings. Ideal self was entered as the dependent variable, and real self was used as the independent variable. In effect, an attempt was made to predict the adolescents' ideal self from their real self octants. Since we are dealing with discrete data, however, interpretations about prediction must be made cautiously.

The multiple r-squared value (0.0496) tells us the percent of variance accounted for by the equation. Since less than 5.0% of the variance is explained, though the correlation is significant, prediction will be questionable at best. An analysis of variance was performed on the regression equation which was subsequently found to be significant (p < 0.034).

Age. The mean age of the participating adolescents was 15.63 years. The subjects ranged from 12 to 19 years of age. Pearson Chi Square and Kruskal-Wallis tests of significance were performed to see whether adolescents of different ages varied from one another in the kinds of real self and ideal self ratings they selected. The statistics indicated that age did not affect the teenagers' selection of real self and ideal self.

Sex. Of the total number of respondents, 728 indicated whether they were male or female. There were 296 boys (40.7%) and 432 girls (59.3%) who indicated their sex. An analysis of variance was performed on both real self and ideal self ratings to determine whether boys and girls were different in their selection of personality orientations. Both analyses of variance yielded indicative results. Selection of real self personality type was significant at the p < .0418 level. Selection of ideal self personality type was significant at the p < .0331 level.

More specifically, boys gave themselves a power-oriented real self rating more frequently than did the girls. Girls rated their real selves in the conforming and responsible categories more often than did the boys. Boys also more frequently rated their ideal selves in the power-oriented octant than girls. The girls more often than boys placed their ideal self ratings in the responsible type.

Denomination. A wide range of denominations was represented in the sample of teenagers who responded. A total of 683 indicated the denomination to which they belonged. Chart 9 shows the denominations, the number of participants belonging to each denomination and the percentage of the sample belonging to each denomination.

Chart 9
Research Sample By Denomination

Denomination	Number	Percent
Assembly of God	2	.3
Baptist	92	13.5
Catholic	83	12.1
Congregational	20	2.9
Episcopalian	8	1.2
Lutheran	119	17.4
Methodist	178	26.1
Nazarene	11	1.6
Non-Denominational	55	8.1
Presbyterian	76	11.1
Protestant	10	1.5
Reformed	26	3.8
United Church of Christ	3	.4
Total:	**683**	**100.0**

Pearson Chi Square and Kruskal-Wallis tests of significance were applied to see whether denominational affiliation had any affect on the participants' real self and ideal self ratings. No significance was found among these denominational groups.

Geographic Region. The teenagers who participated in this study were from throughout the United States. Of those who responded, 703 reported the state in which they lived. The states were divided into nine regions. These regions, the number of teenagers from each region and the percent of participants from each region are reported in Chart 10.

Chart 10
Research Sample By
Geographic Region

Geographic Region	Number	Percent
New England	12	1.7
Mid-Atlantic States	24	3.4
Southern States	71	10.1
Midwest States	462	65.7
Rocky Mountain States	51	7.3
Pacific Coast	58	8.3
Southwest	20	2.8
Alaska	5	0.7
Hawaii	0	0
Total:	**703**	**100.0**

Pearson Chi Square and Kruskal-Wallis tests of significance were performed to determine whether teenagers from different geographic regions in the United States were different from each other in the way they selected real self and ideal self orientations. No significant differences were found in the real self and ideal self ratings.

■ Conclusions, Applications and Suggestions

These conclusions are considered preliminary because further research is needed to replicate the same results and broaden our understanding. The conclusions of the research are limited by the sample at the National Christian Youth Congress. It may be possible that this sample represents a more Christ-motivated type of young person than might be found in the general population of Christian adolescents. Variables such as socio-economic status and level of motivation to Christian belief were not tested. These variables could have been significant.

Our research did, however, discover important information on the personality types of Christian teenagers. Based on this information, we make these preliminary conclusions:

1. As a group, these Christian teenagers tend to perceive their real self as similar to the perception of their ideal self.

2. Christian teenagers most often describe their real self in terms of dominance, affection and competition.

3. Christian teenagers most often describe their ideal self in terms of dominance and affection.

4. Christian teenagers least often describe their real self in terms of submissiveness and aggression.

5. Christian teenagers least often describe their ideal self in terms of submissiveness, aggression and dependence.

6. Male Christian teenagers most often see themselves as power-oriented personalities.

7. Female Christian teenagers most often see themselves as responsible personalities.

8. Age, denomination and geographic location do not affect how Christian teenagers view their real self and ideal self.

The following points offer applications and suggestions based on the research project. We encourage youth workers, teachers, counselors and parents to use these applications and suggestions. Psychologists, therapists and graduate students preparing to do their dissertations or theses may be able to generate more research from the following suggestions.

1. Ministers to youth, teachers, counselors and parents can help their young people better understand their personality type. Gradually help your teenagers recognize how they have developed their personality traits. Be more aware of what they *really* express through their behavior.

2. Caring adults can help their young people to realize the psychological and theological implications of their behavior. We can assist them to move toward healthier interpersonal adaptation.

3. An item analysis might be done on the Interpersonal Check List to better determine the possible correlation between real self and ideal self scores. Finding some cause-and-effect relationship between real self and ideal self ratings would be particularly valuable.

4. The current study found that the sex of the teenager affected the way he or she completed the Interpersonal Check List. Further research might study how and why boys and girls are different from each other in the way they rate their real self and ideal self.

5. The present research did not find any significant effect in real self and ideal self ratings from the adolescents' age, geographic region and denomination. Further research on these and other variables such as ordinal position, socio-economic level, size of community and whether the young person is from a broken or intact family should be done to more fully understand the causes of our various styles of personality development.

6. To better understand the effects of family dynamics on personality development, family members could be tested with the Interpersonal Check List, rating their real self and ideal self, then comparing each other's ratings.

7. Testing of other cultural and national groups would provide further information about how people's personality development is affected by their culture.

8. Testing groups of Christian and non-Christian teenagers who are similar to each other in other variables would help us to understand the impact of faith in Christ on personality development.

9. Testing groups of teenagers who have been Christians for different lengths of time might help us to better understand the impact of faith development on personality development.

10. Longitudinal studies of young people as they mature from early through late adolescence would help us more fully understand how adolescent development affects personality orientation.

The author trusts that this research will stimulate interest for further study into adolescent personality development from a philosophical base that integrates psychological and theological perspectives. The value of the present research will be greatly enhanced if it stimulates others to do more evaluation of this fascinating area of study.

■

Notes

Chapter 1

[1]Bruce Narramore, *Adolescence Is Not an Illness* (Old Tappan, NJ: Fleming H. Revell, 1980).

[2]J.B. Phillips, *Your God Is Too Small* (New York: Macmillan, 1969).

Chapter 2

[1]Thomas D. Gagney, *How to Put Up With Parents: A Guide for Teenagers* (Ottawa, IL: Facilitation House, 1975).

[2]Peter Buntman and Eleanor Saris, *How to Live With Your Teenager* (Pasadena, CA: Birch Tree Press, 1979).

[3]John Powell, S.J., *Why Am I Afraid to Tell You Who I Am?* (Chicago: Argus Communications, 1969).

[4]Kevin Leman, *The Birth Order Book* (Old Tappan, NJ: Fleming H. Revel, June, 1986).

[5]G. Keith Olson, *Counseling Teenagers* (Loveland, CO: Group, 1984) p.105.

[6]Erik Erikson, *Childhood and Society* (New York: Norton, 1950).

[7]David Elkind, *The Hurried Child* (Reading, MA: Addison-Wesley, 1981).

Chapter 3

[1]Abraham H. Maslow, ed., *Motivation And Personality* (New York: Harper and Row, 1954).

[2]G. Keith Olson, *Counseling Teenagers* (Loveland, CO: Group Books, 1984) pp. 34-36, 399-452.

[3]M. Scott Peck, *The Road Less Traveled* (New York: Simon and Schuster, 1978).

[4]Olson, pp. 293-311.

Part Two-Introduction

[1]T. Leary, *Interpersonal Diagnosis of Personality* (New York: The Ronald Press Company, 1957).

[2]R. LaForge and R. Suzek, "The Interpersonal Dimension of Personality: III. An Interpersonal Check List," *Journal of Personality* 24, Supplement no. 1 (1955): pp. 94-112.

[3]This illustration has been adapted from R. LaForge, *Using the ICL* (Mill Valley, CA: 1976) p. 48 and Leary, p. 65.

Chapter 8

[1]W.E. Vine, Merrill F. Unger and William White, *The Expository Dictionary of Biblical Words* (Nashville: Thomas Nelson Publishers, 1984) pp. 727-28.

Chapter 10

[1]G. Keith Olson, *Counseling Teenagers* (Loveland, CO: Group, 1984).

[2]Peter Buntman and Eleanor Saris, *How to Live With Your Teenager* (Pasadena, CA: Birch Tree Press, 1979).

Make your ministry more effective with

■ *Training Volunteers in Youth Ministry,* Video Kit

Give your volunteer youth workers a deeper understanding of youth ministry. You'll get expert, in-depth education with the **Training Volunteers in Youth Ministry** video kit. The nation's top authorities on teenagers and youth ministry provide solid, practical information.

Design a complete training program to meet your needs using helpful tips from the 128-page leaders guide and four 30-minute VHS videotapes . . .

Video 1: Youth Ministry Basics

Video 2: Understanding Teenagers

Video 3: Building Relationships

Video 4: Keys for Successful Meetings

You'll use this valuable resource again and again, sharpening the skills of your volunteer team. You'll discover how to find, motivate and keep volunteers. Plus, you'll strengthen your youth ministry team spirit with practical, affordable youth ministry training.

ISBN 0931-529-59-X, $98

■ *Instant Programs for Youth Groups 1, 2, 3* by the editors of Group Publishing

Get loads of quick-and-easy program ideas you can prepare in a flash.

Each meeting idea gives you everything you need for a dynamic program. Step-by-step instructions. Material lists of easy-to-find items. Dynamic discussion starters. And ready-to-copy handouts to involve kids.

Each book gives you 17 (or more) meeting ideas on topics that matter to teenagers . . .

1—Self-image, pressures, living as a Christian
2—Me and God, responsibility, emotions
3—Friends, parents, dating and sex

With all three books, you can keep a year's worth of program ideas at your fingertips—ready to tap instantly.

Instant Programs for Youth Groups 1, ISBN 0931-529-32-8, $7.95
Instant Programs for Youth Groups 2, ISBN 0931-529-42-5, $7.95
Instant Programs for Youth Groups 3, ISBN 0931-529-43-3, $7.95

■ *Training Teenagers for Peer Ministry,* by Dr. Barbara Varenhorst with Lee Sparks

Train your young people how to reach out in Christian faith. Use this step-by-step program to help kids minister effectively to their friends.

The easy-to-follow, activity-rich format equips young people with important life skills . . .

● Making responsible decisions
● Assertive communication
● Effective listening
● Respecting confidences
● Knowing how to deal with typical teenage concerns, such as family problems, substance abuse, sexual concerns, suicide, death and dying

Teach your young people how to turn their faith into real caring with peer ministry training.

ISBN 0931-529-23-9, $8.95

Creative, Innovative Programming Ideas from Group Books

■ Youth Ministry Care Cards

Keep in touch with your group members—with **Youth Ministry Care Cards.** Each inspiring, attention-getting post card includes a colorful cartoon, a meaningful Bible verse and a place for your personal message.

Visitor Follow-Up—colorful post cards let visitors to your group know they were appreciated, and are welcome back!

Affirmations—positive messages to let your kids know you're thinking about them.

Attendance Builders—unforgettable reminders to attract more kids to your meetings, retreats and special events.

Birthday Greetings—quick, lighthearted cards to remember kids' birthdays.

Your kids will love these crazy, colorful post cards. Each 30-card pack contains 6 different messages. Order your **Youth Ministry Care Cards** today. $3.95/pack.

Affirmations ISBN 0-931529-28-X
Attendance Builders ISBN 0-931529-36-0
Birthday Greetings ISBN 0-931529-80-8
Visitor Follow-Up ISBN 0-931529-88-3

■ Youth & Parents Together: Facing Life's Struggles, A 13-week curriculum for junior high kids and their parents by Mike Gillespie

Strengthen junior high families with the NEW scripture-based curriculum that brings young people and their parents together. Use 13 action-packed sessions to help parents and kids address important life issues . . .

- Discouragement
- Impatience
- Anger
- Communication
- Doubt and fear
- Loneliness
- Forgiveness
- Faith, and more

Your easy-to-use leaders guide gives you everything you need to prepare and teach 13 fast-moving sessions with confidence. Parents and kids each use their own participants book, loaded with fun activities to do both in class and at home.

Help junior high young people and their parents improve communication. Develop greater trust and understanding. And share important moments of Christian growth—with **Youth & Parents Together: Facing Life's Struggles.**

Leaders Guide, ISBN 0931-529-27-1, $10.95
Participants Book, ISBN 0931-529-29-8, $3.95

These and other Group Books are available at your Christian bookstore or direct from the publisher. Group Books, Box 481, Loveland, CO 80539. Please add $2.50 postage/handling to all direct orders. Colorado residents add 3% sales tax.